African Americans in the Human Sciences

African Americans in the Human Sciences

Challenges and Opportunities

Edited by
Vanessa P. Jackson, Jacqueline M. Holland,
and Julia R. Miller Arline

LEXINGTON BOOKS
Lanham • Boulder • New York • London

Published by Lexington Books
An imprint of The Rowman & Littlefield Publishing Group, Inc.
4501 Forbes Boulevard, Suite 200, Lanham, Maryland 20706
www.rowman.com

6 Tinworth Street, London SE11 5AL, United Kingdom

British Library Cataloguing in Publication Information Available

Library of Congress Cataloging-in-Publication Data

Names: Jackson, Vanessa P., 1956- editor. | Holland, Jacqueline M., 1953 editor. |
  Miller Arline, Julia R., 1943- editor.
Title: African Americans in the human sciences : challenges and opportunities / edited
  by Vanessa P. Jackson, Jacqueline M. Holland and Julia R. Miller Arline.
Description: Lanham : Lexington Books, 2021. | Includes bibliographical references
  and index. | Summary: "This book highlights significant contributions of
  African American women in education, their successes and challenges in the human
  sciences/family and consumer sciences profession, and the impact of historically
  Black colleges and universities throughout American history"— Provided by
  publisher.
Identifiers: LCCN 2021018582 (print) | LCCN 2021018583 (ebook) |
  ISBN 9781793648945 (cloth) | ISBN 9781793648952 (epub) |
  ISBN 9781793648969 (pbk)
Subjects: LCSH: African American women in the professions—United States. |
  Women social scientists—United States. | African American women—Education—
  United States.
Classification: LCC HQ1410 .A357 2021 (print) | LCC HQ1410 (ebook) |
  DDC 305.48/896073—dc23
LC record available at https://lccn.loc.gov/2021018582
LC ebook record available at https://lccn.loc.gov/2021018583

Contents

Preface

African Americans in the Human Sciences: Challenges and Opportunities provides reflections on various transformations of knowledge and experiences that have evolved over time These transformations come together to form symbolic relationships, in a pattern that is relevant for preprofessionals and professionals. As one looks through the prisms of this book, there are specifically designated, ever-changing reflections that represent opportunities and challenges. Many of these evolving opportunities and challenges offer reflections not only for human sciences professionals but also for professionals in other disciplines.

Multiple disciplines and multiple professions are brought together to configure and reconfigure knowledge. A major question that comes to the forefront is: What and how can information related to a wide range of concepts, topics, and issues be further integrated in a manner that is accessible, meaningful, and useful to the current and next generation of leaders? An option is to expand upon knowledge in the field to explore more diverse perspectives.

This book represents an important and timely contribution to the field, exploring topics divided into five sections: *Women, Education, and Careers*; *Historically Black Colleges and Universities: Opportunities and Challenges*; *Internationalization and the Human Sciences*; *Human Sciences Foundations for New Career Paths*; and *Technology: Wave of the Present and Future*. Captured in these sections are the perspectives and work of authors who have conducted research; engaged in teaching, outreach, and service; and been shaped by personal and professional experiences. The information in these sections is not intended to totally fill the absence of knowledge available from other resources. It will, however, contribute to a range of untold knowledge that the authors consider relevant. Our intent is to capture some of the vitality and diversity of knowledge that has, over time, assisted in transforming the field, and to share this knowledge with other professions.

We are indebted to the authors and reviewers who have been tenacious, highly motivated, and steadfast in assisting with the development of this important treatise. Their expertise will contribute to the accessibility of significant knowledge within the profession.

Vanessa P. Jackson
Jacqueline M. Holland
Julia R. Miller Arline

Part I

WOMEN, EDUCATION, AND CAREERS

Women's education and pursuit of career paths remain in the forefront of educational agendas. The chapters in this section provide evidence of the intersectionality of social exclusion, racism, and gender that create barriers to success for women (particularly women of color) in education. It further discusses raising families and working while facing challenges such as breaking the glass ceiling, health issues due to stress, examining the needs of the future generation of leaders called the millennials, and biographies of those who have helped others along the way to receive recognition and rewards for their hard work and accomplishments.

Gains in educational attainment and career development for women, particularly for African Americans and other women of color, have been attributed to their perseverance and to educational political movements.

From the beginning, African American women in the human sciences have worked hard to improve quality of life and education within the African American community. Some African American women have done so by seeking upper and middle levels of leadership in the human sciences. While some, not many, have achieved those upper- and mid-level leadership positions, they have faced barriers that led to negative experiences along the way.

Chapter 1 examines how women in general, and specifically women of color, have taken pathways to and through education that ultimately impacted their empowerment in American society.

Chapter 2 explores the intersectionality of racism and gender as a barrier to growth and development for human sciences leaders. Oral history adds to the literature the evolution of African American women's sustainability as leaders in the human sciences, using mentors outside the academic arena and their spiritual foundation.

Chapter 3 provides an in-depth look at the experiences of a group of Black, middle-aged women and the understanding of what it means to mother and work at the same time. It also emphasizes the importance of how we envision and define women of color, particularly African American women, and speaks to how we view and analyze these women individually and collectively.

Chapter 4 elaborates on an analytical perspective of the challenges, struggles, obstacles, and successes faced by African American women as described in the book, *African American Women: Contributions to the Human Sciences*. The chapter sheds light on the need to fill the gap in the history of the profession related to the collective inclusion of professionals who are African American women. These are women who made significant contributions to the growth and development of the field of human sciences.

Chapter 5 describes the strengths and potential of a new group of professionals who will become the next leaders in our profession and beyond. Ethel G. Jones provides an excellent discussion on the importance of understanding the next generation of professionals known as the millennials.

Chapter 6 explains how the reproductive and sexual health of African American women has been negatively affected by a traumatic history filled with coercion and oppression. The work explores how education related to African American women's reproductive and sexual health can counteract the media industry's perspective that often perpetuates negative stereotypes of African American women and describes how they are influenced by the media across their lifespan.

African American women have a long history of living with chronic stress, which has contributed to their susceptibility to chronic disease. African American women have survived the terrorizing reproductive and sexual maltreatment of slave owners, and continue to overcome oppressive societal barriers to accessing education that makes a difference in understanding culturally competent preventative healthcare.

Chapter 7 shares the personal story of a woman whose life illustrates academic concepts as her objective reality. This chapter celebrates a woman who contributed to the fight for human rights and chronicles her lifelong contributions to the human sciences. This personal story demonstrates the determination needed to excel within challenging and sometimes hostile environments.

Chapter 1

Quest for Education

Empowerment of Women of Color

Julia R. Miller Arline, Debra L. Mayfield,
and William H. Whitaker Jr.

INTRODUCTION

American society has grappled with the education of women for centuries. For several decades, the phenomena of the education of women have transitioned from exclusivity to gradual access across various parameters. Once coined by Charles Darwin, "universal education is the pathway to human improvement of women and was considered to be sound social policy." Furthermore, international consensus emerged in developing countries that mass education, particularly for women and girls, not only had beneficial effects for women and girls but also for individuals, families, and society at large (LeVine, LeVine, and Schnell 2001). Regardless of educational levels across decades and globally, there are common themes pertaining to the empowerment of women. Some of these themes are (1) social interactions, relationships, and attitudes; (2) gender; (3) culture; (4) race; (5) ethnicity; (6) injustices and inequality; (7) religion; (8) access and opportunity; (9) political ideology and laws; (10) economic growth; (11) human capital development; and (12) nation building (Tembon and Fort 2008; Sheykhjan, Rajeswari, and Jahari 2014).

Sheykhjan, Rajeswari, and Jahari (2014) stressed the importance of empowerment as the basis of human rights, development and implementation of laws, education and employment that result in equality with men, nation building, and personal development. These researchers stressed that societies are becoming cognizant of the powerful trust that girls and women are not the problem but the solution to the development of an economically and socially developed society. Sundaram, Sekar, and Subburaj (2014) emphasized that education is a critical factor in the empowerment of women, leading to the prosperity, development, and welfare of a culture as a whole. Their concept of empowerment provides capacity to establish gender equality, rather than domination (Sundaram, Sekar, and Subburaj 2014).

A visionary Ghanaian educator emphasized, "The surest way to keep a people down is to educate the men and neglect the women. If you educate a man you simply educate an individual, but if you educate a woman you educate a family" (Tembon and Fort 2008). The education of women is not just a women's issue, but it is critical for their development, which provides economic empowerment. The education of women and girls provides poverty-reducing synergies and gains that are intergenerational. According to these same researchers, there is a positive correlation between economic productivity and higher earnings that subsequently improve health and well-being (Tembon and Fort 2008).

Stromquist (2011) wrote:

> Pervasive social beliefs about women's and men's proper places in society still shape people's conceptions of their possible life and career trajectories. Schools tend to reproduce these gender ideologies, and educators rarely problematize content taught to girls and boys. Meanwhile, men continue to fill more varied and numerous roles in the public sphere, while women often remain relegated to the private sphere and its domestic responsibilities. Traditional gender ideologies are stronger and more resistant to change in countries with limited wealth and weak infrastructural capacity. Conservative religious beliefs are also influential in constraining women's roles. In addition, gender interacts with other social variables such as socioeconomic status, ethnicity, race, and location to compound the effects of disenfranchisement.

THEORETICAL FRAMEWORKS RELATED TO WOMEN IN EDUCATION

From a theoretical and historical perspective, there are several theoretical frameworks and theories that are useful to explore related to empowerment of women of color in education (Tembon and Fort 2008; Shanyanana and Ndofirepl 2014). Those discussed are not exhaustive but relevant to this phenomenon. Some of the same issues that American society addressed in the twentieth and twenty-first centuries related to education, gender equality, and empowerment of women have been given global attention today. Tembon and Fort (2008) encapsulate four main dimensions: equality of access, equality in the learning process, equality of educational outcomes, and equality of external results.

In order to receive equality of educational access in the United States, girls and women had to overcome biological and social stereotypes. These biological and social stereotypes pertained to whether girls and women have the intellectual capacity for any form of education as compared to men. There were struggles, discussions, and debates related to single-sex education, coeducation between the sexes, and education of people of color. This dilemma resulted in males, females, and people of color being educated separately, which in turn resulted in a hindrance to equality of access. There was a transition in education for White males and females. This transition was less apparent in higher education of single sex, religious, military institutions, and colleges for people of color. From a similar emerging perspective, particularly in the developing world, equality of access is viewed through the lens of females and males gaining admission to formal and nonformal education on various levels (USAID, United States Agency for International Development 2008).

Shanyanana and Ndofirepl (2014) discussed Morrow's theoretical position on women's access to higher education from two perspectives: (1) formal access and (2) epistemological access. Formal access relates to the number of students provided opportunities to be admitted to higher education institutions. Epistemological access involves the number of institutions that provide a knowledge-shared system to those that they admit. These concepts not only apply to access for students in general but also for women (particularly women of color) who are students, faculty, and staff. In essence, there are formal and epistemological accesses that are fully exemplified to the extent that women and women of color have the opportunity to contribute knowledge to decision-making and problem-solving (Shanyanana and Ndofirepl 2014).

Equality of learning processes and external outcomes reflect the potential for women to have equality in learning that provides positive external outcomes. For many decades, women's education was less inclusive and primarily in disciplines that did not generate high wages. Women were relegated to designated "women's courses" or "female curricula" (Aleman and Renn 2002). Female exposure to decision-making and problem-solving strategies to select courses and programs was not possible and was more often for men. While doors to equality in education are more open than they were in the past, this is not always true for women of color.

Equality of educational outcomes for men and women is necessary due to the proven academic performance of girls. According to Stromquist (2011), in some countries the academic performance of girls exceeded that of boys, with the exception of math. This substantiates that there are no differences in cognitive ability; thus, lack of ability is not the cause of women and girls' marginalization in the educative process. This is also an issue for women and girls of color. Educators and policymakers need to have a clear understanding of education's role in both reproducing and transforming gender relations and ethnicity, and to consider the totality of schooling experiences. In addition, we should examine curricula, instructional methodologies, peer relations, extracurricular activities, and hidden messages about authority, power, and culture. Unfortunately, there is reluctance on the part of both governments and international development agencies to address these issues. Until these concerns are addressed, gender parity, ethnicity, and culture related to access will not translate into full social, political, and economic equality.

The theory of symbolic interactionism is relevant to the empowerment of women of color in the educative process. Crossman (2018a) describes this theory as the subjective meanings that individuals give to objects and behaviors. Subjective meanings are primarily given because people often behave according to beliefs, rather than what is objectively factual. Consequently, meanings are socially constructed based on human interpretation. This interpretation of one another's behaviors forms social bonds that become the "definition of the situation" (Crossman, 2018a). This definition of the situation is often formed by the majority population and has been a hindrance in education for women of color and people of color in general.

Lastly, according to Crossman (2018b) female perspectives are fundamental; unlike male perspectives that typically employ an analytical, topical focus. From this viewpoint, feminist theory highlights social problems, trends, and issues that are often overlooked or misidentified by male culture. Areas of focus include discrimination and exclusion based upon sex and gender, objectification, structural and economic inequality, power, oppression, gender roles, ethnicity, culture, religion, stereotypes, exclusivity, and inclusivity (Crossman 2018b). Women of color often experience the double jeopardy of being a female and an ethnic minority.

Theoretical frameworks are windows for viewing the education of women, particularly women of color, through analytical lenses. As education for women of color is investigated, one can conceptualize the challenges and opportunities that were transcended and are still being transcended. There were and continue to be similarities in issues and themes that pertain to the education of women and women of color at various levels, as they transcend the educational pyramid. It is most noteworthy to further peer through analytical lenses more closely to determine what were and can still be the complexities of progress in higher education in its various forms. Ultimately, higher education continues to be the gateway to improvement of the human condition within diverse societies.

WOMEN OF COLOR IN HIGHER
EDUCATION: A DIVERSE PERSPECTIVE

African American Women

African American women have faced many barriers to education, from simply reading and writing to accessing knowledge that would assist them in understanding the society in which they were embedded (Bates 2007). One of the most crucial issues facing African American women in higher education is that they function at the intersection of two forms of oppression: racism and sexism. One must be immersed in a higher education experience where gender discrimination and racism exist to fully understand its impact (Jayakumar, Vue, and Allen 2013). The major focus of education in American society was for White men. When the education of women began to be considered, the purpose was for the socialization of White women. These women were placed in subservient roles to White men (Coleman-Burns 1989). At the same time, the education of African American women was not even discussed. Generally, African American women were expected to take a subordinate role to all White males and females, regardless of age, and to Black men (Coleman-Burns 1989).

Zamani (2003) emphasized that there is a deep cultural and historical belief that education is of critical importance and has been sought in every conceivable manner. Prosper (2004) further elaborated: In the middle and late years of the nineteenth century, a new dialogue began regarding women and education. Social theorists focused on the extension of higher education to women and African Americans. Black women were often dissuaded from entering degree programs, but they forged ahead nonetheless. By the turn of the century, African American women were defying society's expectations and attending coeducational integrated institutions. The 1954 *Brown v. Board of Education* decision gradually led to an increase of Black women at traditionally White colleges and universities across America. Today the oppression, hostility, and disapproval that Black women face when applying to graduate programs are covert but still present.

Historically Black and Black private single-sex women's colleges and universities, along with White public and private single-sex women's colleges, established educational environments for African American women to flourish. According to Hughes and Howard-Hamilton (2003), coeducational historically Black colleges and universities do a better job of encouraging African American women to major in math and science programs. These programs are usually associated with men. Encouragement and exposure at these institutions are associated with a greater likelihood that graduates will eventually earn doctoral degrees.

According to Watson (2004) and Bates (2007), despite the historical fact African American women have been prohibited in advancing to higher education top leadership positions at mainstream colleges and universities, there have been some slow advancements. Reid (2012) reports that, more than ever before, the pathway to the presidency in higher education institutions is chair, dean, then provost. Toutant (2017) stated it has been proven that African American women are more than capable to lead institutions to educational attainment. The reason these women are marginalized is they are faced with not only what is called the *glass ceiling*, but with a *concrete ceiling* that affects not only upper mobility of women of color in higher education but also their ability to coexist within a system that works against them (Toutant 2017).

The researchers' overview of the literature suggests themes that have inhibited African American women from upper mobility in higher education. These themes include myths and stereotypes about Black women and their ability to work with others, boards of trustees who prefer to work with people who look like them, a system of higher education that is not built for African Americans to succeed, college and university presidencies that often require 70-hour weeks that may conflict with familial lives, and organizational barriers that are sexist and racist (Toutant 2017).

Latino American Women

This ethnic group self-identifies using the terms Latino or Hispanic. Cuellar (2018) differentiates these terms in the following manner: Hispanic has been used to refer to individuals with heritage from Spanish-speaking countries, regardless of race. The federal government uses the term Hispanic when it first appeared in a limited version of the 1970 Census and later adopted broadly in subsequent versions. Latino is another commonly used term to refer to individuals with ancestry in Latin America. As Latino in Spanish is a masculine term, Latina/o is often used to simultaneously recognize feminine and masculine versions of this identity. Preferences for identification as Hispanic or Latino vary by region as well as by national origin.

There is conclusive evidence in the literature that the Latino population is the fastest growing ethnic group in the United States. Jackson (2013) and Krogstad (2016) stressed that even though the Hispanic high school dropout rate has declined, there remains a lag for other ethnic groups: African Americans (7%), Whites (5%), and Asians (1%). Moreover, Krogstad (2016) found that higher education enrollment for Hispanics ages 18–24 increased from 22% in 1994 to 35% in 2014 at two- and four-year colleges (an increase of 13 percentage points). The same study showed enrollment for African Americans increased eight percentage points to 33% in 2014, while White enrollment increased five points to 44%. Asians saw a nine percentage point increase from 1999 (earlier data was not available) to 64% in 2014 (Krogstad 2016). Interestingly, over half of Hispanics attending college were enrolled in two-year institutions.

Garcia (2016) observed that Hispanic women's college academic goals and aspirations are very connected to their families. Latinas in college view their experiences as a strategy to not only improve themselves but also elevate their families (Garcia 2017). In analyzing Latina educational attainment, Jackson (2013) found that college graduation for Latinas has increased faster than any other group of women. In 2012, Latinas held only 7.4% of degrees earned by women, even though they constituted 16% of the female population. Similarly, only 3% of Hispanic women are represented in science, technology, engineering, and mathematics (STEM) fields. While women in total make up 24% of the STEM workforce, Latinas represented 49% of all Hispanics who matriculated into medical school in 2004. From 1980 to 2004, the number of Latina medical school graduates jumped from 93 to 485.

Lastly, Becerra (2017) noted that most first-generation university students are Black or Hispanic, and that overall, 59% of students whose parents had no college experience enrolled in some type of postsecondary education versus 93% if the parents had a bachelor's degree. In other words, students with parents who attended college are more likely to attend themselves. For Hispanic females, only 15% had parents with a bachelor's degree. This explains, in part, why only 8.8% of all women with bachelors' degrees were Hispanic, and that while one in five women in the United States is Hispanic, there were only 8,000 Hispanic women with doctoral degrees compared to about 100,000 White women in 2010.

Fewer Hispanic women earning a bachelors' degree leads to a smaller pool of educated Hispanic women who qualify for higher-paying jobs. In 2010, 64% of Hispanic children (about half female) under the age of 18 lived in poverty. These trends reveal that enrolling and preparing Hispanic women with higher education degrees provides opportunities for higher-paying jobs that will influence future generations. Empowering Latinas to graduate from college will also lead to personal, familial, and societal benefits as more children grow up with mothers who have a strong belief in getting a college education (Becerra 2017).

Asian American Women

According to Smith (2013), Asian American women surpassed White women in actual graduation rates in 2004. College graduation rates for White women and Asian American women were 45.8% and 59.4%, respectively. In 2013, Asian American women held 8.36% of bachelors' degrees held by women while only constituting 5.14% of the female population. Asian American and White women earned a number of science and engineering degrees equal to that of their male counterparts in 2010. Compared to other women of color, Asian American women are as likely to have received four years of college as their White American female counterparts, though they faced cultural and socioeconomic barriers to higher education similar to those of Asian American males (Fong 1997).

The traditional Asian American value system is characterized by filial piety, obedience to authority, a quiet and passive acceptance of one's situation, subjugation of the individual to the group, self-control, self-abasement, and a strong sense of family solidarity (Fong 1997). In contrast, American women's values overall are characterized by individualism, egalitarianism, independence, future orientation, and mastery over one's environment.

People often hold stereotypical views of Asian Americans. One such false image or stereotype is that they are "model minorities." This myth is often problematic for Asian students because they are expected to excel academically (Mekouar 2016). In contrast, there are income gaps and growing poverty among different nationalities of Asian Americans, which erases the myth of them being "model minorities" (Massie 2016). Ho and Jackson (2001) and Lin and colleagues (2005) report that Asian American stereotypes about being highly competent can make them appear threatening in the workplace, and stereotypes about Asian Americans lacking social skills can make them seem unfit for leadership. Still more problematic is the inconsistency between Asian American stereotypes and the traits people tend to value in leaders. While business leaders are expected to be competent, intelligent, and dedicated, they are also expected to be charismatic and possess certain social skills, along with being masculine and dictatorial or authoritarian (Johnson and Sy 2016). This puts Asian Americans at a disadvantage, who, like African American women, are often seen to fit low- to mid-level management positions, but not top-level leadership. It's even harder for Asian women—they comprise only 3.1% of executives at Google, Hewlett-Packard, Intel, LinkedIn, and Yahoo while Asian men comprise 13.5%.

Hassan (2018) stated a similar finding in a *New York Times* article: "Asian-Americans fall behind in earnings. College educated; U.S.-born Asian men earn 8 percent less than White men. Although Asian-American women are likely to earn as much as White women, they are less likely to be in a management role."

Native American Women

When conceptualizing the education of Native Americans, one must look not only at issues of language, ethnicity, and social class but also at other characteristics including tribal sovereignty (McCarthy and Lee 2014). In their research, McCarthy and Lee (2014) defined the concept of tribal sovereignty as the right of a people to self-governance, self-education, and self-determination. This also includes the rights of Native Americans to their language and their diverse ways of cultural expressions according to tribal traditions (McCarthy and Lee 2014). The researchers further expound that tribal sovereignty predates the U.S. Constitution but is also included in the Constitution, treatises, and case law. This concept was intended to imply a tribal-federal relationship that was based on "trust responsibility." This trust responsibility was presumed to be both voluntary and contractual. Implied in this tribal-federal relationship was the protection and enhancement of tribal assets, including fiscal, natural, and cultural resources through policy decisions and management actions (McCarthy and Lee 2014).

McCarthy and Lee (2014) and other researchers also state that Native Americans' desire for tribal sovereignty, tribal autonomy, self-determination, and self-identification is interwoven with historical legacies of colonization, ethnocide, and linguicide in the Western education of native peoples. These legacies impact their desire to have separate ways of maintaining their tribal identities. Historically, learning became a mechanism to eliminate Native American sovereignty, rather than to educate the indigenous peoples (Almeida 1997).

Europeans' efforts to educate Native Americans were based on Western values and beliefs, with the intent to eliminate Native American society. The U.S. government continued this effort, disguising Native American educational attainment through the establishment of boarding schools. Removing young children and often entire families from reservations to boarding schools was common practice, without any consideration for geographical locations or ethnic and cultural backgrounds. Moreover, Waterman and Lindley (2013) expressed the positions of several researchers that the intentional Europeans' ideology implemented through the boarding schools eroded how traditional gender roles were valued and attempted to destroy native family and social structures. Some of the most prestigious universities, including Harvard University and Dartmouth College, provided for the education of Native Americans in their charters (Almeida 1997). During that period, Hampton College (now Hampton University) educated Native American men.

Native American women in higher education are described as resilient, with the endurance to adapt to a contemporary education within their own traditional cultures (Waterman and Lindley 2013). Foxworth (2016) states that Native American women attend college and gain advanced degrees at higher rates than Native American men, also noting that they lead the way in private sector business development.

Data related to the representation of Native Americans in higher education reveals that they account for less than 1% of the U.S. college student population (Soria 2015). Some higher education challenges Native Americans face include a lack of role models, and feelings of isolation and racial discrimination. For many Native Americans, these challenges and barriers are coupled with being the first to attend college in their families, being employed while attending college, having dependents, having low incomes, and having issues related to language, ethnicity, and social class. Other characteristics may also differ, including tribal sovereignty (McCarthy and Lee 2014).

Waterman and Lindley (2013) emphasized the research of Shield (2009) in a qualitative study of educational experiences conducted with eight indigenous women. Four data clusters were identified. Spirituality was the first cluster, defined as "an entire way of being" that provided strength for degree completion. The second cluster related to how participants filtered their higher education experiences through their culture. Traditional cultural roles, family, and community comprised the third cluster, while the fourth was "family loyalty" because family was central for these women. Family provided the resiliency needed to make difficult decisions related to educational experiences. In general, research has found that family, cultural, and community supports are critical for Native American women's attainment in higher education (Waterman and Lindley 2013).

CONCLUSION

In this chapter, historical, conceptual, and theoretical frameworks are used to discuss the barriers, challenges, and opportunities that women (particularly women of color) have experienced in their quest for education and empowerment. Demographic and educational statistical data related to the general population of African Americans, Latino Americans, Asian Americans, and Native Americans are presented to establish the context in which women of color are embedded. The major emphasis of this chapter transitions from more general statistical data to specific issues that women from various ethnic groups have faced and continue to grapple with as they strive to gain achievements in higher education. The information presented clearly demonstrates that, despite struggles encountered, women of color have made unbelievable advancements in their educational journeys. Personal attitudes, families, and communities have significantly supported women of color in reaching the heights of their educational visions. These factors have also enabled women of color to hold on to generational beliefs, and their passion for education as the pathway to human improvement through the implementation of sound, nondiscriminatory social policies.

REFERENCES

Aleman, Ana. and Kristen Renn. 2002. *Women in Higher Education: An Encyclopedia.* Santa Barbara, CA: ABC-CLIO.

Almeida, Deidra A. 1997. "The Hidden Half: A History of Native American Women's Education." *Harvard Educational Review 67*, no. 4: 757–771.

Bates, Gerri. 2007. "These Hallowed Halls: African American Women College and University Presidents." *The Journal of Negro Education 76*, no. 3: 373–390.

Becerra, Irma. 2017. "Empower Young Hispanic Women to be Tomorrow's Leaders." Miami Herald. Accessed December 2020. https://www.miamiherald.com/opinion/op-ed/article180703011.html.

Coleman-Burns, Patricia. 1989. "African American Women—Education for What?" *Sex Roles 21*, no. 1–2: 145–160. https://link.springer.com/article/10.1007%2FBF00289733.

Cuellar, Marcela. 2018. "Understanding Latinx College Student Diversity and Why it Matters." Higher Education Today. Last modified January 29, 2018 https://www.higheredtoday.org/2018/01/29/understanding-latinx-college-student-diversity-matters/.

Crossman, Ashley. 2018a. "Learn about Symbolic Interactionism" ThoughtCo. Last modified January 30, 2020. https://www.thoughtco.com/symbolic-interaction-theory-3026633#:~:text=Symbolic%20interaction%20theory%20analyzes%20society,objects%2C%20events%2C%20and%20behaviors.&text=Thus%2C%20society%20is%20thought%20to,that%20form%20the%20social%20bond.

Crossman, Ashley. 2018b. "Feminist Theory in Sociology: An Overview of Key Ideas and Issues." ThoughtCo. Last modified February 25, 2020. https://www.thoughtco.com/feminist-theory-3026624.

Fong, Lina Y. S. 1997. "Asian-American Women: An Understudied Minority." *Journal of Sociology and Social Welfare 24*, no. 1: 91.

Foxworth, Raymond. 2016. *Native American Women, Leadership and the Native Nonprofit Sector.* Longmont, CO: First Nations Development Institute.

Garcia, Katherine. 2016. "4 Obstacles for Latinas in Higher Education- And Why it's Time for a Change." Everyday Feminism. Accessed December, 2020. https://everydayfeminism.com/2016/03/latina-women-higher-education/.

Hassan, Adeel. 2018. "Confronting Asian American Stereotypes." The New York Times. Accessed December, 2020. https://www.nytimes.com/2018/06/23/us/confronting-asian-american-stereotypes.html.

Ho, Collin and Jay W. Jackson. 2001. "Attitude Toward Asian Americans: Theory and Measurement." *Journal of Applied Social Psychology 31*, no. 8: 1553–1581.

Hughes, Robin L., and Mary F. Howard-Hamilton. 2003. "Insights: Emphasizing Issues that Affect African American Women." *New Directions for Student Services 104*, no. 5: 95–104. https://doi.org/10.1002/ss.110.

Jackson, Mareshah. 2013. Fact Sheet: The State of Latinas in the United States. *Center for American Progress.* Accessed December, 2020. https://www.americanprogress.org/issues/race/reports/2013/11/07/79167/fact-sheet-the-state-of-latinas-in-the-united-states/.

Jayakumar, Uma, Rican Vue, and Walter Allen. 2013. "Pathways to College for Young Black Scholars: A Community Cultural Wealth Perspective." *Harvard Educational Review 83*, no. 4: 551–579. https://doi.org/10.17763/haer.83.4.4k1mq00162433l28.

Johnson, Stephanie K. and Thomas Sy. 2016. "Why Aren't There More Asian Americans in Leadership Positions." *Harvard Business Review*. https://hbr.org /2016/12/why-arent-there-more-asian-americans-in-leadership-positions.

Krogstad, Jens Manuel. 2016. "5 Facts about Latinos and Education." Pew Research Center. Accessed December, 2020. https://www.pewresearch.org/fact-tank/2016 /07/28/5-facts-about-latinos-and-education/.

LeVine, Robrt, Sarah LeVine, and Beatrice Schnell. 2001. "Improve the Women: Mass Schooling, Female Literacy, and Worldwide Social Change." *Harvard Educational Review 71*, no. 1: 1–51. https://doi.org/10.17763/haer.71.1.154550 622x3225u7

Lin, Monica H., Virginia SY Kwan, Anna Cheung, and Susan T. Fiske. 2005. "Stereotype Content Model Explains Prejudice for an Envied Outgroup: Scale of anti-Asian American Stereotypes." *Personality and Social Psychology Bulletin 31*, no. 1 (2005): 34–47. https://doi.org/10.1177/0146167204271320.

Massie, Victoria M. 2016. "Asian Americans Are the Highest Wage Earners. They Still Face Racial Discrimination: Higher Wages don't Necessarily Shatter the Glass Ceiling." Vox. Accessed December, 2020. https://www.vox.com/2016/7/6/120810 82/wage-gap-race.

McCarty, Teresa, and Tiffany Lee. 2014. "Critical Culturally Sustaining/Revitalizing Pedagogy and Indigenous Education Sovereignty." *Harvard Educational Review 84*, no.1: 101–124. https://doi.org/10.17763/haer.84.1.q83746nl5pj34216.

Mekouar, Dora. 2016. "Why Asian Americans are the Most Educated Group in America." *NOV News*. Accessed December, 2020. https://blogs.voanews.com/ all-about-america/2016/04/11/why-asian-americans-are-the-most-educated-group -in-america/.

Prosper, Tasha. 2004. "African American Women and the Pursuit of Higher Education." *Encounter: Education for Meaning and Social Justice 17*, no. 3: 16–18.

Reid, P. T. 2012. "Black and Female in Academia." American Council on Education. Accessed December, 2020. https://www.acenet.edu/Pages/default.aspx.

Shanyanana, Rachel Ndinelao, and Amasa Philip Ndofirepi. 2014. "The Place of Women in Higher Education: A Philosophical-Historical Perspective." *Mediterranean Journal of Social Sciences 5*, no. 23: 2168–2177.

Sheykhjan, Mondi Tohid, K. Rajeswari, and Jabari Kamran. 2014. "Empowerment of Women through Education in Twenty-First Century." ERIC Clearinghouse: ED 555571.

Shield, Rosemary White. 2009. "Identifying and Understanding Indigenous Cultural and Spiritual Strengths in the Higher Education Experience of Indigenous Women Utilizing a Culturally Intrinsic Research Paradigm Model." *Wicazo Sa Review 24*, no. 1: 47–63. https://www.jstor.org/stable/40587765.

Smith, Marcus T. 2013. "Fact Sheet: The State of Asian American Women in the United States." Center for American Progress. Accessed December, 2020. https:/

/www.americanprogress.org/issues/race/reports/2013/11/07/79182/fact-sheet-the-state-of-asian-american-women-in-the-united-states/.

Solomon, Barbara M. 1985. *In the Company of Educated Women: A History of Women and Higher Education in America*. New Haven and London: Yale University Press.

Soria, Krista and Alkire, Brandon. 2015. "Elevating Native American College Students' Sense of Belonging in Higher Education." ACPA College Student Education International. Accessed December, 2020. https://developments.myac pa.org/elevating-native-american-college-students-sense-of-belonging-in-higher-e ducation/.

Stromquist, Nelly P. 2011. "Social Cartography of Gender in Education: Visualizing Private and Public Spheres and Interconnecting Forces." *Beyond the Comparative* 173–192.

Sundaram, M. Shunmuga, M. Sekar, and Alagarsamy Subburaj. 2014. "Women Empowerment: Role of Education." *International Journal in Management and Social Science 2*, no. 12: 76–85.

Tembon, Mercy and Lucia Fort (Eds). 2008. *Girl's Education in the 21st Century: Gender Equality, Empowerment, and Economic Growth*. Washington, DC: The International Bank for Reconstruction and Development/The World Bank.

Toutant, Sarah M. 2017. "Underrepresentation of Black Women as College and University presidents." EdSurge Independent. Accessed December, 2020. https ://edsurgeindependent.com/underrepresentation-of-Black-women-as-college-and -university-presidents-10038d7e3325.

Waterman, Stephanie J., and Lorinda S. Lindley. 2013. "Cultural Strengths to Persevere: Native American Women in Higher Education." *NASPA Journal About Women in Higher Education 5*, no. 2: 139–165.

Watson, Jamal E. 2004. "Black Women in Higher Education." *New York Amsterdam News, 95*, no. 25: 4–49.

USAID—United States Agency for International Development (2008). "Education from a Gender Equality Perspective." UNGEI – United Nations Girl's Education Initiative. Accessed December, 2020. http://www.ungei.org/resources/1612_1926 .html.

Zamani, Eboni M. 2004. "African American Women in Higher Education." *New Direction for Student Services 2003*, no. 104: 5–13.

Chapter 2

African American Women's Pathway to Leadership Success

Resilience to Challenges Built on Mentoring and Spirituality

Vanessa P. Jackson and Julia R. Miller Arline

I have learned that success is to be measured not so much by the position that one has reached in life as by the obstacles overcome while trying to succeed.

—Booker T. Washington

INTRODUCTION

African American women are the least likely to hold a position of power in industry board rooms and academia. In 2014, women of color held only 3.2% of board seats among Fortune 500 companies, and more than two-thirds of Fortune 500 companies had no women of color as directors on their boards (Warner and Corley 2014). In 2020, there are no women of color reported as leaders of Fortune 500 companies (Hinchliffe 2020). Many still do not see women of color as a force in the U.S. economy. As they continue to generate $1 trillion as consumers, women of color are projected to make up the majority of all women by 2060, which means they'll also likely become the majority of the U.S. workforce (Pace 2018). While Black female professionals are more likely to seek top leadership roles, they are treated as virtually invisible (Purdie-Vaughn 2015). African American women leaders in the human sciences have experienced role incongruity as they seek to be successful leaders. Their untold historical contributions parallel the history of many of their ancestors who provided leadership in educational, political, and social movements (Miller, Mitstifer, and Vaughn 2009).

As African American women continue to be strong and powerful contributors to the human science profession, they face many challenges that differ from those that other women leaders face. Literature provides limited documentation of their challenges, or the methods they employ to sustain themselves as leaders.

This mixed-method study documents their struggles, methods of resiliency, and sustainability as leaders in the human sciences. This study was conducted in two parts: The first provides a content analysis of the types of leadership positions African American women hold at historically Black Colleges and Universities (HBCUs) and at predominantly White institutions (PWIs); the second consists of interviews with African American women who have contributed to success in teaching, research, and outreach/services in the human sciences.

This study explores and documents the challenges, struggles, and obstacles faced by African American women in human sciences leadership positions. It also describes the leadership styles they employ to be successful, along with the types of mentors they are able to access while climbing the leadership ladder. Spirituality is discussed as a method of sustainability for African American women in positions of leadership.

THE INTERSECTIONALITY OF RACISM, GENDER, AND LEADERSHIP

As women attempt to move up to leadership positions, they face barriers described as a glass ceiling, racism, sexism, a concrete wall, or sticky and labyrinth (Bell and Nkomo, 2001; Eagly and Carli 2007; Wingfield 2020). Branche (2014) quotes Warren Bennis (2009, 64): "Leaders, whatever their field, are made up as much of their experiences as their skills, like everyone else. Unlike everyone else, they use their experience rather than be used by it."

Many researchers have written about the intersectionality of race and gender on leadership success and how it provides privilege to some and marginality to others (Branche 2014; Engerman and Luster-Teasley 2017; Moorosi, Fuller, and Reilly 2018; Pratt-Clarke and Maes 2017; Tarr-Whelan 2011). Tarr-Whelan (2011) notes that "women have to push for their rights" and should expect to be scrutinized no matter how they behave. Pushing for rights is a daily challenge for African American women. The 2010 *Women Matter* study indicates that just 28% of companies surveyed by McKinsey cited "achieving gender diversity" among their top 10 priorities (Desveaux, Devillard and Sancier-Sultan 2010). Although White White women face issues in attempting to climb the leadership ladder, there are clear differences between the issues they face and those faced by African American women. Madden (2005) notes that the intersection of race with leadership leads to racial and sexual stereotyping, token status, inaccurate assessment of work productivity, and unrealistic expectations that mitigate attainment of higher-level positions. African American women also experience lower promotion rates, more occupational job segregation, pressures to modify gender and occupational roles, different predictors for advancement than African American men, early pressures to work, and negative career expectancies due to racism and sexism (Combs 2003).

Dovidio and Gaertner (2000) investigated differences over a 10-year period in Whites' self-reported racial prejudice and bias in selection decisions involving Black and White candidates for employment. Researchers report aversive racism, or subconscious feelings of prejudice, that alter how individuals relate to women and minorities, and whom they recommend for leadership roles in the business world. White men, who typically hold the highest positions of leadership, report more acceptance of White women than African American women (Golden 2002).

HOW HIGH UP THE LEADERSHIP LADDER WILL THEY LET US GO?

Administrative positions in higher education are divided into levels of authority and power. Twombly and Rosser (2002) identify these levels of power as executive, midlevel, and professional positions. Within the executive level are those with the highest level of power: presidents, chancellors, vice presidents, provosts, and deans. The second level of power in colleges and universities includes midlevel administrative positions such as directors, associate directors, and department chairs.

The last classification includes professional positions that have no designated power. This is where women are more highly represented. As stated by Tyson (2002), African American women in PWIs are most likely to be found in custodial and service-oriented assignments such as assistant or special assistant to the president or provost, director of minority affairs, affirmative action and compliance officer, human resource manager, and student affairs administrator. Tyson (2002) also indicates that women of color are prominent in administration at HBCUs while being less visible in these positions at PWIs.

LEADERSHIP STYLES OF WOMEN

Bass (1990) and Bass and Riggio (2006) wrote that transformational leadership (TL) occurs when leaders broaden and elevate the interests of their employees, when they generate awareness and acceptance of the group's purposes and mission, and when they stir employees to look beyond self-interest for the good of the group. Aryee, Walumbwa, Zhou, and Hartnell (2012) describe Transformational Leadership as a style of leader behavior by which the leader helps followers to exceed initial performance expectations by elevating their values, norms, and personal interests (e.g., from pursing stable employment to sharing expertise and knowledge to improve organizational effectiveness).

Yukl (2002) asserted that the transformational leader articulates the vision in a clear and appealing manner, explains how to attain the vision, acts confidently and optimistically, expresses confidence in followers, emphasizes values with symbolic actions, leads by example, and empowers followers to achieve the vision. This description is in line with Bass's components of TL. As reported in Zhu, Sosik, Riggio, and Yang (2012), transformational leaders display individualized consideration because they pay special attention to specific followers' needs for personal growth and achievement, then try to meet those needs and satisfy expectations for future development (Bass 1985). They are known to tie employee self-interest to the goals of the organization; to focus on relationships; to believe in persuasion; to encourage, motivate, and cooperate; and to use indirect communication styles (Winters 2012).

Eagly and Carli (2007) suggest that women are associated with communal qualities that convey concern for the compassionate treatment of others. They include being affectionate, helpful, friendly, kind, and sympathetic, as well as interpersonally sensitive, gentle, and soft-spoken. Kandalec and Robertson (2010) report that women in high-level leadership positions often apply a relationship style of leadership by empowering others and creating a consensus among subordinates. Cheung and Halpern (2010) report that women do not acknowledge their power when discussing their leadership styles; rather, women emphasize their ability to create consensus within the organization and to empower individuals. They are also more likely to promote team building (Cheung and Halpern 2010).

Despite possessing these desirable and beneficial leadership qualities, women continue to be undervalued as leaders—even by themselves. McGill (2014) explored the experiences of 10 African American female directors in North Carolina government. The researcher reported African American women lacked confidence and are not recognized and respected as leaders.

MENTORING AND LEADERSHIP DEVELOPMENT

Mentoring is "the process whereby a more experienced individual provides counsel, guidance, and assistance to another person and serves an essential function in helping younger or newer employees develop their leadership skills and advance within the organization" (Lanna-Lipton 2009).

Scholars have conducted research reporting the importance of mentorship in promoting leadership development. Lester, Hannah, Harms, Vogelgesang, and Avolio (2011) suggest that having a good mentor is essential to one's success as a leader. Allen et al. (2004) suggest that guidance and coaching provided by a superior/mentor helps subordinates to learn special skills that enhance competencies. Their study also suggests that a positive relationship between mentee and mentor creates a more efficacious worker who is confident in performing a job. Taking from their findings, a more efficacious person is likely to have a greater level of self-efficacy and leadership self-efficacy (LSE) in a leadership position.

As reported in Balkundi and Kilduff (2006), mentored individuals can reap rewards both in terms of their own personal performance and in terms of organizational unit performance (Sparrowe, Liden, Wayne, and Kraimer 2001). If an individual has access to a contact in the work world, that individual is supplied with a social network of friends, colleagues, and other contacts through whom the individual receives opportunities to use financial and human capital (Burt 1997).

Other studies affirm the importance of mentoring, particularly in the career development of women and minorities (Cox and Salsberry 2012; Touchton, Musil and Campbell 2008). Women and minorities, however, are found to have less access to influential mentors than their White male colleagues (Sandberg 2013). African American women are typically more isolated, without mentors or a network of support, and are less able to garner the help they might need when faced with extraordinary challenges (Haslam and Ryan 2008).

The social networks and mentors available to African American women are different from those of White women. Jackson and Miller (2014) reported social capital or networks for African American women primarily consisted of family members and fictive kin such as ministers, teachers, and family friends. Mentoring agents of this social network also included parents, grandmothers, siblings and other family members, fellow professionals, and teachers. These support groups can provide motivation to strive for success, but they may be limited in opening the network or organizational doors that lead to high efficacy, LSE, and upper mobility to leadership positions.

SPIRITUALITY AND LEADERSHIP SUSTAINABILITY

Spirituality can serve as a coping mechanism, promoting psychological resistance and fostering identity development (Watt 2003). Van Der Walt and De Klerk (2014) reported that there is a significant workplace correlation between personal spirituality and positive outcomes. Positive outcomes included performance (Thompson 2000) and emotional intelligence and self-efficacy (Hartsfield 2003). African American women often turn to spiritual beliefs to cope with the everyday struggles associated with living in a socially and politically oppressive system (Patton and McClure 2009). African American women also use their faith and spiritual grounding as a motivational force in their present leadership position in higher education (Sherman 2002). Sherman (2002) identified spirituality and spiritual advice as the fundamental weapon in the arsenal of African American women for surviving corporate culture.

In Jackson and Miller (2014), faith and spirituality were reported as methods of sustaining workplace resilience when African Americans struggled in their careers. The study also found that some human science leaders participated regularly in biblical text about the nature of the relationship between humans and God. The participants all had a deep faith in God and used their faith to overcome negative experiences in the education and work environments. Their faith in God helped to disrupt and resist oppression related to racism and enabled them to sustain resiliency.

Bacchus and Holley (2008) reported that African American professional women use spirituality as a coping mechanism to address stress resulting from "stained glass ceiling" effects of discrimination, denied opportunities, and exclusion from informal networks in the workplace. Spirituality for these women was not an escape mechanism but served as an effective coping mechanism for directly confronting the realities of their situations.

CONCEPTUAL FRAMEWORK

The role congruity theory of prejudice suggests that women leaders experience prejudice because people tend to perceive incongruity (or discrepancy) between the female gender role and the leader role (Eagly and Carli 2003; Eagly and Karau 2002). This discrepancy between the female gender role and the leader role is referred to as the role incongruity principle (Ritter and Yoder 2004).

Per the role congruity theory, prejudice arises from the relations that people perceive between the characteristics of members of a social group and the requirements of the social roles that group members occupy or aspire to (Eagly and Karau 2002). The theory suggests that women leaders experience prejudice because people tend to perceive incongruity (or discrepancy) between the female gender role and the leader role (Eagly and Carli 2003; Eagly and Karau 2002). This discrepancy between the female gender role and the leader role is referred to as the *role incongruity principle* (Ritter and Yoder 2004). Women are not considered to have certain leadership characteristics, while men are considered to have the characteristics of a leader. Therefore, gender-based stereotyping and discrimination contributes to defining men and women's ability to be leaders.

This study extends the theory of role congruity to include prejudice structured from attitudes, values, and norms of the general population. African American women are included in the stereotyping of women as potential leaders. However, they are further excluded as potential leaders because of prejudice built on the intersectionality of racism, gender biases, and stereotypes (Sanchez-Hucles and Davis 2010; Zacharakis and Flora 2005).

Incongruity leads to exclusion from potential positions for which women of color qualify, and if they make it into a position, they are excluded from networking, mentoring, and training privileges that are afforded to White women. Exclusion from networking and mentoring in a leadership position (or while seeking one) can lead to lower LSE. When women of color are not afforded the opportunity to build relationships through important networks and experienced mentors, their LSE may be negatively influenced.

Paglis and Stephen (2002) defined LSE as "a person's judgement that he or she can successfully exert leadership by setting a direction for the work group, building relationships with followers in order to gain commitment to goals, and working with them to overcome obstacles to change" (217). LSE enhances accomplishments as a leader, influences the ability to persevere when confronting obstacles as a leader, and can indicate how resilient a leader will be when faced with adverse situations. This confidence is expressed in positive outcomes in accomplishing a task. Professional mentors, particularly those who are privy to networks and professional development for African American leaders, can enhance this critical LSE.

RESEARCH METHODS

A qualitative assessment was conducted on the intersectionality of race, gender, and leadership positions among 10 African American women in the human sciences who held leadership positions. These women were identified and interviewed using the snowball effect. The snowball sampling may be defined as a technique of gathering research subjects through the identification of initial participants who provide names of other potential participants

(Lewis-Beck, Bryman and Liao 2004). These participants may themselves open possibilities for an expanding web of contact. The positions held by the participants were vice president (1), associate vice president (1), dean (1), interim dean (1), associate dean (1), director (2), assistant director (2), and department chair (1). The mean number of years of service in their position was 5.2, with a mean age of 66.5 years. Seven participants were employed at PWIs and three at HBCUs.

RESULTS

Participants were asked to indicate their negative experiences while in a leadership position, describe their leadership style, reflect on their mentoring resources, and describe methods used to sustain themselves in their leadership positions. Factors revealed negative experiences related to issues of acceptance as leaders, trust as a leader, being overlooked for positions of leadership, and selectivity as an African American.

Race, Gender, and Leadership Positions

The women in this study experienced a lack of acceptance by some White colleagues because they were African American, even though they were qualified for positions of leadership. Participants stated the following:

- White people would not accept an African American as a dean. The White people would walk pass our Black dean and not speak to her.
- "When I serve on search committees, I have to advocate for women. I have to really work on how to get my point across so that I do not seem like just an angry Black woman."
- "When we would conduct phone interviews of women and women from foreign countries, one of the men would say, 'I don't know, I don't think she would be a good fit.'"
- "When I push back on a decision, I am seen as an angry Black woman."
- "I have experienced sexism from both male and female supervisors."
- "The political atmosphere in the work environment prevents obtaining more leadership experience."
- "I have worked in environments characterized by hostility."
- "Clique behavior among women leaders has been very detrimental many times. You are in or out of the circle of favor therefore get the abuse."
- "PWI is where I worked. The Dean seemed to have felt threatened by me. When it was time for the department chair reviews, she gave me extra requirements in my portfolio. I asked the other department chairs if they

had to do these things and they said 'No.' I asked [the dean] why I had to do these things and she had no response."

African American women seem to also face lack of trust in their ability to be a leader. Comments expressive of this included:

- "Why do women need to be leaders?"
- "She is a woman, what does she know?"
- "They see me as a woman first and not a leader first."
- "The cleaning lady would stop by to talk to another Black person, and people from the office would start walking by us. Then my boss would walk by and look at me off and on. When we would be talking to each other and ask, 'What are you two talking about?' The next thing I know, they moved her to another building. Racism is alive and well today."
- "Four of us were standing outside the administration building talking. A White person passed by and said, 'My goodness, is this a coup?'"
- "A White man quit because he said there were too many Black people in the office and they (Blacks) did not know what they were doing."

Participants also observed White males and females moving through the ranks without problems, while they were skipped over for a position even when they had the qualifications. Sometimes their position was given to White women who were less qualified. Supportive statements of this experience were as follows:

- "A White person told me she caught the tail-end of an elevator conversation where two White women were saying the organization was 'not ready for a Black executive director.'"
- "I applied for a high-level position and they hired a WhiteWhite woman with less qualifications."
- "Just because White people like you does not mean they like all Black people."

Human Sciences Leadership Style Assessment

Leadership is a practice used to convince members of a workforce to accomplish goals established by a business. The process of enabling individuals and groups to accomplish a shared goal can be influenced by the leader's style. Participants in this study were asked to describe their leadership style, with results compiled based on TL categories developed by Bass and Riggio (2006). A new descriptive, empowerment, was also identified. Managers with *idealized influence* can be trusted to make good decisions for the organization. Some of the participants described their leadership style to include being honest as a leader and letting people know the reality of the situation.

Inspirational motivation (IM) describes managers who motivate associates to commit to the vision of the organization. Managers with IM encourage team spirit to reach goals of increased revenue and market growth for the organization. Some participants saw themselves as leaders who inspire workers by embracing change, creating and promoting a vision, being a forward-thinker, developing and using a strategic plan, seeing the big picture, and working backward to achieve goals.

Intellectual stimulation (IS) describes managers who encourage innovation and creativity by challenging the beliefs or views of a group. Manager's use IS to promote critical thinking and problem-solving to make the organization better. Some participants were categorized as IS-type leaders because they promoted the sharing of ideas, maximized skills by providing necessary training, provided training with love, and expected quality.

Individual consideration (IC) describes managers who act as coaches and advisors, so associates can reach goals that help both the associates and the organization. According to descriptions of their leadership styles, some study participants could be categorized as providing IC. Their leadership styles included nurturer of individuals, inclusiveness, importance of knowing how to treat people by learning about them, and helping people do their jobs by investing in them.

Empowerment is an added descriptive. Participants exhibiting this style reported that it is important to allow autonomy with high standards, to employ group decision-making, and to promote teams to create quality and provide people with what they need to do their job.

Mentoring

Mentoring was found to serve as a method of sustainability in leadership and as an enhancer of self-efficacy. Women of color use mentoring agents to create the resiliency necessary to stop interference with or disruption of goal achievement. Participants were asked to talk about their mentors before, during, and after college. Prior to college, some indicated high school teachers with good character served as motivators. Participants described precollege mentors as follows:

- "I adored their lifestyle and the way they dressed. So, I followed their way of doing things and they always gave me good advice. They taught me to dress properly and no cussing."

- "I was a poor farm girl and my parents were pro-education. They had no money to help us. My father would borrow against his land to help us out when we ran short."
- "Church members and my pastors serve as mentors prior to attending college."

Mentors during college were listed as parents, sister, faculty member, doctoral committee chair, and public relations persons. Participants described mentors/mentee relationships as follows:

> I was a first-generation college student. My parents wanted me to get an education. My father was my best mentor. Before I went off to college, he said to me, "No matter what happens, never let White folks see you sweat. If you do, they will take advantage of you."

Others indicated professors/faculty served as mentors for them while in college. One stated that a professor

> told our class to be forward thinkers, don't be afraid of anything; always be professional. Professional means, "Does, is, and looks like." The professor had rules: If the class started at 11, you needed to be in your seat 15 minutes prior to class or do not come to class, especially if you had not done the work. She never told anyone who was going to speak about a topic or oversee a project, so you better . . . be prepared.

One person who did not have a college mentor described a negative experience while trying to get her education:

> When I went to college, the college of education did not want Black people to be teachers. I had a low GPA, so they put me out of school. I did not even know it. So when I went to register, the lady pulled up my account and said, "Oh, you can't come back to school because you have to have a GPA of 2.5 or higher." Well, I had received the letter indicating the situation. But the letter said 2.0 and I had a GPA of higher than that. I showed the lady the letter and she said, "DAM." I changed my major and went on and I got my degree.

Once the participants completed college, some continued to have mentors while others did not. Those that did not have mentors expressed how they maintained resiliency while working in a leadership position.

- "I watched people to see what they did and encountered people who made a difference in their life."

- "A university president, provost, dean, pastor, men who worked at church, and a Black lady who was vice president of student life that acted as a mentor. A dean took me under his wing, mentored me, helped me move up, made me an associate dean, and provided input when I needed help."

Leadership Self-Efficacy

Leadership self-efficacy (LSE) deals with an individual's belief that he or she can successfully exercise leadership over a group. Some participants indicated they were confident in themselves and their leadership abilities. LSE seemed to build upon relationships with mentors. Examples of experiences that may have influenced participants' LSE included:

- "I knew that I had to do my job five times better than a White man. My confidence was seen as arrogance. I was over a major event and I asked this White lady to move some chairs. I went about my business doing other things. When I returned, I asked her, 'Didn't I ask you to move those chairs?' She said, 'Yes, but I am not doing that. Get some students to do it.' It literally messed up my day. But I never let on about it. When I got to my car and closed the door, I screamed and cursed like crazy. But no one ever knew how the situation influenced me."
- "I am very confident in myself, but sometimes when I am not taken seriously, I feel my confidence being attacked."
- "I doubt myself. Sometimes my confidence is questioned, but I know I am doing a good job."
- "I was fired . . . and this rocked my world and made me question myself. I started thinking about all the things I did. I helped people learn their jobs; I felt I was doing a good job. Others encouraged me that I was doing a good job. Then I found out it was very political. I could not make sense of the politics. But I began to get back to my old self."

Spirituality as a Method of Resiliency

In this study, faith and spirituality were reported as methods to sustain their resilience while surviving struggles throughout their lives and careers. Here, a most profound method of resiliency was their spiritual foundation. Participants expressed their ability to be resilient while facing struggles as a leader as follows:

- "Lots of prayer."
- "Stay prayed up all the time."
- "My God provides me a foundation."

- "I felt I had an obligation to do what is right, but it was really hard. I prayed and reflected on whether I wanted to maintain my character. So, I decided to treat others with respect even when others did not respect me."
- "Anything that is for me, I will be blessed to get it."
- "I am who I am because of God. I believe in 'Do unto to others as you would want them to do unto you.'"
- "I am very confident in my leadership abilities due to my strong faith in God."

DISCUSSION

It seems that times have not changed for African American women seeking and achieving leadership positions. In this study, we discuss how African American women in leadership positions still face barriers influenced by the intersectionality of race and gender that questions their ability as leaders. If you reflect on the experiences of those in this study, there was prejudice that took away the feelings of acceptance, there was no trust in their abilities as a leader and as an African American woman leader, and there was prejudice that closed the doors to networking and training for a leadership position.

They have experienced negative barriers due to prejudice created by societal norms. These barriers are the same as in the past, fueled by racial and gender stereotyping, token status, lower promotion rates, inaccurate assessment of work productivity, unrealistic expectations that mitigate against the attainment of higher-level positions (Madden 2005), and negative career expectancies due to racism and sexism (Branche 2014; Combs 2003; Dovidio and Gaertner 2000).

Who helped them to survive? These women continued to utilize external mentors such as their parents, professors, siblings, and ministers. Their mentors were persons who lacked any power to help open doors to networks and training needed to be successful as leaders in academia. However, mentors provided these women with words of affirmation that led them to sustainability in the workforce. These women have survived on their spiritual foundation and that of mentors who were often powerless in their ability to help them maneuver the barriers put before them.

Although some experiences seem bleak, those in this study use experience to guide them, not become them. Their descriptions of their leadership styles reflect the traits of transformational leaders. It is now clear that transformational leaders help an organization to achieve change. This study provides evidence of African American women being change agents in the human sciences. Who better to spearhead change than those who have endured the barriers and the feelings of oppression experienced during their careers?

African American women must continually examine themselves to position themselves as leaders of change.

They must set their mind and spirit to accomplish success. This begins with a continual assessment of their leadership style to determine if it fits the job requirements or if it needs to be adjusted. Many leaders become stagnant and refuse to enhance their abilities, then they cannot contribute to the success of others. Adaptation, learning, and growth can be achieved through outside leadership training, and through training programs provided by institutions and others. African American women must continue to enable themselves by seeking out mentors who are willing to help them. They must keep strong mentoring relationship with family members, pastors, and others. They must also watch others who are potential mentors to see how they carry themselves, to understand what kind of influence they have on upper administration, and to model how they work with others in their areas.

Lastly, as African American women, we are our own best critics when faced with barriers built upon the intersectionality of race and gender. We have times when our inner critic takes control of our self-efficacy and our LSE. That inner critic needs to be controlled. How you do it is up to you, but a solid Christian foundation followed by an acceptance of who you are will guide you down the right path to success. Times have not changed, but we have to change to be a force for those who come behind us. Once you are in the circle of successful leadership, it is not about you anymore, it is about those who come behind you. Therefore, when you feel you have reached your pinnacle of success, turn around and reach back and pull another sister up with you. Find people you can help, even if they are not in your field. That is the only way doors will be opened for others like you! As Morrison (1992) said, "Be Able, Be seen as Able, Know what you want, and help others!"

REFERENCES

Aryee, Samuel, Fred O. Walumbwa, Quin Zhou, and Chad A. Hartnell 2012. "Transformational Leadership, Innovative Behavior, and Task Performance: Test of Mediation and Moderation Processes." *Human Performance 25,* no. 1: 1–25. https://doi.org/10.1080/08959285.2011.631648.

Allen, Tammy D., Lillian T. Eby, Mark L. Poteet, Elizabeth Lentz, and Lizzette Lima. 2004. "Career Benefits Associated with Mentoring for Protégés: A Meta-Analysis." *Journal of Applied Psychology 89,* no. 1: 127.

Bass Bernard M. 1985. *Leadership and Performance Beyond Expectations.* New York: A Division of Macmillan.

Bass, Bernard. 1990. "From Transactional to Transformational Leadership: Learning to Share the Vision." *Organizational dynamics 18,* no. 3: 19–31.

Bass, Bernard., and Ronald E. Riggio. 2006. *Transformational Leadership*. Mahwah, New Jersey: LEA.

Bacchus, Denise N. A. and Lynn C. Holley. 2008. "Spirituality as a Coping Resource." *Journal of Ethnic and Cultural Diversity in Social Work 13*, no. 4: 65–84. https://doi.org/10.1300/J051v13n04_04.

Balkundi, Prasad, and Martin Kilduff. 2006. "The Ties that Lead: A Social Network Approach to Leadership." *The Leadership Quarterly 17*, no. 4: 419–439.

Bell Smith, Ella L. J., and Stella M. Nkomo. 2001. *Our Separate Ways: Black and White White Women and The Struggle for Professional Identity*. Boston: Harvard Business School Press.

Branche, Donovan. 2014. "Transformational Leadership and Resilience, African-American Women Nonprofit Leaders: A Mixed-Methods Study." PhD diss., James Madison University.

Burt, Ronald S. 1997. "The Contingent Value of Social Capital." *Administrative Science Quarterly 42*, no. 2: 339–365.

Cheung, Fanny M., and Diane F. Halpern. 2010. "Women at the Top: Powerful Leaders Define Success at Work + Family in a Culture of Gender." *American Psychologist 65*, no. 3: 182–193. https://doi.org/10.1037/a0017309.

Combs, Gwendolyn M. 2003. "The Duality of Race and Gender for Managerial African-American Women: Implications of Informal Social Networks on Career Advancement." *Human Resource Development Review 2*, no. 4: 385–405.

Cox, Kelline S. and Trudy Salsberry. 2012. "Motivational Factors Influencing Women's Decisions to Pursue Upper-Level Administrative Positions at Land Grant Institutions." *Advancing Women in Leadership 31*: 1–23.

Desveaux, Georges, Sandrine Devillard, and Sandra Sancier-Sultan. 2010. "Women at the Top of Corporations Making it Happen." McKinsey & Company. Accessed December 2020. https://www.mckinsey.com/business-functions/organization/our-insights/women-at-the-top-of-corporations-making-it-happen.

Dovidio, John F., and Samuel L. Gaertner. 2000. "Aversive Racism and Selection Decisions: 1989 and 1999." *Psychological Science 11*, no. 4: 315–319. https://doi.org/10.1111/1467-9280.00262.

Eagly, Alice H., and Linda L. Carli. 2003. "The Female Leadership Advantage: an Evaluation of the Evidence." *The Leadership Quarterly 14*, no. 6: 807–834. https://doi.org/10.1016/j.leaqua.2003.09.004.

Eagly, Alice H. and Linda L Carli. 2007. *Through the Labyrinth: The Truth About How Women Become Leaders*. Boston: Harvard Business Press.

Eagly, Alice H. and Steve J. Karau. 2002. "Role Congruity Theory of Prejudice Toward Female Leaders." *Psychological Review 109*, no. 3: 573.

Engerman, Kimarie, and Stephanie Luster-Teasley, 2017. *Women Called to Lead*. Santa Barbara, CA: Fielding University Press.

Golden, M. 2002. White White Women at Work. *Essence Magazine*. October, 190–198.

Hartsfield, Michael. 2003. "The Spirit of Transformational Leadership: Emotions or Cognition?" Paper presented at the Christian Business Faculty Association Conference.

Haslam, S. Alexander and Michelle K. Ryan, 2008. "The Road to the Glass Cliff: Differences in the Perceived Suitability of Men and Women for Leadership Positions in Succeeding and Failing Organizations." *The Leadership Quarterly 19,* no. 5: 530–546.

Hinchliffe, Emma. 2020. "A New Low for The Global 500: No Women of Color Run Businesses on This Year's List." Fortune. Accessed December 2020. https://mi micnews.com/a-new-low-for-the-global-500-no-women-of-color-run-businesses-o n-this-years-list.

Jackson, Vanessa P. and Julia R. Miller. 2014. "Getting and Staying in the Mainstream: African-American Women's Contributions to the Human Sciences." *Family and Consumer Sciences Research Journal 43,* no. 1: 78–91.

Kandalec, Patricia, and Robert W. Robertson. 2010. "Perspectives on Women in Leadership." *Ethics & Critical Thinking Journal* no. 4: 95–107.

Lanna-Lipton, L. 2009. "The Relationship Between Mentoring and Career Advancement of Millennial Generation Women in Leadership." PhD diss., University of Phoenix.

Lester, Paul B., Sean T. Hannah, Peter D. Harms, Gretchen R. Vogelgesang, and Bruce J. Avolio. 2011. "Mentoring Impact on Leader Efficacy Development: A Field Experiment." *Academy of Management Learning and Education 10,* no. 3: 409–429.

Lewis-Beck, Michael S., Alan Bryman, and Tim Futing Liao. 2004. "Snowball sampling." *The Encyclopedia of Social Science Research Methods.* http://dx.doi.org/10 .4135/9781412950589.n931.

Madden, Margaret E. 2005. "2004 Division 35 Presidential Address: Gender and Leadership in Higher Education." *Psychology of Women Quarterly 29,* no. 1: 3–14.

Patton, Lori D. and Michelle L. McClure, 2009. "Strength in the Spirit: A Qualitative Examination of African American College Women and the Role of Spirituality during College." *The Journal of Negro Education 78,* no. 1: 42–54.

McGill, Larrisha. 2014. "The Lived Experiences of African-American Female Directors in North Carolina Government." PhD diss., University of Phoenix.

Miller, Julia R., Dorothy I. Mitstifer, and Gladys Gary Vaughn. 2009. *African American Women: Contributions to the Human Sciences.* East Lansing, MI: Kappa Omicron Nu.

Moorosi, Pontso, Kay Fuller, and Elizabeth Reilly. 2018. "Leadership and Intersectionality: Constructions of Successful Leadership Among Black Women School Principals in Three Different Contexts." *Management in Education 32,* no. 4: 152–159. https://doi.org/10.1177/0892020618791006.

Pace, Cindy. 2018. "How Women of Color Get to Senior Management." Harvard Business Review. https://hbr.org/2018/08/how-women-of-color-get-to-senior-man agement.

Paglis, Laura L., and Stephen G. Green. 2002. "Leadership Self-Efficacy and Managers' Motivation for Leading Change." *Journal of Organizational Behavior 23,* no. 2: 215–235. https://doi.org/10.1002/job.137.

Pratt-Clarke, Menah and Johanna B. Maes. 2017. *Journeys of Social Justice: Women of Color Presidents in the Academy.* New York: Peter Lang.

Purdie-Vaughns, Valerie. 2015. "Why so Few Black Women are Senior Managers in 2015." Fortune. https://fortune.com/2015/04/22/Black-women-leadership-study/.

Ritter, Barbara. A., and Janice. D. Yoder. 2004. "Gender Differences in Leader Emergence Persist even for Dominant Women: An Updated Confirmation of Role Congruity Theory." *Psychology of Women Quarterly 28*, no. 3: 187–193. https://doi.org/10.1111/j.1471-6402.2004.00135.x.

Sanchez-Hucles, Janis V., and Donald D. Davis. 2010. "Women and Women of Color in Leadership: Complexity, Identity, and Intersectionality." *American Psychologist 65*, no. 3: 171. https://doi.org/10.1037/a0017459.

Sandberg, Sheryl. 2013. *Lean in: Women, Work, and the Will to Lead.* New York: Random House.

Sherman, Richard. 2002. "The Subjective Experience of Race And Gender in Qualitative Research." *American Behavioral Scientist 45*, no. 8: 1247–1253. https://doi.org/10.1177/00027642002045008008.

Sparrowe, Raymond T., Robert C. Liden, Sandy J. Wayne, and Maria L. Kraimer. 2001. "Social Networks and the Performance of Individuals And Groups." *Academy of Management Journal 44*, no. 2: 316–325. https://doi.org/10.5465/3069458.

Tarr-Whelan, Linda. 2009. *Women Lead the Way: Your Guide to Stepping up to Leadership and the Changing World.* San Francisco: Berrett-Koehler.

Thompson, William David. 2000. "Can You Train People to be Spiritual?" *Training and Development 54*, no. 12: 18–19.

Touchton, Judith G., Caryn McTighe Musil, and Kathryn Peltier Campbell. 2008. *A Measure of Equity: Women's Progress in Higher Education.* Association of American Colleges and Universities.

Twombly, S. B. and V. J. Rosser. 2002. "Women Administrators: Overview." *Women in Higher Education: An Encyclopedia*, 459–465.

Tyson, V.K. 2002. 'African-American Administrators." In *Women in Higher Education: An Encyclopedia*, edited by Alemán, Ana M. Martínez, Kristen A. Renn, and M. Elizabeth Tidball, 466–468. Santa Barbara, CA: ABC-CLIO.

Van der Walt, Freda, and Jeremias J. De Klerk. 2014. "Workplace Spirituality and Job Satisfaction." *International Review of Psychiatry 26*, no. 3: 379–389. https://doi.org/10.3109/09540261.2014.908826.

Warner, Judith, and Danielle Corley. 2014. "The Women's Leadership Gap: Women's Leadership by the Numbers." *Center for American Progress*, 1–7.

Watts, Sherry K. 2003. "Come to the River: Using Spirituality to Cope, Resist, and Develop Identity." In *Meeting the Needs of African-American women. New Directions for Student Services*, edited by Mary F. Howard-Hamilton , 29–40. San Francisco, CA: Jossey-Bass.

Wingfield, Adia Harvey. 2020. "Women Are Advancing in the Workplace, but Women of Color Still Lag Behind." The Book Institution. Accessed December 2020. https://www.brookings.edu/author/adia-harvey-wingfield/.

Winters, Mareisha. 2012. "Leadership Styles: Men Verses Women." Accessed December 2020. http://diversitynowbyegloballearning.blogspot.com/2012/08/leadership-styles-men-vs-women.html.

Yukl, Gary. A. 2002. *Leadership in Organizations.* Upper Saddle River, NJ: Prentice Hall.

Zacharakis, Jeff, and Jan Flora. 2005. "Riverside: A Case Study of Social Capital and Cultural Reproduction and Their Relationship to Leadership Development." *Adult Education Quarterly 55,* no. 4: 288–307.

Zhu, Weichun, John J. Sosik, Ronald E. Riggio, and Baiyin Yang. 2012. "Relationships between Transformational and Active Transactional Leadership and Followers' Organizational Identification: The Role of Psychological Empowerment." *Journal of Behavioral & Applied Management* 13, no. 3.

Chapter 3

Professional Working Women

A Qualitative Look at African American Mothers

Nina Lyon Bennett

INTRODUCTION

For many years, there have been increasing calls to understand the experiences of African American females from their own perspectives (Collins 2000; Giddings 1984). To fully understand African American female experiences in relation to motherhood, it is important to understand the context in which motherhood is defined for Black women. Historically, the characterization of black women has been basically depicted in terms of their maternal role, a defined role which has been imposed on women as their sole source of identity by the society in which they live (Ghasemi and Hajizadeh 2012). Black maternity has culturally and historically been mythologized and black mothers stereotyped because, as Barbara Christian asserted some 40 years ago, such idealized images have served as "a content for some other major dilemma or problem the society cannot solve" (Christian 1980). Not much has changed since Christian asserted this claim in her book, *Black Women Novelists: The Development of a Tradition*. Compared with other women in the United States, black women have always had the highest levels of labor market participation regardless of age, marital status, or presence of children at home. However, despite and in the face of discriminatory employer and government policies against black men and women, black mothers have always been more likely to be in the labor force compared with other mothers (Banks 2019). Black working mothers work more hours than their White and Hispanic counterparts, and are more likely to work, period (Wilson 2017). Contrarily, when looking at stay-at-home rates for Black mothers, according to Census data:

Black women were about half as likely as White women to be a stay-at-home mother," and ". . . married black women have always been employed outside of the home in large numbers, even following World War II, when many of their White counterparts had withdrawn from the labor force.

Additionally, "more than four in five Black mothers (3.0 million of 3.7 million women or 81.1 percent) are breadwinners, with most Black mothers (60.9 percent) raising families on their own. There are three times as many single Black mother breadwinners as married Black mother breadwinners" (Anderson 2016). With the large majority of U.S. mothers in the labor force and a steady decline in the real earnings of all workers over recent decades, families are increasingly relying on mothers' earnings for economic stability (Anderson 2016). Moreover, among White, Hispanic, and Black mothers with children under 18, a higher share of Black mothers are breadwinners than White or Hispanic mothers in every state across the United States (Anderson 2016).

Although there is continued interest in mothering and motherhood as subjects of scholarly inquiry, African American middle-class mothers remain understudied in family and gender studies research. Whereas numerous studies investigate the parenting strategies of low-income African American women living in socially disadvantaged neighborhoods, feminist sociological research on U.S. women's work and family decisions tends to focus on the experiences of White middle-class mothers (Dow 2019). Until now relatively little was known or written about the ideologies, experiences, and practices of African American middle-class mothers. The performance of middle-class Black womanhood includes a particular set of precepts that determine how Black women may construct or present themselves (Thompson 2009). This research aims to reconceptualize how race, class, gender, and motherhood are represented, performed, and lived for middle-class professional Black women. It explores the rich diversity of the motherhood experience for a group of professional, middle-aged Black women between the ages of 50 and 60. It explores how they define motherhood, their self-definitions and conceptions of themselves as mothers. It explores the meanings of motherhood by the women themselves and the impact of motherhood on their personal identities. This research indicates the importance of looking at the experiences of Black women on their own terms, not simply as part of a larger group of mothers, people of color, or as women. However, before reading their experiences in their own voice, it is important to understand the context from which Black mothers in general have been viewed.

MYTHS AND STEREOTYPES

The myths and stereotypes often used to characterize Black mothers have mostly focused on matriarchal figures, superbly strong and protective, and at the same time, selfless, all embracing, demanding nothing or little, and totally self-sacrificing creatures whose identities are inseparable from their nurturing services (Ghasemi and Hajizadeh 2012). These stereotypes about Black women—which include the Mammy, Jezebel, the Black Matriarch, the welfare mother, and the Sapphire (Bobo 1995; Collins 2000; West 1995)—highlight some important implications for black mothers. While space does not allow for an in-depth discussion about each of these stereotypes, it should be noted that "the first controlling image applied to U.S. black women is that of the mammy—the faithful, obedient domestic servant" (Collins 2015, 72). The mammy figure is typically presented as an older woman who is heavier set, has a dark complexion, and minimizes the needs of her family to be the loyal servant of the needs of her "superiors" (Ayee et al. 2019). The Sapphire was developed in the mid-twentieth century and represented the angry, nagging, emasculating black wife (West 1995). Sapphires are typically loud and verbally aggressive engaging in behavior that is typically seen as masculine (Thomas, Witherspoon and Speight 2004). A more recent typecast image of Black women is that of the Black Lady, who is a more modern mammy who did everything "right"; she went to school, earned her degree, started a career, and achieved professional success. The problem with the Black Lady is that she competes with men and drives them away and is therefore unable to be successful in her personal life (Collins 2000).

In their article "White House, Black Mother: Michelle Obama and the Politics of Motherhood as First Lady," Ayee et al. (2019) look at Michelle Obama's role as wife and first lady by critically examining how the model of motherhood she embraced and exhibited, a model firmly rooted in the African American community, was designed to challenge negative stereotypes of Black women, maternity, and families. Consciously or subconsciously, in her role as first lady, Michelle Obama made the institution of Black motherhood more transparent to those living in the United States and around the world. In so doing, she defied the long-standing dominant and oppressive stereotypes of black women and mothers while simultaneously redefining black motherhood and black families on the nation's most public stage (Ayee et al. 2019). Unfortunately, but not without surprise, perceptions of first lady Michelle Obama were deeply steeped in the context of the four dominant and oppressive stereotypes of black women in the United States mentioned above: mammy, matriarch, welfare queen, and sexual siren, Jezebel (Bobo 1995; Collins 2000). Although Obama countered the mammy image by being fiercely protective of her children and family (Brown 2012), disappointingly her "right to bear arms" became a point of discussion throughout her tenure as first lady (Ibanga 2009), and she was criticized on numerous occasions for exposing her arms when she wore sleeveless dresses, which was a further direct attempt to paint her as hypersexualized Jezebel as opposed to a respectable "lady" (Ajee et al. 2019). Michelle Obama also effectively challenged the stereotype of black women as welfare queens (Ajee et al. 2019), which is particularly pernicious because it places the blame of the nation's socioeconomic deterioration on black women. According to Ajee et al. (2019) the "'Welfare queen' is a phrase that describes economic dependency—the lack of a job and/or income." As the only first lady in history with two Ivy League degrees, Obama's educational attainment contrasts sharply with the image of the black welfare queen as uneducated and lazy. Moreover, having worked in corporate America as an attorney, and later in important administrative positions at both the University of Chicago and the University of Chicago Medical Center, Obama effectively challenged these negative stereotypes that are often ascribed to black women (Ajee et al. 2019).

The stereotypical images of black women are pervasive and popular and, as Emerson (2002) argues, the images are one-dimensional, ensuring that "black women are not represented in their full range of being" (123). Challenging these images and revising the concept of Black motherhood conflicts with the prevailing notion that tends to idealize motherhood and questions the social construction of matriarchy and maternity which often fails to perceive the identity and individuality of a mother apart from her child (Ghasemi and Hajizadeh 2012). Given that it is difficult for people to accept and respect those whom they view negatively, it is plausible that former first lady Michelle Obama increased the effectiveness of her messaging by countering these oppressive and controlling images through both her intentional presentation of self and her unrelenting work to ensure that she and other black women would be viewed more accurately (Ajee et al. 2019).

CHALLENGING NEGATIVE IMAGES
OF BLACK MOTHERHOOD

This research is particularly important because it focuses on an aspect of Black family life that is often devalued, misunderstood, and/or negatively portrayed. It challenges the standards by which Black mothers are measured, critiques the way in which Black women's stories are told, and sheds light on the experiences of black women who do not conform to popular stereotypical images of motherhood. This research places Black mothers at the center of analysis by taking an in-depth look at the experiences of a small group of Black middle-aged, middle-class professional African American mothers who have advanced degrees and successful careers in various fields and were willing to share their lived motherhood experiences of giving birth to and raising Black children in America. Unfortunately, Black women are held to slightly different standard and find themselves more often than not counteracting the negative labels placed on them from a myriad of sources.

Historical womanist theory, which situates Black women as a unique racialized and gendered laboring class in the United States, explores ways in which images of Black women's reproduction and parenting are manipulated in order to justify ongoing regulation and dominance of Black labor, particularly as it relates to biological, reproductive, and productive policies that disproportionately impact Black women in the United States. In a society where the evening news, TV sitcoms, and social media define motherhood, particularly for Black women, this discussion is relevant, timely, and an important part of the family discourse. Black motherhood has always been judged by the standards of the dominant Eurocentric ideology of motherhood (Ajee et al. 2019). As such, "motherhood in the United States is intersectional in nature and highly racialized" (Carew 2019, 144).

Ella Bell (2004) argues that myths and stereotypes about black women can flourish because there have been so few biographical accounts written about the lives of modern-day black women. The lives and experiences of Black women are incredibly rich and diverse, yet the media and popular culture continue to use the same stereotypes to tell the stories of Black women's lives (Fannin 2013). For example, of the many stereotypes that exist as controlling images in the public psyche, "the matriarch" or "angry black woman" is perhaps the one to which Michelle Obama was most often subjected because of her own esteemed legal career (Ajee et al. 2019). Obama was well aware that she was perceived as an angry black woman, and in her memoir, she shared some of the implications and dangers of such a stereotype. "I was female, black, and strong, which to certain people . . . translated only to 'angry'" (Obama 2018, 265). How we choose to see and listen to the ways in which Black women define motherhood speaks to how we view and analyze their experiences individually and collectively. Black women's reactions to motherhood and the ambivalence that many Black women feel about mothering reflect motherhood's contradictory nature (Ghasemi and Hajizadeh 2012).

For many Black mothers, work and familylife balance isn't a new concept. It was simply what you did. Stories of prior generations of Black mothers who worked outside the home are very similar to this:

After Emancipation, those black women fortunate enough to pursue higher education took advantage of the professional opportunities available to them. Many of these middle-class, college-educated women embodied the "lifting as we climb" motto coined by the National Association of Colored Women (NACW) in 1896. (Brevis 2012)

African American communities value motherhood, but the Black mothers' ability to cope with race, class, and gender oppression should not be confused with transcending those conditions. Black motherhood can be rewarding, but it can also extract high personal cost.

MEANINGS OF MOTHERHOOD

Motherhood is often presumed to be a largely personal and private matter. Disputed meanings of motherhood and family are central to some of the most hotly debated social and political issues in contemporary North America (McMahon 1995). Michelle Obama is a prime example. Although many people lauded her marriage to Barack Obama and acknowledged that she was a "good mother" to her daughters Malia and Sasha, she still faced immense public scrutiny and was discredited for her dedication to her husband and children (Ayee et al. 2019). Biological and psychological discourses are used to perpetuate the notion of motherhood and mothering as self-sacrificing and self-fulfilling acts (Mamabolo, Langa and Kiguwa 2009). The social constructionist perspective defines motherhood as a socially constructed identity whereby women are socialized into this role through pervasive discourses of biology and psychology (Burr 1995; Kruger 2006). Thus, motherhood, as a social construct, can therefore also change through social and political processes (Mamabolo, Langa and Kiguwa 2009). In many instances, these constructs are influenced by prevailing concept of "motherhood" as a practice and as an identity, making the assumption that motherhood is both natural and desirable; that having children is regarded as proper and the role of a 'good woman' "is rewarded by social approval and social acceptance" (Richardson 1993; Mamabolo, Langa and Kiguwa 2009).

For Black women, however, the notions of motherhood and womanhood as a socially constructed identity contribute to the stereotypical images that have come to define Black women's identities. Black motherhood has always been judged by the standards of the dominant Eurocentric ideology of motherhood (Ajee et al. 2019). However, black womanhood and mothering are grounded in, and informed by, African traditions of community-based child rearing and care: "Black motherhood consists of a series of constantly renegotiated relationships that African American women experience with one another, with black children, with the larger African-American community, and with self" (Collins 2005, 152). Black women in the United States have mothered differently than White women to ensure the survival of their own. The primary black family unit includes not only the nuclear family but also a collection of individuals who work to keep the family and community intact. This different conceptualization of motherhood has direct implications for the ways in which black American women develop their rhetoric and "perform maternity" to strengthen and protect their families and communities (Boris 1989; Carew 2019; Hayden 2017; Kahl 2009). Following the inauguration of President Barack Obama, Michelle Obama began characterizing herself as the "mom in chief." She described herself first and foremost as a mother to Malia and Sasha and was clear that her priority was to make sure that her young daughters settled happily and adjusted to their highly scrutinized life in the White House (Ajee et al. 2019). Some White feminists expressed negative reactions to Obama's decision to prioritize motherhood, which is part of a broader critique of prevailing ideologies that suggest that maternity is the primary and most important role that a woman should play (Hayden 2017, 12). Black feminists were quick to reject this type of criticism targeting Obama, pointing to the "progressive potential" of her persona and emphasizing that black women need to actively challenge oppressive stereotypes that suggest that the primary purpose in a Black woman's life is to reproduce (Hayden 2017, 12). Collins (1991) argues, "African American mothers place a strong emphasis on protection, either by trying to shield their daughters as long as possible from the penalties attached to their race, class, gender, status or by teaching them skills of independence and self-reliance so that they will be able to protect themselves" (126). Michelle Obama affirmed: "Is there anything more powerful than a mom?" (Doll 2012).

It is important therefore to critically examine the social and cultural constructions of motherhood and their meaning for Black women. Race, political history, gender, class, and motherhood are interconnected for women of color in general and Black women in particular. The life situations of Black mothers, depending on their socioeconomic status, are different from White mothers. This is not to say that the experiences are good or bad, better or worse. They are simply different. Although motherhood for all mothers is hard work, mothers' cultural and historical background as well as current environment affects their ability to mother and their style of mothering (Magwaza 2003). Also, beliefs and cultural constructions of motherhood have a bearing on how mothers' mother (Magwaza 2003). "Black motherhood as an institution is both dynamic and dialectical. An ongoing tension exists between efforts to mold the institution of Black motherhood to benefit systems of race, gender, and class oppression and efforts by African-American women to define and value our own experiences with motherhood" (Collins 2005, 152).

CONCEPTUALIZATIONS OF MOTHERHOOD

Conceptualizations of motherhood are to be understood not only as a socially defined and biological role but also as a social and cultural identity. Motherhood has different meanings for those who experience it, how they experience it, and even when or under what circumstances they experience it. Explorations of motherhood for Black women must take into account the historical-contextual perspective. Context is important and relevant to understanding Black motherhood because "one cannot understand contemporary patterns of Black family life without placing them in the broad historical, societal, and cultural context" (Billingsley 1992; Collins 1991; 2005). Claims about black motherhood, tied to philosophies of black respectability, had long been articulated by some of the most influential thinkers in the black American community, including Nannie Helen Burroughs, Anna Julia Cooper, Mary Church Terrell, Ida B. Wells, and Lucy Diggs Slowe (Ajee et al. 2019). The institution of Black motherhood, as Patricia Hill Collins (2005) notes,

> consists of a series of constantly renegotiated relationships that African-American women experience with . . . the larger African American community. . . . These relations occur in specific locations such as the individual households . . . as well as in Black community institutions. (151–52)

The narratives of the six mothers in this study are fundamentally unique. Common themes emerged in retelling their stories—themes that are useful in presenting the rich, thick descriptive data in a logical and concise manner. Each woman's story was carefully sifted and resifted for insights about how they think about their role as mother. Specific areas of interest guiding this process were (a) the decision to parent and the transition to motherhood; (b) how life changed as a result of motherhood; and (c) the meaning of motherhood as described by the women themselves. Other important areas of interest included self-identification, socialization toward motherhood, challenges of being a mother, unique challenges of being a Black mother, and the impact of relationship status at the time of pregnancy on a woman's feelings about becoming a mother.

RESEARCH METHODS

Six Black professional mothers were selected and interviewed for this study based on the following criteria: (1) self-identification as African American; (2) biological mother of at least two children; (3) at least 50 years of age;

(4) a minimum of a bachelor's degree; (5) working professional in a chosen field; and (6) self-identification as middle class based on education, occupation, and income (either personally and collectively with spouse). Sexual orientation or marital status were not factors considered for participation. Qualitative research methods were used to collect data, conduct interviews to gather in-depth insights about the mothering experiences of a small group of professional Black women, and generate new ideas for future research. The emphasis is on the validation of divergent versions of reality and intersubjective agreement between researchers, rather than on validity and a definitive version of reality (Angen 2000). As such, no claim is made of arriving at any universally valid statements regarding the experiences of motherhood among professional, middle-class, middle-aged Black women, but instead this research seeks only to present a credible picture (Angen 2000; Lincoln and Guba 1985) of the experiences of the women in this study.

Participants were selected using snowball sampling. Snowball sampling is where research participants recruit other participants for a test or study (Levin 2014). It is used where potential participants are hard to find. It is called snowball sampling because (in theory) once you have the ball rolling, it picks up more "snow" along the way and becomes larger and larger (Glen 2014). The initial invitation for participants was given at a Jack and Jill Athens Chapter meeting. Jack and Jill of America, Inc. is a membership organization of mothers with children ages 2–19, dedicated to nurturing future African American leaders by strengthening children through leadership development, volunteer service, philanthropic giving, and civic duty (https://www.jackandjillinc.org/).

MEET THE PARTICIPANTS

Six African American women participated in this study. Two have been married once, two have been divorced and are currently remarried, one has been married twice and divorced twice (and is currently not in a relationship), and one is a widow. All the women have at least two biological children and one woman is currently a foster mother to a developmentally challenged child. Two of the women each have two children, while the remaining four women each have three children. Each woman has at least one daughter and one son, making it easier for all the women to address the differences in raising sons and daughters and what it means to have "the talk" with their Black sons. The average age is 51.5 years, with an average of 17.5 years of education beyond high school. Four of the women are professional educators, with three of these women having college degrees in elementary

education or early childhood education. The fourth educator of the group
has a master's degree in business education and teaches high school business at a predominantly Black high school. One woman who holds an MBA
in finance is retired from a multinational telecommunications conglomer-
ate where she had a career in corporate administration. One woman has a
PhD and is an agricultural science researcher at a historically black college/
university. Each woman chose a pseudonym for this study. Each woman
was interviewed at least twice and open-ended questions were used. Each
participant was asked the same series of questions, with follow-up questions
based on information gathered during the initial 1-hour interview. All interviews were taped with the permission of each participant and transcribed by
the interviewer. Transcriptions were analyzed using narrative analysis and
coded based on emergent themes. Below is an introduction to each of the
women who participated in this study.

Rose—a Lena Horne look-alike—is a strikingly beautiful, elegant, and a
graceful 51-year-old woman. She was interviewed in her meticulously stylishly decorated home, at a round glass table fully decorated with placemats,
in her eat-in kitchen:

I'm 51 years old. I was born in Los Angeles, California. Lived there very,
very briefly. Grew up in the Midwest. Have been in Atlanta for more than 20
years and love the place. I think it's a wonderful place to raise a family. I did
my undergraduate at Southern Illinois University in English literature, which
I love, and my MBA in finance here at Georgia State University. Most of
my professional life has been in marketing with a major telecommunications
company doing new product development and market research and professional kinds of services like that. I have three children. My oldest son finished
Wharton and started out in the corporate world and then tried his own business.
Now he's gone back to the corporate world and soon will be working on his
master's degree. And he has a daughter. My second son finished Florida A&M
University in business also, and he joined his brother in a small business that
they had here in Atlanta. I was just so proud of that; that the two of them got
together to do that and they tried everything that they could to make it work in a
disadvantaged community. I was right in there with them from beginning to end
with that business. He is now working for a software development company in
Louisville. And then I have my daughter, Diane, who is 16 years old, a junior in
high school. That's my baby girl. She's the only one still at home, so, you know
in a year, I guess I'll be an empty nester. . . . My husband died of a massive
heart attack about three years ago and he and my daughter were very, very, very
close. So, it's been difficult for her. But I think that she has gotten herself pretty
much back on track now. So, I'm optimistic about her future as well. She's got
two great examples in her brothers.

Jackie is a brown-skinned, slender 50-year-old woman who has taken very good care of herself. She is athletically toned, very articulate, warm, inviting, and engaging. Her speech is purposeful, and she chooses her words very carefully. She is an educator by training. She was interviewed in the living room of her very airy, picturesque, old southern-style Atlanta home:

> I have two children. My daughter is 30, my son is 21, and I have a grandson who is 15 months old. I'm 50 years old and I grew up in Washington, D.C., so from kindergarten through high school, that's where I went to school. I have a bachelor's degree from Oglethorpe University here in Atlanta and a master's degree in elementary ed and physical education from Georgia State University, and I have a specialist degree in administrative and early childhood education from [Clark] Atlanta University. I work with children. I'm an educator. I teach school now.

Tessa is a short, pecan-brown woman with dyed blond/orange-colored hair, fluffy, and coiffed by the wind. She speaks quietly, slowly, and softly, often searching for just the right words not readily on her tongue. She was interviewed in a conference room on the college campus where she works:

> I'm from on the Eastern Shore of [Maryland], a little place called Jacksonville. . . . I'm 55 and I have three children: 21, 22, and 30. My experience as a child is totally different to the response as a mother today, because. . . . I had one brother who was older, and I virtually grew up by myself. My parents did not relate as parents. My mother, unfortunately, was dominating, and to get me set for motherhood I feel that I didn't have that experience from my mother. But I did get some mothering from my aunt, which I stayed with during the summer; the loving, the caring, the non-judgmental type of responses I received from her. The relationship between my parents was really stressed. My parents just did not get along. . . . Just before I finished high school my mother and father separated. So, between . . . 11 and 17 years old, there was a lot of stress, a lot of animosity, bickering, and hateful things. So, I was in quiet mode from about 11 because I was grieving for my aunt . . . to 17 when there was the divorce.

Yvonne is a tall, slender, fair-skinned 54-year-old woman with shortly cropped, neatly "Halle Berry-styled" hair. She was talkative, assertive, and assured, and was interviewed in the kitchen of her very large southern-styled home located in a suburban planned community in Athens, Georgia:

> I'm married to Russell Studivant, has a Ph.D. He's an educator and I'm an educator. We came from Pennsylvania, small suburb, south side of Philadelphia. I came from Yaden and he came from Glen Alden. We moved to Atlanta in

the early 1970s to attend graduate school. And we have two children that are young adults. One is in Atlanta and one is in New Orleans. . . . Nicole is 24 and Marc is 25. I'm . . . in school administration; assistant principal at Winterville Elementary School here in Clarke County. . . . I've been in education for 32 years . . . looking forward to retiring. I've taught in public school systems of Philadelphia and Dekalb County, and Clarke County. . . . My degree is in elementary education with a special education minor. I got started working on my first masters in Pennsylvania. And that was in library science, media, and communication. And then we moved south. They had a different set of rules here. They didn't have the same type of program. They had library science media, and I didn't want to really be a librarian . . . so then I switched majors and I went into elementary education for my master's degree. I got an add-on certificate in administration. . . . My family was unique in the fact that I'm a descendant of Richard Allen [founder of the African Methodist Episcopal Church].

Susan has a very quiet demeanor. She is a light-skinned, short, pleasingly plump, demure, and a reserved 50-year-old woman who was interviewed in the living room of her home in the Athens suburbs:

I'm Susan. I'm 50 years old and I have three children; a son that's 27, a daughter that's 22, and a daughter that's nine. I have a BS degree in elementary education and I've been teaching about 18 years. . . . This is home; Athens [Georgia] is my home. I'm a teacher, elementary. . . . I like working with the kids. I like kids. . . . I was the oldest and I had four brothers. My parents were real . . . they were very disciplined. Um . . . we grew up under a discipline, not a harsh discipline. My father, he would talk to us. My mom did the spanking. I probably was a smart person because it only took a couple of spankings, then I learned.

Carolyn is a tall, dark-skinned, deep-mahogany-colored woman whose locks are shoulder-length and stylishly adorned with cowry shells. She's a full-figured woman, very talkative, engaging, and warmly inviting. She was interviewed in her classroom at the professional development high school where she teaches business and keyboarding classes:

My name is Carolyn Jones. Jones is not my last name. My name is Carolyn Smith Cottman Jones. I chose to keep Jones because that was an identity with my son. I'm a mother, I'm grandmother of seven, I'm a teacher, a minister of music, and also a prophet. . . . My degree is in business education on the master's level, [with a] focus in business education. Graduated from the University of Maryland Eastern Shore. Graduate credits at University College and other schools in Baltimore, Maryland. I graduated from Washington High School in Princess Anne, Maryland, and attended Somerset High School the last year of segregation in Somerset County, and was in the first graduating class of the integrated system in Somerset County [Maryland].

Carolyn has three children two girls and one boy. She was married twice and divorced twice. When asked how long she was married, she replies, "If you put the two marriages together, uhh . . . let's say eight."

The self-introductions provide important salient identifiers. For example, Rose begins by laying out a geographic map of her upbringing and the significance of location for raising a family. On the other hand, Yvonne establishes her relationship status by stating she is married and to whom she is married. Her statement begins with identifying her husband and his credentials. She identifies herself and her husband as "educators." She then tells where both she and her husband are from. She concludes her statement by establishing her family roots and a family identity as a descendent of Richard Allen.

Richard Allen (The Internet African American History Challenge. n.d.) founded the African Methodist Episcopal Church and the Free African Society. He was born a slave in Philadelphia and with his family was sold to Stockley Sturgis, the owner of a plantation near Dover, Delaware. Richard Allen, along with 11 other members, was committed to the principles of Methodism and formed the Bethel African Church. On April 11, 1816, Richard Allen was named the first bishop of this church. This connection is important for Yvonne and lays the foundation for understanding her self-conception as a Black woman and Black mother.

Jackie begins the conversation describing her children and immediately establishes her role of mother as an important one. Like Yvonne, her profession is a part of how she defines herself. She too labels herself as an educator. As both of their narratives reveal, their role as mother influences their profession. Rose, Tessa, and Yvonne all lay a foundation for better understanding their narratives by providing historical context and geographical roots.

Tessa, unlike the others, states that her "experience as a child is totally different to the response as a mother today, because. . . . I had one brother who was older, and I virtually grew up by myself." She goes on to share about her volatile family background and the relationship she had with her aunt, with whom she stayed during the summer, and who provided her with a positive model of motherhood. As her narrative reveals, when her aunt passed away, she silenced herself for six years and spent it grieving the loss of her aunt. Her early experiences were painful ones, characterized by "a lot stress, a lot of animosity, bickering, and hateful things."

Carolyn and Susan begin by describing themselves first. Susan states her name, age, then how many children she has and their ages. She speaks about her educational background, profession, and her love of children. Carolyn clearly establishes who she is by stating the relevance of her name and why she has chosen to keep it. She makes it clear that keeping her last name was a choice made consciously to maintain a connection with her son, not about a husband to whom she is no longer married.

These seemingly unimportant statements are significant revelations about what is most salient in how each of these six women consciously or unconsciously choose to identify themselves. Their statements offer powerful indicators and descriptors, which offer some insight into how they define motherhood and themselves. In the following section, the women offer their thoughts on the meaning of motherhood. Each woman was asked the same question, "How do you define motherhood?" Their responses to this question are presented below.

MEANINGS OF MOTHERHOOD

There is no one definition of motherhood. That is, there is no sole connotation or unified experience of motherhood (McMahon 1995) and no single emotion that children inspire in their mothers (Arendell 1999). Rather, motherhood is an accumulation of so many things. It is a combination of raw emotions, experiences, hopes, and dreams. Because there is no single meaning or given experience of motherhood, becoming a mother changes a woman's life and roles perhaps more than any other single event (Lutz and Hock 2002). As Arendell (1999) notes, "mothering is neither a unitary experience for individual women nor experienced similarly by all women" (1196). Motherhood may be a font of personal fulfillment, pleasure, love, pride, contentment, and joy (Arendell 1999) while simultaneously being a realm of distress, helplessness, frustration, hostility, and disappointment, as well as an arena of oppression and subordination (Donath 2014). The women in this study define motherhood in terms of their own situated but interactive relationship with their social worlds, and the material and cultural resources available to them (McMahon 1995). Their answers reflect their own personal experiences of motherhood and include common descriptors such as "biological," "loving," "instinct," "nurturing," "patient," "spiritual," "role model," "kind," "challenging," "responsible," and "supportive."

For example, Rose states:

> When it comes to my definition of mother, I think of my grandmother and my mother. . . . I admire so much about my grandmother and so much about my mother that I try to aspire to portions of their character and their way of doing things. . . . My grandmother was strict, stern, disciplinarian, somewhat controlling . . . my grandmother, as grandmothers will do, was always very affectionate, patient. I can't remember ever hearing her raise her voice.

She goes on to say that motherhood is

nurturing, guiding gently, loving unconditionally, and what that really says is
that mothering can be done by either a mother or a father. And that it can be
done by someone who is not necessarily of blood relation. I think it also means
saying no when you need to say no . . . there was some discussion recently about
some kids . . . the parents were working long hours to give the kids everything
that they could possibly need materially, but not enough time and not enough
guidance, not enough limitations being placed on them, not enough discipline.
No consequences for their actions. So, from my perspective, they may be legally
mothering those children but in reality, the children are not getting what they
need. They're probably getting a lot of what they want but not what they need.
So, I think that that is a distinction that's important. That it's not just a biological connect; it's not just a physical proximity; it's not simply providing for. It's
more than that. It's a lot more demanding than maybe a lot of people appreciate
and it's an ongoing process.

Carolyn agrees that mothering is not just about biology but is a role that
can be performed by either a mother or a father. She states:

Motherhood does not necessarily mean biological, but one who has the nurturing instinct knows the value of an individual that is sent to this earth, the
purpose of destiny, and being able to protect that individual and challenge that
individual in the right direction. Nurturing includes clothing and shelter, but also
understanding the spiritual aspect of every individual that comes through your
life, and then looking for spiritual help to help that individual develop into the
person that God would have them to be.

Yvonne, the descendent of Richard Allen, states:

Motherhood to me is just such a spiritual experience. I guess from the first
day of conception in the womb now that you're carrying the life of someone
else, you start to put your own life in order. And . . . you think and you raise a
child, you're just . . . you want the best for a child. You want to make sure that
they make the correct choices and do service to people. So, you sort of know
that you're going to be that model and you're going to be there to reinforce, to
relieve things. So, to me I think that was the best experience that I ever had . . .
have had, and that was becoming a mother. I think it made me have a different
perspective in my job. As I looked at other people's children, I saw them from
the perspective of being a mother. . . . So I think it [motherhood] opened up
many doors. . . . It just made me change the way I thought about certain things.
I just love my children. I like being a mother. Even now my role is different
because now I'm more of a listener and give advice when asked for it.

Carolyn, who is a minister of music, says:

I guess motherhood is sort of like . . . it's kind of a love. It's a bond that sort of
grows apart. Not that you love each other less, but you grow apart from each
other. You're preparing that child to go off and be independent.

Susan responded to the question by saying:

Motherhood . . . entails a lot. For me, some of it is instinct, I think. They're just
some things that I do, not knowing. I can hear them if they cry, move or. . . .
And its busy making sure that I'm making them comfortable. Also giving them
some guidance of being independent; teaching them how to do things for themselves rather than depending on me. So, I guess I work with their emotions, and
spiritual, and educational, molding and trying to set an example.

Jackie stated:

That's a pretty broad question. Well initially you think of the biological aspect
of motherhood, carrying and bearing children. And then you think of a lot of
other things. I think of motherhood as being supportive of my children; being
a support system, being a counselor for my children, being a friend to my children. . . . I reflect on when they grew up; when they were growing up and I think
about being concerned about what they were doing and what they were involved
in; nurturing them and caring for them and just being here for them. I think of
being . . . someone who is bonded in some way—in a very special, loving, caring way to another person that you can't be bonded to—to anyone else.

Tessa very simply and matter-of-factly says:

Motherhood means to me a sense of responsibility, of caring, loving, and a role
model for my children. Motherhood is biological or can be through adoption. To
me mothering is being a loving, supportive person.

Like Jackie, Tessa explains motherhood from a biological perspective, but
her answer is brief, direct, succinct, and straight to the point. As a researcher,
this gave me reason for pause. In other words, it isn't so much what she does
say that poses a challenge, it's what she doesn't say (and why) that piques my
curiosity. Do I need to dig deeper, probe more? I wondered if there is more to
her answer than the simplistic, to-the-point answer she provided. Is there more
below the surface that may be influencing how she answered the question?
Three short sentences compared to the somewhat lengthy answers provided by
the other women. Perhaps the short answer doesn't mean anything and can be

attributed to her personality or the fact she is a researcher. Maybe there is more to it. Perhaps a clue to addressing the why may be found in her introduction. Tessa discusses how volatile her family life was as a child. She states:

> I virtually grew up by myself My parents did not relate as parents. My mother unfortunately was dominating, and to get me set for motherhood I feel that I didn't have that experience from my mother. But I did get some mothering from my aunt, which I stayed with over the summer; the loving, the caring, the non-judgmental type of responses I received from her.

It is in this statement about herself that we might find clues to her definition of motherhood. Unlike the other women, Tessa in her introduction describes her family life as a child. She does not mention her relationship status as Yvonne and Carolyn do. However, there is one word that stands out in her statement, "nonjudgmental." In interviewing Tessa, I found her to be quite reserved. The interview process was somewhat strained—almost a forced conversation. She was very careful about what she said. Tessa tended not to elaborate on her answers; she simply answered the questions asked and did not offer any additional information; neither did she give any details, context, or a "back story" for her answers as many of the other women did. She simply answered the questioned asked, offering nothing more. Perhaps her early family experiences and the feeling of constantly being dominated and judged by her mother may have influenced how she mothered and how she defines motherhood.

Rose defined motherhood based on images she received as a child from both her mother and her grandmother. She mentioned the importance of unconditional love, which is quite a contrast to Tessa's experience with a judgmental, controlling mother. Rose stated:

> I think the unconditional love is very important. I think a child needs to know . . . that no matter what there will be this person who is going to love you. I mean . . . you could be a murderer on death row, but your mother is the one that you can count on to be there for you on earth . . . your best friend; this is the person who you can count on absolutely to do whatever is required. This is one person you can count on who will be there for you. So unconditional love I think is a big part of it. But then there is the tender part of being a mother as well. The nurturing part; the one that's gonna' rub your back when you don't feel well. The one who's going to hold you when you're sad. Be there for you emotionally. The love, the support, the affection. It's a real giving kind of love that mothers do, I think. It's very self-sacrificing.

Rose's childhood experiences growing up with both her mother and grandmother influenced her definition of motherhood and may provide the basis for her image of a mother. Like Rose, Tessa's childhood experiences influenced her definition of motherhood.

From the answers provided by these six very diverse women, we learn that motherhood is about being—being an example for your children to emulate. It is also about responsibility, nurturance, care, love, and consequences. Motherhood is also about doing, as evidenced by the answers given by the women to the question, "How do you define motherhood?" It is both an identity and a role they perform. It's about behaviors that demonstrate unconditional love, acceptance, and nurturing. For example, Rose states:

> The mother's role is very important in nurturing the child to be self-confident and independent and to be able to face issues and challenges. And respond in a way that lets you know that they at least thought through the situation.

Motherhood is demanding. It is an ongoing process of change, not only in terms of the relationship between mother and child but also in terms of the changes experienced by the woman herself and the ongoing relationships she may have with others. Motherhood is dialectic, reflecting both a biological and spiritual experience, as Carolyn and Yvonne point out. Motherhood is, as Yvonne stated, about putting "your life in order." Motherhood is a sacrifice; "a giving of one's self." Motherhood is

> a spirit of love, something that's inside that would make you kill if you had to defend them. . . . It's just a special kind of love. It's the kind of love that I'd be willing to sacrifice everything for . . . when they are a young child. As an adult, I would sacrifice things for my child if they needed it. And if I had to give them any part of me that they needed, I would. . . . It's something I wouldn't trade for anything in the world.

For several of the women, however, motherhood is more than biological. Rose, for example, stated

> It's not just a biological connect; it's not just a physical proximity; it's not simply providing for. It's more than that. It's a lot more demanding than maybe a lot of people appreciate and it's an ongoing process. Mothering is not just limited to women. It's not simply a matter of biology or being a woman who has given birth. Mothering encompasses actions, behaviors, and ways of thinking, doing, and being.

TRANSITION TO MOTHERHOOD

The transition to motherhood begins antenatally and is one of life's more complex and challenging transitions. For many women, motherhood may or may not be a welcome transition. It involves taking on new roles and entering new relationships. These new roles and emerging relationships represent some of the greatest changes and challenges women may experience in their lives. Several factors may influence whether motherhood is a welcome transition, including timing in the life cycle, relationship status at the time of pregnancy, the response of others, and preconceived ideas about marriage and family. Other factors may include the life circumstances of the parents, the social environment, and the circumstances of conception. It is also influenced by the level of support provided by the woman's partner and family, as well as the physical health of the mother and her unborn baby, her past or current mental health issues and any current or unresolved conflict, loss or trauma can also affect, and sometimes disrupt, this transition (Mares, Newman and Warren, 2011; Symes 2017).

Tessa describes her feelings about becoming a parent:

Well, it was excitement, because I had lost my first child . . . it was a miscarriage . . . my husband wasn't as happy as I was because that's not what he wanted. When we were going together . . . his intentions were very different from mine. We did get married and then I was pregnant. I think he wanted children, but not at that time.

Carolyn says:

I was ecstatic, because of the limited experience and knowledge of really what was available to me, really the only thing that I thought was necessary to be successful was to be married and then after you married, to get pregnant and then have a baby. So that's what I planned to do, get married and then have a baby. . . . So, in my first pregnancy, I was ecstatic. I was just excited because I wanted to be pregnant, and I wanted to have a baby. My husband, he was excited.

Yvonne was also "very excited." She stated:

When I became pregnant it was grand and it was great, and I enjoyed it . . . there was a different kind of emotion there. But I was extremely excited. Seems like from the very first moment I knew I was pregnant I started talking to the baby and just saying little things. . . . I guess that was the best. . . . I think that was the grandest feeling I've ever had was the fact I was pregnant; that I was going to raise a child . . . this child was a part of me and a part of my husband. And it came out of a bond of love.

However, not all women reported being excited or feeling ecstatic about becoming a mother. For some women, their relationship status may impact or influence how they feel about motherhood. It was Adrienne Rich (1976) who expressed this conjunction of deprivations and abundances so profoundly: "My children cause me the most exquisite suffering of which I have any experience. It is the suffering of ambivalence: the murderous alternation between bitter resentment and raw-edged nerves, and blissful gratification and tenderness" (21). Yet while it has been well acknowledged that the landscape of mothering may be replete with dialectical tensions (Arendell 1999), there has been little recognition that these tensions may lead women to foreground an emotive and cognitive stance of regret toward their motherhood. In mainstream and media discourse, this stance of regretting the transition from being a nonmother, and the wish to undo motherhood, tends to be seen as an abject maternal experience and an object of disbelief (Donath 2015).

Two mothers share very different accounts about becoming mothers. Rose, the Lena Horne look-alike, shares her experience:

> I was devastated. I was devastated because I was not married yet. My husband and I started dating when I was 15. He was my first date and then I had my second date with him when I was 16. . . . I was a virgin until I was 18. . . . I had to interrupt my schooling to get married . . . so it was traumatic for him and for me. . . . I felt I had let my mother down, embarrassed everybody, including myself. . . . My father was furious beyond words. Literally, I mean he would not speak [to me]. So, it was difficult, very difficult in the early years of our marriage . . . in my first motherhood experience.

Motherhood itself is rarely associated with regret, and the potential presence of regret is disregarded. Women considering motherhood do not have to reckon with discourses that intimidate them with future regret if they become mothers (Morell 1994), since maternal experience is institutionalized as a rewarding and worthwhile experience despite the difficulties, come what may (Donath 2015).

Historical and cultural context is important in understanding what it means to be pregnant and not married. For some women, the transition to motherhood was not initially an exciting time. Jackie shares here perspective.

> Well I wasn't married initially. So, I was scared, of course. I felt like I should have been married 'cause that had been drilled into me all along. I wanted to be married. You feel a little lonely and depressed, along with being scared, but I think the fact that I had to nourish this child and care for this child and find out so much about taking care of this child overwhelmed that aspect. I felt scared, depressed, and lonely. I was sorry I wasn't married, but I didn't dwell on it a lot. As time went on, I felt it was just a wonderful feeling to feel . . . life inside your body. That's just indescribable. And then I felt, wow, I have to do a lot because I am going to have

to teach this baby lots of things. . . . What I remember feeling is a special feeling. I loved the attention that I got. You get a lot of attention when you're pregnant. . . . It was a good feeling. Of course, I told the dad first and we talked about options and choices. . . . I was away at school. . . . I remember being really concerned about missing school and when I'd get back to school to finish my degree.

Inundated with images of motherhood and messages about the appropriate circumstances under which to create a family, many women, as Jackie and Rose did, find themselves in situations that contradict the images, values, and personal ideas they have about motherhood and that society has about them. The marriage-and-motherhood imperative was reinforced by severe social and religious sanctions. Indeed, social mores at the time provided little latitude in gender roles (Barnett and Hyde 2001).

Although times have changed and society has become more tolerant of nontraditional family roles, Black women receive subtle but very potent messages from parents, significant others, media, and mainstream society about what it means to be a Black woman and a mother. Sometimes these messages are contrary to the meanings Black women define for themselves. Consider Michelle Obama. Graceful, elegant, intelligent, empowered, and confident, yet challenged by her critics in various media outlets about what it means to be the First Lady of the United States. The first Lady made choices of sleeves or no sleeves; baring shoulders, showing arms; giving her husband a fist bump; and bangs or no bangs. At times, she was even characterized as an "angry Black woman." Depending on who is doing the analyses, sometimes insignificant, meaningless actions can somehow take on very different meanings for Black women. Unfortunately, "these counter-opinions threaten to attack the new self-perceptions" and many Black mothers, in light of limited social support, may not "possess the ability to combat these external voices" (Cooper 1990, 31).

Although times have changed, how much have our attitudes changed about Black women, motherhood, single mothers, and absent fathers? To what extent do we place the character of Black mothers on trial when we microscopically examine the inner sanctums of their mothering experiences and the circumstances under which they become mothers?

Jackie stated:

I grew up with the Cinderella complex. You know, find Mr. Right and he's Prince Charming and he'll marry you and you'll have this big, gorgeous home. And you'll be able to stay at home and raise your kids. That's when you have a baby.

Rose received a very similar message. She was socialized to understand the value of being married *before* getting pregnant:

[It was] my upbringing; my parents. I was concerned about being able to give a proper home and upbringing to my child. I was concerned about what I was doing to my own life and what I was doing to the life of my soon to-be-husband. It wasn't what was supposed to happen. I guess in my mind I was going to have children much later in my life and by that time, I would have been a woman. I didn't feel that I was a woman yet. I felt I was still a girl; that I was still a college student and there was so much that I didn't know. I knew I didn't know; that I just didn't feel prepared to handle it. I wasn't sure I even wanted to have children. . . . I didn't feel emotionally ready. I didn't feel that I had the information or the emotional readiness to deal with that. . . . I remember feeling just kind of in a state of shock; just lost and afraid.

For these two women and perhaps countless others, conformity to social norms and roles for African American women plays a significant role in how they perceive themselves and how society perceives them. In twenty-first-century America, how much has changed?

Carolyn's story represents a powerful dichotomy. It represents the need to be loved and to belong, and the need for family formation as a means of validation. At the same time, her decisions, she admits, were careless and represented a lack of concern for herself or for her daughters. Carolyn stated it did not matter if she was in a happy situation (i.e., relationship) or not, she needed to have a family. When asked why having a family was so important, she stated:

I was the product of a broken home, mother and father divorced when we were. . . . I guess I was in the sixth grade and my sister was in the fifth grade and we had a baby sister that may have been in the second grade. Watching my absent father and feeling the rejection and resistance of a mother to little girls, I vowed that my children would never have to go through a situation like that, no matter what I had to go through.

Carolyn's statement reflects the powerful impact of childhood experiences on adult decisions. It demonstrates how inner vows made as children or teens manifest themselves in our adult lives. Her statement also reflects how important socialization is to the survival of positively functioning families. How women are socialized can have a significant impact on their decisions as women and as mothers. It also influences those unspoken inner vows women make to themselves to never repeat the dysfunction of their own families.

Susan's story represented a different scenario from the other five women. When asked about how she felt about conceiving her first child, she smiled a very broad smile and simply says, "ah yes, I remember. I felt real special." However, the birth of her second child is what presented a challenge for her.

Her second child was not planned. As a matter of fact, she and her husband thought they were done having children and had planned to purchase a Corvette.

> At the time, my husband and I were buying a Corvette. He was going to Atlanta; that was the day I found out [I was pregnant]. He was going to Atlanta and he was getting a Corvette. His dream car. He tried it out. . . . I wasn't excited about it because being short, I really couldn't drive it. The accelerator was too far down. And while we were there, I said, "The doctor said it was positive." And he was kind of laughing and looking, saying yeah, yeah, because then he knew he couldn't get that two-seater. So, after that we decided on not really a family car, but a larger car.

She described her first-time mothering experience as "special but scary." When asked why it was special but scary, she replied that it was

> an experience that I had never had carrying a baby. Being a mother; thinking about the responsibility. There's a difference when you raise your . . . brothers and sisters . . . your mother's children, but when it's yours, all that responsibility lies with you.

Susan was 40 years old when her youngest daughter was born. When asked about the birth of her daughter, she became teary-eyed and somewhat emotional as she recalled her experience. She said her third child was a surprise. There is a 13-year difference between her second child and her third. Not only was she totally unprepared, but she didn't think she could have any more children. Getting pregnant for a third time was not an idea that she even entertained. As far as she was concerned, her childbearing days were over. Her two older children were young adults living on their own. She had great concern about raising a child later in life.

> I knew when my other two. . . I just knew when it happened, but with her I had no intentions; no desire. I guess I was questioning God as to why me, why this, but sometimes He has a way; that was His gift to me because she really keeps me young. Keeps me happy. I keep up probably with what's going on in the young people's world more rather than getting set in my ways and not seeing the whole picture. . . . She keeps me active and involved. So that's been a plus.

Susan was facing a dilemma that many women who wait to have children face. Her identity as a woman was being challenged by the fact that she was about to reenter a stage in her life she had left 13 years earlier. With a baby on the way at age 40, she would have to change and restructure her life, and redefine or rethink how she defines herself. Instead of getting ready to become a grandmother, she entering motherhood . . . again. She had questions. Do you parent the same way you did when you were in your late 20s? Would society deem her too old to become a mother . . . again? Pregnancy and birth can be a period of intense reorganization of identity, leading to reflections on the way the woman herself was parented (Symes 2017).

The most important task any woman can undergo is the process of identity formation. Female identity formation is critical to the female individual because the way in which she defines herself and what she bases her sense of self upon will ultimately serve as the foundation for her life (Marcelin 2012). The interaction between the identity development process and having to deal with contradicting perceptions of female gender roles within the American culture and the culture of their heritage can best be understood within the assimilist and ethnic pluralist perspectives, respectively, because "in real life, ethnic/racial or cultural identity and gender are not separable, but intersect and influence each other" (Goodenow and Espin 2003). Crenshaw (2011) noted that explorations of race and gender (female identity) tend to be addressed as two distinct experiences and identities. Yet, when discussing issues affecting Black women, including identity development, an intersectional approach is most appropriate for examining the unfolding complexities of Black womanhood. Crenshaw (2011) explained that there is a "multi-dimensionality of black women's experience[s] and single-axis analysis [erases black women theoretically" (25). Crenshaw (2011) urges us therefore to reconsider the ways we have framed our ideas on racial and female identity development, as we currently assume that their experiences one-dimensional. Unfortunately, the preponderance of theoretical literature compartmentalizes identity development; however, in order to obtain clarity on the lived experiences of Black women, these perspectives should be consolidated, creating a single lens that reflects multiple identities (Patterson 2016). The experiences of Black mothers are not monolithic. The range of Black women's reactions to motherhood and the ambivalence that many Black women feel about mothering reflect motherhood's contradictory nature (Ghasemi and Hajizadeh 2012).

UNIQUE CHALLENGES AND RESPONSIBILITIES OF BEING A BLACK MOTHER

The importance of Black women's role in the socialization of their children cannot be underestimated. The family is the first and probably most important socializing agent. It is in the family that children learn about gender roles, about parenting, about responsibility, acceptance, and validation. The family teaches us how to respond to challenges. It teaches us values and strategies for navigating a sometimes cold world. Families offer a sense of identity and a place to belong. Its importance and relevance to the survival of the Black community is sometimes underestimated.

Rose stated that motherhood

> is essential to the well-being of our people. I mean it's just so basic that motherhood today is similar in a lot of ways to mothering during slavery. I mean because there are so many single Black mothers. And that's the way we were back then. And so, I see some parallels in that, in that you have to, Black women, Black mothers have to continue to have a strong sense of self, because you aren't going to get a lot of validation from outside. You have to have that strength from God and within—that you are valuable. You have to be comfortable with yourself in order to be effective as a mother. I think that because there are so many negative messages for Black women, it makes it difficult to be an effective mother. . . . You have all these distractions and negative messages come from everywhere about Black women from within the race and from outside of the race. I guess the negative messages from the race distress me the most. When you hear . . . Black women tearing down other Black women; that really disturbs me. All of that combined makes it essential that we stay in touch with God and then make sure that we keep ourselves healthy, physically and emotionally, in order to be effective as mothers. That's not simple to do. The other thing about motherhood, Black motherhood, is that, even though we are spread out and do a lot more moving around geographically, we still manage to use extended family as a resource and a network. That's why I love "Jack and Jill" so much, because that has been my extended family here in Atlanta. It's a mother network. But even if you don't have organizations like "Jack and Jill," we tend to use our churches and our community organizations to support each other in rearing our children.

Kinship systems and extended families, particularly for the Black community, represent a source of strength and are particularly important to the survival and resiliency of many Black families. Support systems are significant and can represent of network of resources for positively rearing Black children. It seems noteworthy to mention the link between Black motherhood and support systems. As Rose stated, support systems in the Black community helped her to succeed as a mother. They are part of the history of Africans in America.

Yvonne puts it this way:

> We don't know our history. First of all, the Black family was hardly in existence because we were always being ripped apart and pulled apart, during slavery. . . . We came from a history of people having to nurture somebody else's children.

A history of the village raising the child. In our community, anybody's mother could talk to you and fuss at you, and it was ok, because they were an adult and they were looking out for you. White society just doesn't understand what they have done. They've created this, and they don't want to accept the fact that they've created it. I don't think it's the Black mother. The Black mother is the victim. She's the victim because she's the one who can't get the job that pays money she can raise her children on. . . . We are victims of what society has created. Black mothers owe it to their children to tell them where they came from. I think it's important to know who you are and where you came from. I think it's . . . the black mother's responsibility to make sure that their child understands what happened to Black people as a race in this country and that times are changing.

Times have changed, and according to Yvonne, there is no attempt to connect the struggles of former generations of Blacks in America to the advantages Blacks have today. Yvonne, who is a school principal, is concerned that the values that were once embraced by the Black community are no longer being embraced, like the value of an education:

Some of our downfall as Black Americans is that we are turning more complacent, relaxed with our discipline. I see more and more of our kids having their way. I think you have to be tougher on them as a Black mother and let them know that life is not always going to be easy. That you're going to have stumbling blocks. . . . You always have to do a little bit more than mother, you have to go that extra mile with it comes to being Black. Going back to my childhood . . . it was segregated, and everyone was pretty much in the same boat. Pretty much everyone was poor. We didn't have the opportunities that kids have now. And our parents instilled education in us. They taught us values, good and bad. And I guess that's probably where I got some of those close-knit values. They were real controlling as to where we went, what we did, which wasn't much. They instilled education and I guess that why I see the importance of it. . . . This generation, they have a little more, better than what we had but they are valuing education. You don't need to necessarily have gone to college, but you have to have some type of ability to read; being able to think, being able to make good decisions. You just don't get that by osmosis. We don't value it anymore. Blacks . . . are getting away from that value or valuing a good education.

She says that Black mothers

owe it to their children to tell them where they came from as far as our history. I think it's so important to know who you are and where you came from. I think it's a mother's responsibility to make sure that their child understands what's happened to Black people as a race in this country and that times are changing. When they go out there, someone is going to judge them by the color of their skin, and if you don't tell them that, then they won't know how to respond when it happens. So, I think we do have a special responsibility. We have to show them how to get along with various cultures and races of people; that things are not always going to be the way we would like for them to be, but as long as you know from whence you came and that you are made of something good, it's ok, and you can look at those other people and say, you know, I can look forward and I'm not going to let that hold me back. I'm going to let it make me strong.

Rose offered a very poignant view of the challenges faced by Black mothers.

Mothers of Black children have to be aware of some different kinds of threats and issues in a world that perhaps mothers of White children do not. For example, if my son gets a speeding ticket somewhere in South Georgia, that could mean his life. My other son is in New York somewhere and gets pulled over for drunk driving, that could mean his life, his career. It could mean his job. I mean more so I think than would be the case with a White child, a White young man. I think there is a presumption when it is a young Black male that they're automatically guilty. They're automatically wrong. They're automatically suspect. If you're driving a nice car, you're going to get pulled over. So, we can't pretend to our children that they're just like majority children. They have to be prepared with the right kinds of tools to protect themselves. And so . . . having to carry that kind of negative message and yet have them turn out to be positive people is not easy.

Rose's statement paints a very vivid picture of the powerful role Black mothers (and fathers) play in socializing their children. The term *racial socialization* is used to denote the verbal and behavioral practices that parents use to communicate with their children about the social significance of race and to prepare them for life in a racist society (Hughes et al. 2006; Lesane-Brown 2006). Racial socialization is considered to be of particular importance in Black families in which parents must teach their children to succeed despite personal and systemic experiences of racism (Coard and Sellers 2005; Lesane-Brown 2006). One example of racial socialization many Black parents engage in involves having "The Talk" with their children, particularly their young Black sons. "The Talk" represents the "surviving interactions with police or other members of authority" discussion and is largely considered an essential rite of passage in African American homes. "The Talk" was the topic of a *New York Times* video from 2015, explaining how black parents have to prepare their sons for police encounters—out of fear, mainly, that such interactions can go horribly wrong, ending with their son dead (Lopez 2016). As Rose stated previously, the role of the Black mother is "essential to the survival of our people." Yvonne puts it this way:

> Our role is the ultimate role in order for us to survive as a people, as a race. "Cause if it wasn't, I guess I wouldn't be here." Our role is important, but I think for the future of our race, I think our role is becoming more important. We have to perpetuate our race and if we don't get a handle on our own children and give them a sense of who they are and where they came from, then as a people we are going to suffer.

Black parents are required to prepare their children to understand and live in two cultures—Black American culture and standard American culture (Carothers 1990). This phenomenon has been referred to as biculturality, an idea derived from W. E. B. Dubois's' writings in the early 1900s about the idea of double consciousness. He writes that "Blacks have to guard their sense of blackness while accepting the rules of the games and cultural consciousness of the dominant White culture" (Itzigsohn and Brown 2015).

For many Black mothers and their children, the rules of the game change on a regular basis. The lessons and values of the larger society and culture are often contradictory. As Rose stated, "they have to learn how to navigate through a very contradictory system and yet still turn out to be positive people. It's a difficult task but it can be done."

Each woman gave voice to her own mothering experience and provided an insightfully meaningful view of Black motherhood. Their stories, as told on these pages, place each woman at the center of analysis. Their stories provide those of us on the outside looking in, listening to their conversations, with a clear view of why it is important to bring from the margins, from the periphery, from the fringes to the center of discussion, the voices and motherhood experiences of professional Black women.

REFERENCES

Anderson, Julie. 2016. "Mothers by Race/Ethnicity and State". Accessed December 20, 2020. https://www.jstor.org/stable/resrep27253?seq=1#metadata_info_tab_contents.

Angen, Maureen Jane. 2000. "Evaluating Interpretive Inquiry: Reviewing the Validity Debate and Opening the Dialogue." *Qualitative Health Research 10*, no. 3: 378–395.

Arendell, Teresa. 1999. "Hegemonic Motherhood: Deviancy Discourses and Employed Mothers' Accounts of Out-of-School Time Issues." *Center for Working Families Working Paper* 9, no. 1: 32.

Ayee, Gloria Y. A., Jessica D. Johnson Carew, Taneisha N. Means, Alicia M. Reyes-Barrientez, and Nura A. Sediqe. 2019. "White House, Black Mother: Michelle Obama and the Politics of Motherhood as First Lady." *Politics and Gender 15,* no. 3: 460–483.

Banks, Nina. 2019. "Black Women's Labor Market History Reveals Deep-Seated Race and Gender Discrimination." Economic Policy Institute. Assessed December 2020. https://www.epi.org/blog/black-womens-labor-market-history-reveals-deep -seated-race-and-gender-discrimination/.

Barnett, Rosalind Chait, and Janet Shibley Hyde. 2001. "Women, Men, Work, and Family: An Expansionist Theory." *American Psychologist* 56, no. 10: 781.

Bell, Ella Louise. 1992. "Myths, Stereotypes, and Realities of Black Women: A Personal Reflection." *Journal of Applied Behavioral Science 28,* no. 3: 363–376.

Billingsley, Andrew. 1992. *Climbing Jacob's Ladder: The Enduring Legacy of African American Families.* New York: Simon & Schuster.

Bobo, Jacqueline. 1995. *Black Women as Cultural Readers.* New York: Columbia University Press.

Boris, Eileen. 1989. "The Power of Motherhood: Black and White Activist Women Redefine the Political." *Yale Journal of Law and Feminism 2,* no. 1: 25–50.

Brevis, Vita. 2012. "Where Do Women of Color Factor into the "Mommy Wars"." Daily Kos. Accessed December, 2020. https://www.dailykos.com/stories/2012/04 /17/1084142/-Where-Do-Women-of-Color-Factor-Into-the-Mommy-Wars.

Brown, Caroline. 2012. "Marketing Michelle: Mommy Politics and Post-Feminism in the Age of Obama." *Comparative American Studies an International Journal 10,* no. 2–3: 239–254.

Burr, Vivien. 1995. *An Introduction to Social Constructionism.* London: Routledge.

Carew, Jessica D. J. 2019. "Mothers of the Movement: Black Motherhood and the Political Power of Grief in the 2016 Presidential Election." In *Women of the 2016 Election: Voices, Views, and Values,* edited by Jennifer Schenk Sacco, 139–156. Lanham, MD: Lexington Books.

Carothers, Suzanne C. 1990. "Catching Sense: Learning from Our Mothers to Be Black and Female." In *Uncertain Terms: Negotiating Gender in American Culture,* edited by Ginsburg, Faye D., and Anna Lowenhaupt Tsing. Boston, MA: Beacon Press.

Christian, Barbara. 1980. *Black Women Novelists: The Development of a Tradition.* Westport, CT: Greenwood Press.

Coard, Stephanie I., and Robert M. Sellers. 2005. "African American Families as a Context for Racial Socialization." In *African American Family life: Ecological and cultural diversity,* edited by McLoyd, Vonnie C., Nancy E. Hill, and Kenneth A. Dodge, 264–285. New York, NY: Guilford Press.

Collins, Patricia Hill. 1991. "On Our Own Terms: Self-Defined Standpoints and Curriculum Transformation." *NWSA Journal 3,* no. 3: 367–381.

Collins, Patricia Hill. 2000. *Black Feminist Thought: Knowledge, Consciousness and the Politics of Empowerment.* 2nd ed. New York: Routledge.

Collins, Patricia Hill. 2005. "Black Women and Motherhood." In *Motherhood and Space: Configurations of the Maternal Through Politics, Home and the Body,* edited by C. Wiedmer, and Sarah Hardy. Springer.

Collins, Patricia Hill. 2015. "No Guarantees: Symposium on Black Feminist Thought." *Ethnic and Racial Studies 38,* no. 13: 2349–2354.

Cooper, Terry D. 1990. "The Plausibility of a New Self: Self-Esteem from a Sociology of Knowledge Perspective." *Counseling and Values 35*, no. 1: 31–38.

Crenshaw, Kimberle. 2011. "De-Marginalizing the Intersection of Race and Sex: A Black Feminist Critique of Anti-Discrimination Doctrine, Feminist Theory, and Anti-Racist Politics." In *Framing Intersectionality: Debates on a Multi-Faceted Concept in Gender Studies*, edited by Helma Lutz , Maria Teresa Herrera Vivar, and Linda Supik, 25–42. Burlington, VT: Ashgate Publishing Company.

Dickerson, Bette. J. 1995. *African American Single Mothers: Understanding Their Lives and Families.* Thousand Oaks, CA: Sage.

Doll, Jen. 2012. "Michelle Obama and the Power of Mom." The Atlantic. Accessed September 5, 2020. https://www.theatlantic.com/politics/archive/2012/09/michelle -obama-and-power-mom/323963/.

Donath, Orna. 2014. "Regretting Motherhood: A Sociopolitical Analysis." *Signs: Journal of Women in Culture and Society 40*, no. 2: 343–367.

Donath, Orna. 2015. "Choosing Motherhood? Agency and Regret Within Reproduction and Mothering Retrospective Accounts." *Women's Studies International Forum,* Vol. 53, 200–209.

Dow, Dawn Marie. 2019. *Mothering While Black: Boundaries and Burdens of Middle-Class Parenthood.* Oakland, CA: University of California Press.

Emerson, Rana A. 2002. ""Where My Girls at?" Negotiating Black Womanhood in Music Videos." *Gender & Society 16*, no. 1: 115–135.

Fannin, Lauren D. 2013. "They Aren't June Cleaver: Understanding the Experiences and Perceptions of African American Stay-at-Home Mothers." PhD diss., Georgia State University.

Ghasemi, P., and R. Hajizadeh. 2012. "Demystifying the Myth of Motherhood: Toni Morrison's Revision of African-American Mother Stereotypes." *International Journal of Social Science and Humanity 2,* no. 6: 477.

Giddings, Paula. 1984. *When and Where I Enter: The Impact of Black Women on Race and Sex in America.* New York: William Morrow.

Glen, Stephanie. 2014. "Snowball Sampling: Definition, Advantages and Disadvantages." StatisticsHowTo.com: Elementary Statistics for the rest of us! Accessed December, 2020. https://www.statisticshowto.com/snowball-sampling/.

Goodenow, Carol, and Oliva M. Espin. 1993. "Identity Choices in Immigrant Adolescent Females." *Adolescence* 28, no. 109: 173–184.

Hayden, Sara. 2017. "Michelle Obama, Mom-in-Chief: The Racialized Rhetorical Contexts of Maternity." *Women's Studies in Communication* 40, no. 1: 11–28.

Hughes, Diane, James Rodriguez, Emilie P. Smith, Deborah J. Johnson, Howard C. Stevenson, and Paul Spicer. 2006. "Parents' Ethnic-Racial Socialization Practices: A Review of Research and Directions for Future Study." *Developmental Psychology* 42, no. 5: 747.

Ibanga, Imaeyea. 2009. "Obama's Choice to Bare Arms Causes Uproar." ABC News. Accessed December, 2020. https://abcnews.go.com/GMA/story?id=6986019&p age=1.

Itzigsohn, José, and Karida Brown. 2015. "Sociology and the Theory of Double Consciousness: W. E. B. Du Bois' Phenomenology of Racialized Subjectivity." *Du Bois Review: Social Science Research on Race 12*, no. 2: 231–248. doi:10.1017/ S1742058X15000107. Jack and Jill of America, Inc., https://www.jackandjillinc .org.

Kahl, Mary L. 2009. "First Lady Michelle Obama: Advocate for Strong Families." *Communication and Critical/Cultural Studies 6*, no. 3: 316–320.

Kruger, L. 2006. "Motherhood." In *The Gender of Psychology*, edited by Tamara Shefer, Floretta Boonzaier, and Peace Kiguwa, 182–195. Cape Town: UCT Press

Lesane-Brown, Chase L. 2006 "A Review of Race Socialization Within Black Families." *Developmental Review 26*, no. 4: 400–426.

Levine, David M., and David Stephan. 2014. *Even You Can Learn Statistics and Analytics: An Easy to Understand Guide to Statistics and Analytics 3rd Edition.* Pearson FT Press.

Lincoln, Yvonna S., and Egon G. Guba. 1985. *Naturalistic Inquiry.* Beverly Hills, CA: Sage.

Lopez, German. 2016. "Black Parents Describe "The Talk" They Give to Their Children About Police." The Vox. Accessed December, 2020. https://www.vox .com/2016/8/8/12401792/police-black-parents-the-talk.

Lugo-Lugo, Carmen R., and Mary K. Bloodsworth-Lugo. 2011. "Bare Biceps and American (In)Security: Post-9/11 Constructions of Safe(ty), Threat, and the First Black Lady." *Women's Studies Quarterly* 39, no. 1/2 (2011): 200–217.

Lutz, Wilma J., and Ellen Hock. 2002. "Parental Emotions Following the Birth of the First Child: Gender Differences in Depressive Symptoms." *American Journal of Orthopsychiatry* 72, no. 3: 415–421.

Magwaza, Thenjiwe. 2003. "Perceptions and Experiences of Motherhood: A Study of Black and White Mothers of Durban, South Africa." *Jenda: A Journal of Culture and African Women Studies,* 4.

Mamabolo, Itumeleng. Malose Langa, and Peace Kiguwa. 2009. "To Be or Not to Be a Mother: Exploring the Notion of Motherhood Among University Students." *South African Journal of Psychology 39,* no. 4: 480–488.

Marceline, Marleine. 2012. "Female Identity Development in a Cross-Cultural Context. The Woman in the Mirror." *Hofstra Papers in Anthropology* 7, no. 2. https://www.hofstra.edu/academics/colleges/hclas/anthro/hpia/hpia-marcelin. html.

Mares, Susan, Louise Newman, and Beulah Warren. 2011. *Clinical Skills in Infant Mental Health* (2nd ed.). Victoria: Acer Press.

McMahon, Martha. 1995. *Engendering Motherhood: Identity and Self-Transformation in Women's Lives.* New York: Guilford Press.

Morell, Carolyn Mackelcan. 1994. *Unwomanly Conduct: The Challenges of Intentional Childlessness.* London: Routledge.

Obama, Michelle. 2018. *Becoming.* New York: Crown.

Patterson, Shawna M. 2016. "Progression to Womanhood: A Framework on the Identity Development of Black American." *Urban Education Research and Policy Annuals 4,* no. 1.

Rich, Adrienne. 1976. *Of Woman Born: Motherhood as Institution and Experience*. New York: Bantam.

Richardson, Diane. 1993. *Women, Motherhood and Childrearing*. London: The Macmillan Press Ltd.

Symes, Emma. 2017. "The Transition to Motherhood: Psychological Factors Associated with Pregnancy, Labour and Birth." *Psych: The Bulletin of the Australian Psychological Society Ltd* 39, no. 1: 18.

The Internet African American History Challenge. n.d. *"Richard Allen."* Accessed December, 2018. rightmoments.com/blackhistory/nrallen.html.

Thomas, Anita Jones, Karen McCurtis Witherspoon, and Suzette L. Speight. 2004. "Toward the Development of the Stereotypic Roles for Black Women Scale." *Journal of Black Psychology 30*, no. 3: 426–442.

Thompson, Lisa B. 2009. *Beyond the Black Lady: Sexuality and the New African American Middle Class* (Vol. 131). University of Illinois Press.

West, Carolyn M. 1995. "Mammy, Sapphire and Jezebel: Historical Images of Black Women and Their Implications for Psychotherapy." *Psychotherapy* 32, no. 3: 458–466.

Wilson, Valerie. 2017. "African American Women Stand Out as Working Moms Play a Larger Economic Role in Families." Economic Policy Institute. Accessed May 1, 2017. https://www.epi.org/blog/african-american-women-stand-out-as-working-moms-play-a-larger-economic-role-in-families/.

Chapter 4

Getting and Staying in the Mainstream

African American Women's Contribution to the Human Sciences

Vanessa P. Jackson and Julia R. Miller Arline

INTRODUCTION

There is a gap in the history of the growth and development of the profession of human sciences.[1] The gap is related to the contributions of African American professionals and other people of color. Many of the challenges, struggles, and obstacles encountered by African Americans and other people of color are invisible. This is especially true with regard to instruction, research, and outreach/service. African American professionals and other people of color have made overwhelming contributions to the quality of life and well-being of individuals and families within the context of their communities.

This study draws on resiliency theory from an ecological approach. The resilience-enhancing approach is in concert with the ecological, or person-in-environment, perspective of the profession (Bronfenbrenner 1979). Resiliency theory draws from a strength perspective—a philosophical standpoint that recognizes the inherent power and tenacity of individuals and families within the context of their communities (Chapin, Nelson-Becker, and MacMillan 2006; Saleebey 1997). This integrative framework is employed to better understand the obstacles faced by African American women professionals in human sciences. The obstacles were based on societal attitudes and values that prohibited access to resources in culturally relevant ways.

The chapter presents an analytical perspective of the challenges, struggles, obstacles, and successes faced by African American women as described in the book *African American Women: Contributions to the Human Sciences*. This book begins to document the strides made by African American women throughout the growth and development of human sciences. Although African American women have often shared common experiences with White women in the profession, they also possess an individual, yet collective perspective. This perspective suggests the need for additional research and documentation.

Given all of the challenges, struggles, and obstacles faced by African American women as explained in the book, it is worthwhile to examine this question: "Why were these women so resilient?" Hence, this study uses an ecological approach to resilience theory to describe inequities in education due to segregation, the value of education and self-efficacy, the importance of personal mentors and mentoring, commitment to the discipline, and community through faith and spirituality.

LITERATURE REVIEW

Educating Professionals in the Field: A Historical Perspective

According to Ralston (1978), the philosophy of home economics developed by the Lake Placid participants emphasized the importance of home and family life. However, there was a difference between domestic science in Southern Black schools and home economics in White schools. The difference was a result of the political and economic implications of the respective curricula (Miller, Mitstifer, and Vaughn 2009). While programs in both systems focused on the need to improve nutrition, sanitation, and economy of the home, domestic science programs in many Black schools were designed to train domestic workers for White homes. This focus helped to keep educated Blacks in their "appropriate" places in Southern society (Anderson 1973; Enck 1970). The curriculum developed in Black schools was more practical and less theoretical. In White schools, however, the liberal and professional aspects of home economics instruction were emphasized (Fritschner 1977; Ralston 1978). Although American society practiced and was strongly vested in a segregated society, the dividing racial lines in the home economics curriculum became more similar as American women sought more public roles in areas such as education, other professional careers, and social reform (Fritschner 1977; Ralston 1978; Miller, Mitstifer, and Vaughn 2009).

African American Women in Higher Education

African American women began to make gradual strides in the acquisition of formal and higher education and in educational attainments as early as the mid-nineteenth century (Bates 2007; Evans 2007). African American women such as Mary Jane Patterson, Anna Julia Cooper, and Mary McLeod Bethune were among the first to break down the educational barriers and pave the way for generations to come (Bates 2007). The first African American woman to receive a baccalaureate degree was Mary Jane Patterson in 1862 from Oberlin College (Bates 2007; Bennett 2003). The first two African American women to receive their PhD were Georgiana Simpson and Sadie Tanner Mossell Alexander (Fraser 1989). Georgiana Simpson got her PhD a day earlier than Alexander at the University of Chicago (Fraser 1989). Alexander earned her PhD in economics from the University of Pennsylvania.

When the second Morrill Act of 1890 became law, access to education for African Americans increased. This was due to the creation of segregated land-grant colleges in 17 Southern and Border States. The historically African American public colleges and universities demonstrated a remarkable record for innovations. These innovations were seen in such fields as nutrition, agriculture, and animal husbandry. In addition, there were substantial contributions made in teacher education.

Gains in educational attainment and career development for African Americans and people of color have been attributed to their perseverance and educational political movements. Hughes and Howard-Hamilton (2003), for example, report that these gains resulted largely from the civil rights movement and the creation of financial aid programs. Today, political sentiment regarding education has moved away from civil rights and affirmative action ideals. As reported in Orefield (2000), where affirmative action has been removed, there has been a significant decline in the number of African Americans who attend institutions of higher education and a decline in the number of African American professors and graduate students.

Although there were a few major accomplishments made by African American women in higher education, many barriers were constructed based on race, sex, and class (Hughes and Howard-Hamilton 2003). Evans (2007) suggests African American women in higher education experienced (and still experience) racism. Black women must perform twice as well to get recognition, are subjected to unwarranted mediocre reviews, and are isolated by lack of limited women mentors. The demographics of African American women in higher education, both in public and private research universities, reveal they have been excluded and marginalized more than any ethnic group of women. In academia Black women suffered a distinct pattern of educational and intellectual stereotypes and are still subjected to what is referred to as extraordinary scrutiny. An account of a survey of the first Black faculty members at the nation's flagship state universities revealed:

> For Black Women University professors, pay and promotion were unreasonably low. They were relegated to lower ranks, doing much "invisible work," such as counseling, coordinating meetings, stretching meager resources, and organizing

grassroots civil rights campaigns that improved their campuses and communities. (Evans 2007, 132)

THEORETICAL FRAMEWORK

Campbell (2013) describes the ecological approach as follows:

> Also known as the social ecological model is a methodological framework used in the social sciences to examine the dynamic relationships between individuals and includes multiple levels of perspective of the social environment. The ecological perspective is used primarily as a qualitative research perspective borrowed from the natural sciences, where environmental factors are influential and studied in addition to the primary subjects of the research.

When a person faces struggles and challenges, the complexities of this state of being are often predicated on (1) the individual's capacity to navigate the psychological, social, cultural, and physical resources that build and sustain their well-being, and (2) the collective capacity to negotiate for those resources to be provided and experienced in culturally meaningful ways (Ungar 2012). This perspective is linked to an individual's self-efficacy or the belief in one's capacity to execute the behaviors necessary to achieve specific performance attainments (Bandura 1994; Bandura 1977; Bandura and Schunk 1981; Wong, Lau, and Lee 2012). Self-efficacy reflects confidence in the ability to exert control over one's own motivation, behavior, and social environment. Perceptions of self-efficacy influence the choice of activity, task perseverance, level of effort expended, and ultimately the degree of success achieved (Bandura and Schunk 1981). The greater the level of self-efficacy, the potential for resiliency to navigate and negotiate during critical processes increases.

Reflecting on Ungar's view of resilience, the African American participants in this research were often engaged in dual critical processes of navigation and negotiation. Their resilience was demonstrated when they took advantage of the opportunities to capitalize on available resources. Often there were obstacles based on societal attitudes and values that prohibited access to resources that met the needs of this population.

The relationship between obstacles that hindered and resources that facilitated study participants' resiliency in navigating and negotiating systems—resiliency that ultimately led to their successes in making significant contributions to the profession. As figure 4.1 illustrates, the resilience of African American women in higher education was the core that facilitated successful outcomes. Obstacles such as inequities in education were faced by the professionals in this study. These obstacles were based on negative societal attitudes and values during the time of segregation in education. Specifically, in the education of African American women they have included exclusion, neglect, and discrimination (Perkins 2005). However, African Americans valued education and believed it was an avenue for success. They developed a level of self-efficacy that allowed them to execute the behaviors necessary to attain educational desires. To enhance their self-efficacy, they used mentors as resiliency resources. Many were also able to mentor others.

Hill identified five strengths that foster resilience in African American families that were culturally transmitted from their African ancestry. These five strengths include strong kinship bonds, a strong work orientation, a strong achievement orientation, flexible family roles, and a strong religious orientation (Hattery and Smith 2007). These resources were used to defer interruptions to resiliency (Zimmerman 2013). Human science/family and consumer sciences professionals have utilized this approach when working with individuals, families, and communities within the context of their ecological environments. In this study, the professionals provided mentoring to others as they faced struggles and challenges in the field.

The successes of the professionals in this study are grounded in their commitment to the human science/family and consumer sciences discipline and community. These participants maintain their commitment to the discipline and the community through their faith and spirituality. Their commitment to the discipline is evident in their development of educational programs, curriculum, and research. Their commitment to service/outreach activities is demonstrated by their transfer of educational and research programs within communities. From this study, faith and spirituality were a "means of negotiating and understanding the issues, struggles, and forms of oppression" they faced (Patton and McClure 2009). Milner (2006) noted, "Throughout history, particularly during slavery, African Americans have held strong spiritual beliefs and convictions." They had to be in touch with their spiritual selves to survive hate, turmoil, and racism. With resilience balancing and counterbalancing the interactive effect of the obstacles and resources, strides were made toward significant contributions to the profession.

METHODS

Data Collection and Analysis

African American Women: Contributions to the Human Sciences was published in 2009. The authors of this book, Miller, Mitstifer, and Vaughn, were greatly concerned that there was no historical, collective account detailing the contributions of African American women to the human sciences. A content analysis of this book provides a descriptive perspective of the contribution and challenges African American women professionals face when pursuing careers in the human sciences. A content analysis is a systematic, replicable technique for compressing many words of text into fewer content categories based upon explicit rules of coding (Krippendorff 1980; Weber 1990). Stemler (2001) states that it can be a useful technique in discovering and describing a focus of individual, group, institutional, or social attention.

The content analysis was conducted using ATLAS.ti, a program that provides highly sophisticated tools to manage, extract, compare, explore, and reassemble meaningful segments of large amounts of data in flexible and creative, yet systematic ways. Emergent coding was used to identify categories in the data (Haney, Russell, Gulek, and Fierros 1998). First, each researcher reviewed the content of the book and came up with a set of variables to use to conduct the content analysis. Then the authors compared notes and reconciled any differences in their set of variables. The qualitative themes that were identified were (1) inequities in education due to segregation, (2) value of education and self-efficacy, (3) personal mentors and mentoring as a motivator for resiliency and advocacy, (4) commitment to the discipline and community, and (5) faith and spirituality. Each researcher used this set of variables to code the content of the book. Once the content was coded, the researchers compared and consolidated where necessary to complete the data coding.

RESULTS AND DISCUSSION

Demographic Information

Thirty-seven women were included in this content analysis of *African American Women: Contributions to the Human Sciences*. The year of birth for these professionals ranged from 1899 to 1940. Twenty-two percent of these women were born between 1921 and 1930, while 16% were born between 1941 and 1950. Thirty-five percent did not report what year they were born. Twenty-seven percent of the women had been working in the human sciences profession between 31 and 40 years. Most of the women portrayed in the book majored in home economics/home economics education/ family and consumer sciences education (23), while others had degrees in foods and nutrition, chemistry, textiles and clothing, and child development. As reported in Miller, Mitstifer, and Vaughn (2009), Ralston (1978) suggested that the decision by African American women to major in home economics was influenced by social origin (lower family socioeconomic status), significant others (family members such as sister, brother, or other relatives), and previous curriculum-related experiences.

Inequities in Education

Negative societal attitudes and values were evident during the time of segregation in education; these led to inequities in education. The education of African American women has been infused with exclusion, neglect, and discrimination (Perkins 2005). Hughes and Hamilton (2003) suggest that barriers to higher education for African American women include systemic racism, sexism, and classism. As discussed in Perkins (2005), most attempts to educate African Americans occurred when they took matters into their own hands. The civil rights movement helped to rewrite segregation laws, voting obstruction, and discrimination at all levels (Karson 2005).

According to Zamani (2003), "The inequities faced by African Americans as a group have been particularly oppressive for Black women." Lerner (1993) wrote bluntly that

> African American women traditionally have been preceded by White men, White women, and African American men in importance and standing. Moreover, African American men and women, as well as rural and immigrant White women were not afforded the same educational opportunities as the middle- and upper-class White girls. (Lerner 1993; Ogbu 1990)

Subjects of this content analysis reflected on their experiences of segregation in education. The formal education of Black females was not universal throughout the country's first 200 years (Zamani 2003). While working in the profession, women in the study sought to (1) improve quality of life for individuals and families (six participants); (2) engage in programs for women, youth, and the elderly (five participants); (3) serve as role models for students and faculty (six participants); and (4) improve the community by serving as civil rights advocates (six participants).

The civil rights movement showed the resilience of many in the study. One participant stated:

> The Civil Rights Movement had impacts beyond the provisions for basic civil rights for all citizens. The movement touched the very fabric of our system of justice, equality, as well as every aspect of our lives. For example, entities such as professional organizations began to assess and address their posture and positions regarding inclusion. (Miller, Mitstifer, and Vaughn 2009, 134)

Although this movement seemed to release African Americans from racial disparities, segregation still prevailed and existed throughout America.

Women in the analysis expressed facing racism (9), segregated systems/infra-structures (4), inequities in program funding between Black and White public schools and institutions (5), and poor quality of program facilities for Blacks (3). Regarding life during segregation, one professional stated: "The White children rode by on their yellow busses and made funny faces at us. The fathers with farm trucks and cars often stopped to give us a ride, especially on cold days" (Miller, Mitstifer, and Vaughn 2009, 395).

Another stated: "Although we had very experienced and dedicated teachers and administrators, we were deprived of resources to enhance our learning. For example, we had no library or learning labs. Instead of hands-on experiments, science was explained and demonstrated" (Miller, Mitstifer, and Vaughn 2009, 533).

Segregation was also very prevalent in higher education. One professional referred to her years as a graduate student as described in Miller, Mitstifer, and Vaughn (2009, 110): "[African Americans] could not enroll at [the] State University . . . only 28 miles from [her] home and . . . only across town from [the segregated] University." Despite this prohibition, she was "willing to make the sacrifice to leave home to go to Pennsylvania and then to New York in order to prepare . . . for success in the profession."

Another reflected on trying to acquire housing while attending graduate school:

> Upon arrival at the bus station in State College, she asked the White cab driver to take her to the address where she had arranged to live. The cab driver asked her if she was going to work at that address. She said she was going to live there and pursue graduate study for a year. "Maybe so, but I don't believe it." To my dismay, he was correct. The owner of the home, a White woman, informed me that she had no idea that I was a Negro and that I would not be able to live there [because] . . . she provided housing for White girls, some of whom were from the South and would not live with a Negro. She returned my deposit and informed me of two sisters who lived down the street who might provide housing. (Miller, Mitstifer, and Vaughn, 2009, 111)

Another professional further stated:

> Many of the Black colleges and universities had dilapidated and ramshackle buildings with practically no equipment for teaching in laboratories. (Miller, Mitstifer, and Vaughn 2009, 481)

Value of Education and Self-Efficacy

Billingsley (1992, 181) wrote: "The value African Americans place in education has always been extraordinarily high. There is a deep historical and cultural belief in the efficacy of education. Blacks have sought education in every conceivable manner at every level." Parental concerns for the education of Blacks can be traced back to the 1870s. At that time, the Freedman's Bureau, philanthropists, and religious organizations worked with parents and the few Black political officials who existed at that time to establish public schools for Blacks (Johnson and Staples 2005). There were, however, inequalities in the education of Blacks and Whites, as well as in Black teachers' salaries and other resources (Johnson and Staples 2005).

Parents often made the decision to educate their Black daughters as a strategy against their working in the homes of Whites (Johnson and Staples 2005). In this analysis, one of the women was so committed to and resilient in getting her education that "she worked on several different farms in the county earning 40 cents per day toward her college education" (Miller, Mitstifer and Vaughn 2009, 84).

Another woman wrote:

> I have always been committed to my own education and the education of other
> black men and women.

As a result of their achievements in education and professionalism, all of the women studied came to believe they should be a resource to students, helping them to build a level of self-efficacy that would motivate them to achieve. Seven of the professionals in the study worked to enrich the lives of family and consumer sciences students by creating programs that educated individuals to fulfill their roles within the family. Another six revised, developed, and updated curriculum for the field to advance students' knowledge and skills.

These African Americans' self-efficacy was built on a system of motivation and resilience developed from resources such as family, parents, teachers, ministers, and others who supported their educational progress. Many were motivated and resilient in believing that failure was not an option, but success through education was the most important outcome in life. One professional wrote:

> My father worked [in the citrus grove] for fifteen cents an hour for ten hours,
> $1.50 a day [six days a week]. Out of the $9.00 ($144.21 in 2007 dollars) per
> week, he paid thirty cents per day, $1.50 per week ($24.03 in 2007 dollars), for
> . . . us to be taken to school in a taxi . . . [because her father was at work, her
> mother did not drive, and the distance was too great for young children to walk.]
> [T]he remaining $7 50 was all that was available for other necessities. (Miller,
> Mitstifer, and Vaughn 2009, 105)

Personal Mentors and Mentoring

The professionals studied were mentored by many people. According to Johnston (2013) and others, mentoring is the "process whereby a more experienced individual provides counsel, guidance, and assistance to another person, serves an essential function in helping younger or newer employees to develop leadership skills and advance within the organization" (Lanna-Lipton 2009). Further, "it is the role of current leaders in an organization to cultivate future leaders, and mentoring can be used as a strategy for growing leaders" (Davidson and Middleton 2006, 350).

Resiliency theory focuses attention on creating positive contextual, social, and individual variables that stop interference with or disruption of achieving personal goals (Fergus and Zimmerman 2005). In this analysis, mentors provided a strong method of survival and resilience throughout educational and work experiences. Mentors also provided positive feedback to enhance the possibility of accomplishing educational and work achievements. Mentors helped the professionals to recover from negative experiences in their educational and work environment. The content analysis further reveals that professionals in this study were mentored by parents (14), mothers (6), a grandmother (1), siblings (3), other family members (5), fellow professionals (4), and teachers (8). One of the professionals wrote:

> My early life was influenced by my parents, relatives, teachers, and the minister at church. Through these mentors I learned the importance of education to the success of the first generation of freedom and former slaves. (Miller, Mitstifer, and Vaughn 2009, 478)

Another professional stated:

> Our parents instilled within us the importance of always doing our best. They taught us that we were born to make a contribution to this world or we would just occupy space for nothing, having wasted our lives. (Miller, Mitstifer, and Vaughn 2009, 106)

Another professional's passion was described as

> designing successful models that provide a mechanism to reach students. She has coordinated MEMS, Mentoring Multicultural Students for the Health Professions, which began as collaboration with Florida A&M University. She also worked with five historically black colleges and universities (HBCUs) to develop SciencPrep, a program to increase the diversity and quality graduates in the human sciences through enhancement of their scientific preparation for

professional roles and graduate education. (Miller, Mitstifer, and Vaughn 2009, 451)

Yet another professional stated: "My mission in life is about helping people and I particularly like helping young people move forward" (Miller, Mitstifer, and Vaughn 2009, 454).

Commitment to the Discipline and the Community

The professional women in this study were committed to the home economic discipline (7), contributed to curriculum development (11), implemented and improved program development (12), developed and enhanced grant-writing to support program (5), and planned and implemented outreach workshops (4). As stated in her biography, one of the professionals "embraced research, teaching, publishing, outreach, and service on the local, national, and international basis; a loyal and dedicated supporter of her alma mater; and extraordinary service to humanity" (Miller, Mitstifer, and Vaughn 2009, 70).

Another wrote:

> at a point where we must continuously assess as a profession where it is. . . . What would the profession be if those of us and the few persons who are coming along, at this point and time, [were] no longer pushing for the profession we call family and consumer sciences?. . . . If it ceases to be [anymore], is there something else that is going to take its place or is it just simply going to cease to be? (Miller, Mitstifer, and Vaughn 2009, 148)

Many of the professionals in this analysis stated that they were able to achieve many of their goals because of social justice advocacy for African Americans in education. The success of African American communities is and was founded on the advocacy and commitment of those who had been resilient to adversity. Their commitment to the discipline is evident in their passion for the profession. A professional stated:

> I just don't know any other profession that touches as many different bases as home economics . . . the home, the family, the child, the interior decorating, the furnishings, education. . . . I have often said EVERYBODY should go through vocational home economics before they do anything else. . . . [T]here is nothing that you can't do with home economics as a base. (Miller, Mitstifer, and Vaughn 2009, 193)

These words describe how many in the profession felt about what and how home economics influenced their involvement with students.

Ralston (1978) summarized research on Black families conducted by African American academicians in home economics in earlier years, in support of the human sciences and the African American community. The professionals in this study conducted research related to improving the quality of life of Black families in the community. Their research was transferred into service and outreach in the form of serving as leaders on community boards and committees (15), volunteering on quality of life programs (8), conducting teen programs (6), implementing eldercare programs (6), fostering programs to combat illiteracy (2), and facilitating food and nutrition programs (5).

One of the women studied stated that, as a professional in the human sciences, a person should:

> Be dedicated to the profession. . . . Be a person who is people oriented. The love of working with people and helping them to live their lives . . . is one of the joys of home economics. . . . You help people with their quality of life. (Miller, Mitstifer, and Vaughn 2009, 194)

Another stated:

> I firmly believe that the basis of my contribution to the human sciences depends mainly on family origin and heritage, educational background, influence of mentors, membership in organizations, and deep faith in God. Additionally, I believe that setting worthwhile goals and working hard are required to achieve outcomes that greatly benefit mankind. (Miller, Mitstifer, and Vaughn 2009, 404)

Yet another professional shared:

> I believe my biggest contribution . . . is assuring [that] African American women are in positions of leadership or authority. When you have the voice of minorities, it brings a whole new perspective to discussions . . . [about] the decisions that are being made, and it brings to bear some things that I think would never be considered if it were not for those persons around the table or in positions where they could exhibit influence. (Miller, Mitstifer, and Vaughn 2009, 145)

One professional's commitment to the human sciences is demonstrated by this description:

> She is a strong supporter of the family and consumer sciences profession as reflected in her various publications, professional activities, and external funds generated for research and educational programs. She has devoted much of her time to promoting careers in family and consumer sciences and to the

recruitment and retention of minority students in higher education. (Miller, Mitstifer, and Vaughn 2009, 306)

Another wrote:

A goal of mine has been to examine families, just normal families, middle class families, working class families, and place emphasis not only on their strengths, but also on their strategies—for instance the extended family. At the same time, I provide more than just the negative view presented about African American families. I think that this would be one of my contributions. (Miller, Mitstifer, and Vaughn 2009, 391)

Faith and Spirituality as a Function of Success in Higher Education

Milner (2006, 373) notes, "Throughout history, particularly during slavery, African Americans have held strong spiritual beliefs and convictions. They had to be spiritual beings and in touch with their spiritual selves to survive the hate, turmoil, racism and destruction of their 'masters.'"

Patton and Michelle (2009) echo this sentiment, saying, "African American women often turn to spiritual beliefs to cope with everyday struggles associated with living in a socially and politically oppressive system. Spirituality can serve as a coping mechanism, promoting psychological resistance, and fostering identity development" (Watt 2003).

In the words of Mattis (2002):

African American women have engaged in radical rereading's of biblical text and have embraced private beliefs about the nature of the relationship between God and humans that have helped them disrupt and resist the impact of patriarchy and other forms of oppression including racism. For African American women, spirituality is a means of negotiation and understanding the issues, struggles, and forms of oppression that they face on a day-to-day basis. (310)

According to Allison and Broadus (2009), Black educators find spirituality to be a significant foundation of their worldview and a motivational force behind their present course in higher education. In this study, faith and spirituality were cited as methods of sustaining resilience while surviving life and career struggles.

One of the professionals in the analysis shared the following passage from Isaiah (Isaiah 54:17, King James Version): "No weapon formed against thee shall prosper; and every tongue that shall raise against thee in judgment thou salt condemn. This is the heritage of the servants of the Lord, and their righteousness is of me, saith the Lord" (Miller, Mitstifer, and Vaughn 2009, 154). Another said, "I did not know how I was going to finance the rest of my education. I stepped out on faith!" Still another said, "With my strong faith in God and His blessings, I made it through trials and tribulations" (Miller, Mitstifer, and Vaughn 2009, 404).

IMPLICATIONS AND RECOMMENDATIONS

This study used an ecological approach to resilience theory to describe women's experiences as presented in *African American Women: Contributions to the Human Sciences* (Miller, Mitstifer, and Vaughn 2009). The women's experiences related to inequities in education are due to segregation, the importance of advocacy, the value of education and self-efficacy, personal mentors and mentoring as a motivator for resiliency, and a commitment to the discipline and community through faith and spirituality. These African American women realized their struggles and established resiliency strategies to maintain existence in the profession. Their foundation for survival, even in the face of segregation, was grounded in the value of education. The deep and historical efficacy of education provided them with the necessary tools to succeed as an African American woman in the human sciences. They were mentored by family members, parents, ministers, and teachers who wanted them to succeed. Their resiliency built success through faith and spirituality.

This study illustrates that these African American human sciences professionals made significant contributions, despite the societal and institutional barriers and adversities faced. The human sciences profession needs to capitalize on the rich background and diverse experiences, perspectives, and abilities of African American women. These women bring different worldviews that provide a multicultural perspective.

To capitalize on this rich human resource, an ethnically diverse professional taskforce could be developed to plan and implement strategies that are directed toward a more inclusive engagement of African Americans and other professionals of color in problem-solving and decision-making for the profession, and in student education for our current and future workforce. Human sciences professionals could examine the structure and function of the profession to develop more mainstream inclusion of African American women and other professionals of color.

The human sciences profession could be a model for advocacy with local, state, and national legislators, with private and public organizations, and with businesses to assure that all voices are heard relative to families and other social policies. Human sciences could engage with internal and external professionals, legislators, private and public organizations and agencies, and businesses to follow a modified version of Zamani's (2003) recommendations to:

- Develop and maintain programs and policies that recognize and attend to the special concerns, needs, and contributions of African American women and other professionals of color within the context of organizations;
- Create a substantive African American presence in organizations through a firm commitment to attracting African American and other women, other professionals of color, and students as employees (irrespective of the retrenchment on affirmative action in higher education). This effort would reduce marginalization among African American women.
- Allocate financial and human resources to support organizational and institutional efforts to address racial and gender biases;
- Augment organizational and institutional programs and experiences to be more inclusive of African American women and other professionals of color to foster professional development (Zamani 2003).

NOTE

1. Reprinted with permission from the *Family & Consumer Sciences Research Journal,* September 2, 2014.

REFERENCES

Allison, Audrey M. Wilson, and Patreece R. Boone Broadus. 2009. "Spirituality Then and Now: Our Journey Through Higher Education as Women of Faith." *New Directions for teaching and Learning,* no. 120: 77–86.

Anderson, James Douglas. 1973. "Education for Servitude: The Social Purposes of Schooling in the Black South, 1870-1930." PhD diss., University of Illinois.

Bandera, Albert. 1994. "Self-efficacy". In *Encyclopedia of Human Behavior*, edited by V. S. Ramachaudran, 71–81. New York: Academic Press.

Bandura, Albert. 1977. "Self-efficacy: Toward a Unifying Theory of Behavior Change." *Psychological Review* 84, no. 2: 191–215.

Bandura, Albert, and Dale H. Schunk. 1981. "Cultivating Competence, Self-Efficacy, and Intrinsic Interest through Proximal Self-Motivation." *Journal of Personality and Social Psychology 41*: 586–598.

Bates, Gerry. 2007. "These Hallowed Halls: African American Women College and University Presidents." *Journal of Negro Education 76,* no. 3: 373–390.

Bennett, Lerone. 2003. *Before the mayflower: A History of Black America*, 7th ed. Chicago: Johnson Publishing.

Billingsley, Andrew. 1992. *Climbing Jacob's Ladder: The Enduring Legacy of African American Families*. New York: Simon & Schuster.

Bronfenbrenner, Urie. 1979. *The Ecology of Human Development: Experiments by Nature and Design*. Cambridge, MA: Harvard University Press.

Campbell, D. 2013. "What is the Ecological Perspective?" eHow. Accessed September 10, 2013. ehow.com/about_6638441_ecologicalperspective_.html#ixz z2ijl8ODWW.

Chapin, Rosemary, Holly Nelson-Becker, and Kelly MacMillan. 2006. "Strengths-based and Solution-Focused Approaches to Practice with Older Adults." In *Handbook of Social Work in Health and Aging*, edited by Barbara, Berkman and Sarah, D'Ambruoso, 789–796. Boston: Oxford Press.

Davidson, Jeanne R., and Cheryl A. Middleton. 2006. "Networking, Networking, Networking: The Role of Professional Association Memberships in Mentoring and Retention of Science Librarians." *Science & Technology Libraries 27*, no. 1–2: 203–224.

Enck, Henry Snyder. 1971. "The Burden Borne: Northern White Philanthropy and Southern Black Industrial Education, 1900-1915." PhD diss., University of Cincinnati.

Evans, Stephanie. Y. 2007. "Women of Color in Higher Education." *Thought & Action* 23: 131–138.

Fergus, Stevenson., and Mark A. Zimmerman. 2005. "Adolescence Resilience: A Framework for Understanding Healthy Development in the Face of Risk." *Annual Review Public Health, 26:* 399–419.

Fraser, Gerald. 1989. "Sadie T. M. Alexander, 91, Dies; Lawyer and Civil Rights Advocate." The New York Times. Accessed May 1, 2017. https://www.nytimes. com/1989/11/03/obituaries/sadie-t-m-alexander-91-dies-lawyer-and-civil-rights -advocate.html#:~:text=Sadie%20Tanner%20Mosell%20Alexander%2C%20a ,a%20retirement%20community%2C%20in%20Philadelphia.&text=Alexander %20was%20also%20the%20first,nation%20to%20get%20a%20Ph.

Fritschner, Linda M. 1977. "Servants or Ladies: The Differential Implementation of a Federal Mandate." *The School Review* 85, no. 2: 287–296.

Guerra, Maria. 2013. "Fact Sheet: The State of African American Women in the United States." Center or American progress. Accessed May 1, 2017. https://ww w.americanprogress.org/issues/race/reports/2013/11/07/79165/fact-sheet-the-state -of-african-american-women-in-the-united-states/.

Haney, Walt, Mike Russell, Cengiz Gulek, and Ed Fierros. 1998. "Drawing on Education: Using Student Drawings to Promote Middle School Improvement." *Schools in the Middle 7*, no. 3: 38–43.

Hattery, Angela J., and Earl Smith. 2007. *African American Families*. New York: Sage Publications, Inc.

Hughes, Robin L., and Mary F. Howard-Hamilton. 2003. "Insights: Emphasizing Issues that Affect African American Women." *New Directions for Student Services* no. 104: 95–104.

Johnson, Leanor B., and Robert Staples. 2005. *Black Families at the Crossroads: Challenges and Prospects*. San Francisco: Jossey-Bass.

Johnston, Melissa P. 2013. "The Importance of Professional Organizations and Mentoring in Enabling Leadership." *Knowledge Quest* 41, no. 4: 34–39.

Krippendorff, Klaus. 1980. *Content Analysis: An Introduction to Its Methodology.* Newbury Park, CA: Sage.

Lanna-Lipton, Leslie. 2009. "The Relationship Between Mentoring and Career Advancement of Millennial Generation Women in Leadership." PhD diss., University of Phoenix.

Lerner, Gerda. 1992. *Black Women in White America: A Documentary History.* New York: Vintage Books.

Mattis, Jacqueline S. 2002. "Religion and Spirituality in the Meaning-Making and Coping Experiences of African American Women: A Qualitative Analysis." *Psychology of Women Quarterly 26,* no. 4: 309–321.

Miller, Julia R., Dorothy I. Mitstifer, and Gladys Gary Vaughn. 2009. *African American Women: Contribution to the Human Sciences.* East Lansing, MI: Kappa Omicron Nu.

Milner, H. Richard. 2006. "Culture, Race and Spirit: A Reflective Model for the Study of African Americans." *International Journal of Qualitative Studies in education 19,* no. 3: 367–385.

Ogbu, John U. 1990. "Literacy and Schooling in Subordinate Cultures: The Case of Black Americans." In *Going to School: The African American Experience,* edited by K. Lomotey. Albany, NY: Albany State University of New York Press.

Orfield, Gary, Marin, Patricia, and Horn, Catherine. L. 2005. *Higher Education and the Color Line.* Boston, MA: Harvard Education Publishing.

Patton, Lori D., and Michelle L. McClure. 2009. "Strength in the Spirit: A Qualitative Examination of African American College Women and the Role of Spirituality during College." *Journal of Negro Education 78,* no. 1: 42–54.

Perkins, Linda M. 2005. "African American Women Historians Tell Their Stories." *The Journal of African American History,* 424–430.

Ralston, Penny. A. 1978. "Black Participation in Home Economics: A Partial Account." *Journal of Home Economics 70,* no. 5: 34–37.

Saleebey, Dennis. 1997. *The Strengths Perspective in Social Work Practice* (2nd ed.). White Plains, NY: Longman.

Stemler, Steve. 2001. "An Overview of Content Analysis." *Practical Assessment, Research & Evaluation 7,* no. 1: 17. https://doi.org/10.7275/z6fm-2e34.

Tabit, Michelle M. 2004. Remaining Relevant: Home Economics at the University of Idaho, 1902–1980. PhD diss., Washington State University.

Ungar, Michael. 2012. *The Social Ecology of Resilience: A Handbook of Theory and Practice.* New York: Springer.

Watt, Sherry K. 2003 "Come to the River: Using Spirituality to Cope, Resist, and Develop Identity." *Meeting the needs of African American women. New Directions for Student Services 104:* 29–40. https://doi.org/10.1002/ss.105.

Weber, Robert Philip. 1990. *Basic Content Analysis* (2nd ed.). Newbury Park, CA.

Weigley, Emma Seifrit. 1974. "It Might Have Been Euthenics: The Lake Placid Conferences and the Home Economics Movement." *American Quarterly 26,* no. 1: 79–96.

Wong, Martin CS, Tony CM Lau, and Albert Lee. 2012. "The Impact of Leadership Program on Self-Esteem and Self-Efficacy in School: A Randomized Controlled Trial." *PLoS One 7,* no. 12 (2012): e52023. https://doi.org/10.1371/journal.pone.0052023.

Zamani, Eboni. M. 2003. "African American Women in Higher Education." *New Directions for Student Services 104:* 5–18.

Zimmerman, Marc A. 2013. "Resiliency Theory: A Strength–Based Approach to Research and Practice." *Health Education & Behavior 40,* no. 4: 381–383.

Chapter 5

Administrative Acumen in Working with Our Next Generation of Professionals

Ethel G. Jones

The next generation of professionals, known as millennials (born after 1980), operate in a world with a completely different perspective as it relates to loyalty, time, and success. In 2015, millennials became the most populous workforce demographic in the United States. Therefore, they will have a significant influence on the workplace for years to come (Heathfield 2016a). According to the *LinkedIn 2015 Talent Trend Report*, millennials will comprise 50% of the workforce by 2020 (Landrum 2018). By 2025, the millennials will make up the majority of the workforce (Hyder 2014). When it comes to work ethic, they are self-centered and dedicated to completing their tasks, yet they were not taught to look around and determine what needs to be done next; instead, they ask, "what is my job" and proceed to figure out the easiest and fastest way to get the job done (Marston 2018). In order to work with our next generation of professionals, it's imperative to identify the characteristics of the Millennial Generation and their thoughts pertaining to personal work ethic and self-motivation. The list includes being technologically savvy, civic-oriented, conscious, adventurous, global-minded, impatient, special (entitled), entrepreneurial-minded, team-oriented, flexible, pragmatic, nonreligious, authentic, nomadic, multitaskers, transparent, progressive, confident, frugal, liberal, diverse, compassionate, practical, and results oriented. For the purpose of this chapter, the top 10 millennial hallmarks will be explored as follows: technologically savvy, special (entitled), team-oriented, transparent, flexible, multitaskers, diverse, confident, civic-oriented, and progressive.

TECHNOLOGICALLY SAVVY

Millennials are the first generation to grow up with constant technology, and they have embraced it like no other generation. They adapt faster to technology because they have always had it. They do everything tech-related in higher percentages than all other generations, and they have more positive attitudes about technology than any other generation (Abbot 2019; Korobka 2019). Termed "iPhone and internet zombies," millennials often seem oblivious to the world around them (*Top 10 Bad Traits of Millennials, 2018*). Patel (2018) explains that "one study found that the average college student checked either Snapchat or Instagram 11 times per day." Although millennials grew up in a connected world, they don't want just to be connected online but also to be connected with the people and brands that are important to their lives, including organizations that are leading technological innovation (Haskins 2017).

SPECIAL (ENTITLED)

While it may be fair to credit millennials with being the first generation to have unlimited technological platforms, they can and do express themselves in other ways. Anyone trying to work with millennials would be wise to give them tools to self-express and show how much they care (Hyder 2014). This generational group has always been treated as special and important. They feel they are here to solve world problems that older generations have failed to address. They crave attention and have a sense of entitlement with the expectation of frequent positive feedback (Abbot 2019; Howe and Strauss 2003).

TEAM-ORIENTED

Teamwork is something millennials enjoy. They believe that working together is far more effective than working alone (Abbot 2019; Korobka 2019; Patel 2018). Millennials prefer not to stand out among their peers but would rather be seen as a part of the group. They dislike selfishness and are more oriented toward service learning and volunteerism. Millennials prefer egalitarian leadership over hierarchies. Because they appear to be more people-oriented in their working style, establishing relationships in the workplace is very crucial (Howe and Strauss 2003).

TRANSPARENT

To millennials, transparency refers to being clear regarding the reasons behind decisions, and to being open about policies, results, and information. It also means sharing truths about the company/institution, providing truthful feedback on performance, and encouraging two-way communication. Millennials want open and honest relationships with their coworkers and manager (Abbot 2019; Korobka 2019). Maccoby's (2000) study indicated that millennials leaders should increase trust by promoting transparency and involvement, since they like to be kept in the informational loop. Having their views be heard and taken into account is critical.

FLEXIBLE

Millennials prefer flexible working arrangements and freedom as opposed to the typical nine to five jobs. They want to work from remote locations with nontraditional hours. While money is important to millennials, they do not see it as their only source of happiness. They would rather be rewarded through work arrangements that offer flexibility (Lucky Attitude 2018). In the UK, flexible work hours are a legal right for all employees. According to the Bentley University study (2017), millennials indicated that flexible work hours would make the workplace more productive for people of their age and that they would be more loyal to their employer if they were offered flexible working options (flexjobs).

MULTITASKERS

Research suggests that millennials almost never instant message someone without doing some other task(s) simultaneously. They feel multitasking is an efficient and practical use of their time and that doing this helps them to accelerate their learning (Lucky Attitude 2018). However, contrary to what the aforementioned study reveals, Howe and Strauss (2003) indicated that millennials take on too much at one time and think others should be flexible with them when they want to negotiate a scheduling conflict. They believe that multitasking saves time and is the smart thing to do, but are not aware when it contributes to poor quality results.

DIVERSE

Millennials are America's most ethnically and racially diverse cohort. About 43% of millennial adults are nonwhite, which is the highest share of any generation (Taylor and Keeter 2010). A major factor in this trend is the large wave of Hispanic and Asian immigrants who have been coming to the United States for the past half-century, and whose U.S.-born children are aging into adulthood. This generation is more accepting of all kinds of people regardless of color, gender, religion, or how people dress. As this generation attempts to overcome challenging issues like racism, immigration, sexism, homosexuality, and religion, diversity will become even more crucial. One good thing about this generational group is that they are open-minded about diversity.

CONFIDENT

Millennials in the United States today use the word "confident" when asked to describe themselves (Korobka 2019). They are motivated, goal-oriented, and confident in themselves and the future. The 2008 Pepsi Refresh Optimism Report indicated that 81% of millennials chose the word "hopeful" to describe their feelings about the future, 65% chose "optimistic," and 57% chose the words "confident" and "excited." Millennials have been raised to believe they can accomplish anything. They grew up with the saying "if you believe it, you can achieve it." According to the 2015 PwC Millennial Survey, British female millennials are the most confident and ambitious of any generation's females, and 49% of them starting their careers believe they can reach the very top of levels with their current employer. Millennials expect colleges and universities to help them launch their greatness and may even brag about their generation's potential and power to resolve issues. When it comes to achieving, grade point averages are rising and crime rates are falling. They view college as the key to high-paying jobs and success and are likely to have at least a bachelor's degree. Millennials are clearly optimistic that things will change and that future business and entrepreneurs will generate the innovative solutions needed to address the global challenges confronting society.

CIVIC-ORIENTED

Millennials have a strong sense of community at various levels, and on the larger scale they give attention to societal rather than individual needs. They believe in the value of political engagement and are convinced that the government can be a powerful force for the common good (Korobka 2019).

Millennials also believe that the government knows what is best and will take care of them. They support and believe in social rules, and their values are more in line with their parents (Howe and Strauss 2003). During this civic generation's time, economic equality and being more racially and ethnically inclusive will influence their ability to build a powerful legacy because of their high levels of compassion. Overall, they feel obligated to do their part to make the world a better place, and they believe they can (Korobka 2019).

PROGRESSIVE

Studies of millennials indicate that they are a very progressive generation and that many will become more conservative as they age (Korobka 2019; Howe and Strauss 2003). This is a generation that does not accept the status quo and will challenge the system if there is something to be improved. To them, progressive means moving the country forward, advocating for change, and advancing new ideas and policies. In the 2007 Greenberg Millennial Study, one of the top defining characteristics for this generation was the ability to "embrace innovation and new ideas." Millennials hold their most aggressive views on social issues like homosexuality, interracial relationships, gender roles, immigration, marijuana legalization, and religion. More women in this generation are breadwinners and are coparenting with their partners (Korobka 2019).

MILLENNIAL THOUGHTS, WORK ETHIC, AND MOTIVATION

Millennials live in a world where they believe that nothing is guaranteed; therefore, the only thing that really matters to them is the present. Forget about promotions five years from now because, to them, life is uncertain (Marston 2018). Moreover, Marston (2018) explains that parents of millennials thought they were doing a great thing by working long hours and paying their dues to ensure their children didn't experience hardship or adversity, but millennials today are not interested in following in their parents' footsteps. Instead, they are looking at the corporate ladder and saying, "there must be a better way."

Millennials view time as a "valuable currency not to be wasted." They are a generation that wants to get the job done so they can enjoy life. They demand work/life balance and paid time off (Abbot 2019; Marston 2018). Organizations will do well to recognize their priorities and meet their needs (Heathfield 2016a). Bentley University Center for Women and Business

(2017) conducted a study that indicated the top 10 career goals for millennials are (1) making a positive impact on the organization; (2) helping solve social and/or environmental challenges; (3) working with diverse groups of people; (4) working for an organization among the best in their industry or field of study; (5) doing work they are passionate about; (6) becoming an expert in their field; (7) managing their work/life balance; (8) becoming a senior leader; (9) achieving financial security; and (10) starting their own business.

Millennials believe that loyalty and respect must be earned, and when it is earned it is given intensely. Loyalty to individual supervisors is the reason millennials would stay on a job during their first three critical years; conversely, dissatisfaction with the supervisor is the number one reason they would quit (Marston 2018). Millennials want supervisors who are close, caring, and aware while remaining careful not to get too close. What the millennials need is a guide, not a social life. In other words, millennials are eager to learn, but the teaching has to be respectful and engaged (Heathfield 2016b).

According to Twenge (2016), millennials are willing to work long hours and weekends to achieve career success. An Ernst and Young study reported that millennials have begun working more hours than baby boomers within the last five years. However, the trend is attributed to age and career stage rather than generational traits (Twenge 2016).

What does this mean for today's professionals who need to work with millennials?

1. Don't waste your time wishing they were different or like us because they are not and will never be. Moreover, time needs to be spent on understanding and using the information given to reposition how you interact with, motivate, and reward them.
2. Today's youth want to stand out and allow their individuality to shine even though a company may have a consistent standard of service and performance; therefore, balancing the two will take some creative thinking.
3. Supply flexible work schedules, earn their commitment with work that motivates them, and provide leadership that is willing to listen and to teach them.
4. Praise, praise, and praise millennials.
5. If you really want a millennial to accept a job with your company or organization, provide a positive overall interview experience and generous compensation package, along with professional development and opportunities for advancement.
6. Millennials prefer to be their own boss. If they do have to work for another person, employers should make sure they are coached and/or mentored.

REFERENCES

Abbot, Lydia. 2019. "11 Millennials' Traits You Should Know about Before You Hire Them." Linkedin Corporation. https://business.linkedin.com/talent-solutions /blog/2013/12/8-millennials-traits-you-should-know-about-before-you-hire-them.

Bentley University Center for Women and Business. 2017. "Multi-Generation Impacts on the Workplace." Accessed June 10, 2018. https://www.bentley.edu/c enters/center-for-women-and-business/multigenerational-impacts-research-report -request.

Haskins, Christine. 2017. "What Matters to Millennials - 6 Insights You Can't Ignore." Ideas to Go. Accessed June 10, 2018. https://www.ideastogo.com/articles-on-innovation/what-matters-to-millennials-6-insights-you-cant-ignore.

Heathfield, Susan M. 2016. "Working with Generation Y Employees." Accessed December, 2020. https://www.rochester.edu/college/staff/assets/pdf/generational -differences-workplace-myth.pdf.

Heathfield, Susan M. 2016. "5 Tips for Managing Millennials." The Balance Careers. Accessed December, 2020. https://www.thebalancecareers.com/tips-for-managing -millennials-1918678.

Howe, Neal and William Strauss. 2003. *Millennials go the College.* Great Falls, VA: American Association of Registrars and Admissions Officers and LifeCourse Associates.

Hyder, Shama. 2014. "Here's What You Need to Know About Millennials." Forbes. Accessed December, 2020. https://www.forbes.com/sites/shamahyder/2014/03/04/ here-is-what-you-need-to-know-about-millennials/?sh=33b1ba4a311d.

Korobka, Tanya. 2019. "The Ultimate List of Millennial Characteristics." Last updated November 5, 2019. https://luckyattitude.co.uk/millennial-characteristics/.

Landrum, Sarah. 2018. "10 Mistakes to Avoid When You Hire Millennials." Last updated January 17, 2020. https://www.thebalancecareers.com/mistakes-when-hi ring-millennials-1918062.

Maccoby, Michael. 2000. "The Human Side: Understanding the Difference Between Management and Leadership." *Research-Technology Management 43,* no. 1: 57–59.

Marston, Cam. 2018. "Manager Tips for Keeping Millennial Employees." Accessed June 10, 2018. https://www.thebalancecareers.com/tips-for-retaining-millennial-e mployees-1918679.

Patel, Deep. 2018. "7 Surprising Traits That Make Millennials Excellent Employees." Accessed June 10, 2018. https://www.entrepreneur.com/article/306860.

Taylor, Paul, and Scott Keeter 2010. *Millennials: Confident. Connected. Open to Change.* Pew Research Center.

The Top Tens. 2018. "Top 10 Bad Traits of Millennials." Accessed December, 2020. https://www.thetoptens.com/bad-traits-millennials/.

Twenge, Jean. 2016. "Do Millennials Have a Lesser Work Ethic?" Behavior Scientist. Accessed June 10, 2018. https://behavioralscientist.org/millennials-have -a-lesser-work-ethic.

Chapter 6

The Effects of Trauma and Chronic Stress on Black Women's Reproductive and Sexual Health

Quantanise M. Williams

Epigenetics is the study of how our environment influences our genes. Scientists have found that trauma and stress can be passed down from generation to generation through alterations in gene expression (DeGruy 2017). Epigenetics explains how African American women's historic and contemporary exposure to chronic stressors has contributed to their susceptibility to chronic disease over the years (DeGruy 2017). Black women have survived the terrorizing reproductive and sexual maltreatment of slave owners and continue to overcome oppressive societal barriers that restrict access to culturally appropriate preventative healthcare services. This lack of access (among many other social barriers) has contributed to Black women accounting for some of the highest rates of reproductive challenges and diseases in the United States. Maternal mortality (death caused by pregnancy or birth complications) is one example of a common reproductive disparity. According to the Centers for Disease Control and Prevention (CDC), in 2018, the maternal mortality rate (MMR) in the United States was 17.4 per 100,000 live births. In 2018, the MMR for non-Hispanic black women was 37.3 per 100,000 live births, 14.9 for non-Hispanic white women, and 11.8 for Hispanic women. The racial disparities in MMRs experienced today have a similar trend to what was experienced decades ago. Research shows that MMRs for white women declined at a faster rate than Black women between 1935 and 1982 and that the MMR for Black women has consistently been 3–4 times higher throughout history (Singh 2010). This continual racial disparity in maternal morbidity shows that there is underlying structural and systemic racism at play.

This chapter explores how the reproductive and sexual health of African American women has been negatively affected by a traumatic history filled

with coercion and oppression. It explores how the media industry perpetuates negative stereotypes of Black women and describes how Black women
are influenced by the media across their life span. Statistics are presented
to show how Black women are disproportionately affected by reproductive
diseases, along with information on some of the underlying causes that make
Black women more susceptible to these diseases. This chapter also provides
ideas on how culturally appropriate psychotherapy and interventions that
focus on self-care can help Black women and communities heal and improve
their physical, mental, and spiritual wellness. The ideas in this chapter are
greatly inspired by three works—*Post Traumatic Slave Syndrome, Health
First*, and *Our Bodies Ourselves. Post Traumatic Slave Syndrome* explores
how American slavery and continuous societal oppression against African
Americans have impacted Black health and wellness, and outlines recommendations for healing from intergenerational trauma. *Health First* and *Our
Bodies Ourselves* outline how Black women journey through each stage of
life, and the reproductive and sexual health challenges that are relevant during each stage.

HISTORY

The reproductive health of African American women is arguably one of
the most important factors in the survival and well-being of Black communities across the nation. The womb (a woman's life force and vessel for
her reproductive organs) requires exceptional care and loving attention.
Historically, Black women's wombs have been mutilated, brutalized, and
unwillingly operated upon for the advancement of medicine (DeGruy 2017).
During American slavery, women had little control over what was done and
who entered their most sacred possession. This served as the precursor to a
generational cycle of shame and insecurity, unhealthy hygienic practices and
sexual behaviors, and a silence against rape and molestation. Today, Black
women are continuously gaining autonomy and the confidence to demand
control over and respect for their bodies, despite conflicting societal taboos
and cultural norms.

The reproductive health of African American women is and has always
been widely studied by doctors and researchers of Western medicine, but
their overall health is often neglected (DeGruy 2017). Dr. James Marion
Sims of Alabama practiced treating enslaved Black women suffering from
vesicovaginal fistulae between 1844 and 1849 (Flynn 2018). Sims surgi-
cally experimented on these women's delicate reproductive tissues without
anesthesia and possibly against their will (Flynn 2018). His experiments
served two main purposes: (1) to improve the reproductive health of enslaved

women so that they could continue birthing healthy slave labor and (2) to better understand and improve the reproductive health of White women (Owens 2017). Enslaved Black women were expected to cook, clean, garden, and to care for and nurse the children of the slave owners, while also serving as experimental subjects for medical and monetary advances that were not intended to benefit them (Owens 2017). The trend of medical exploitation and experimentation of Black women continued throughout history. For example, Margaret Sanger, a nurse and lead activist for the American birth control and eugenics movement in the early 1900s, was influential to the legalization and open access of birth control to all women, but she also contributed to efforts to decrease African American populations using birth control and reproductive sterilization of Black women (Mundt 2017).

African American women carry stigmatizing stereotypes that were established during slavery. During this time, physicians' medical journals described Black women's bodies as being inferior to those of White women and labeled them with demeaning names like 'Hottentot Venus,' 'fancy girl,' 'humble negro servitor,' and 'breeder' (Owens 2017, 19). These names perpetuated the stereotype that Black women are overly sexual. It is ironic that slave owners (who raped and reproductively coerced their enslaved women) were among the culprits who tagged Black women as hypersexual. These rapists ignited hundreds of years of rape and molestation culture, identity and self-esteem crises, and unresolved sexual trauma within African American families. Another common stereotype emphasized by medical journals of the nineteenth century was that Black women's bodies are naturally abnormal and function improperly. Dr. Eve Paul from the Medical College of Georgia wrote, "The history of diseases among our negro population is generally very imperfect and unsatisfactory, and this is especially true as regards uterine derangements" (Owens 2017, 20). Today, many Black women are working to overcome centuries of oppressor-induced self-hatred by being intentional in learning to love themselves and their bodies, while also acting as positive role models for their children and communities.

As African American women heal from historical bondage and intergenerational reproductive trauma, they also bear the burden of chronic stress. Chronic stress is heightened by a multitude of factors, including Post-Traumatic Slave Syndrome, ' a condition that exists when a population has experienced multigenerational trauma resulting from centuries of slavery and continues to experience oppression and institutional racism today" (DeGruy 2017, 105); vigilance, "a never-ending, daily anticipation of discrimination or prejudice" (Sherburne 2018); actual discrimination; prejudice; and the constant battle to receive equitable access to education, housing, transportation, healthcare services, and healthy nutrition. Stress aggressively affects Black women's physical, mental, emotional, and spiritual health across the life span.

Dr. Bessel van der Kolk (2014) explains that a trauma survivor navigates the world with a different nervous system, constantly trying to maintain control of unrecognizable physiological reactions, which can manifest into chronic disease. Dr. van der Kolk (2014) also writes about how trauma survivors have compromised immune systems that are oversensitive to perceived threats, which can ultimately lead to the immune system attacking the body's own cells. When considering historical and contemporary exposures to trauma and racism, and epigenetics research findings, it is no wonder that Black women are more susceptible to reproductive illnesses such as breast, cervical, and uterine cancers; HIV/AIDS; and other sexually transmitted diseases (STDs). Public health researcher and clinician, Dr. Gwendolyn Norman (2012, 61), writes: "Perceived racism induces racism-specific coping mechanisms . . . found to be related to increased psychological stress, poorer wellbeing and more chronic conditions among African Americans. . . . Racism, like other stressful life events, produces measurable reports of subjective distress. The presence of intrusion and avoidance symptoms suggest a reaction like post-traumatic stress disorder." Similarly, social work researcher, Dr. Joy DeGruy (2017), notes that enslaved Africans were exposed to a lifetime of traumas that are considered as diagnostic criteria for post-traumatic stress disorder (PTSD). Sadly, there was no diagnosis or treatment available for PTSD during American slavery or after enslaved people were freed. Enslaved people would not have even been allowed access to treatment if it was available. The effects of the traumas were never addressed, and additional traumas have been endured throughout history. African Americans today continue to experience traumas comparable to those experienced by enslaved people.

REPRODUCTIVE HEALTH RISKS FOR
AFRICAN AMERICAN WOMEN

Chronic stress determinately impacts reproductive health outcomes. DeGruy (2017) explains that high exposures to stress early in life can damage our ability to manage and control emotions as we develop. She notes that scientists have discovered that the "stress hormone," cortisol, can block our ability to make rational decisions and begin affecting us before birth, as pregnant mothers can pass cortisol to infants through the placenta. This phenomenon explains how chronic stress caused by the trauma of slavery, racism, and other continuous oppressions against African Americans can have lasting negative effects on health and wellness.

The CDC defines health equity as being "achieved when everyone has an equal chance to be healthy regardless of their background" (CDC 2019). African Americans have the highest reported rates of sexually transmitted infections (STIs) than any other group in the United States. Poverty and unjust "social conditions" are among the top risk factors for lack of equitable access to sexual health services (CDC 2019). In 2017, according to the CDC (2019), the Black poverty rate was 21.2% (8.9 million), which is also the highest of any ethnic group in the country. Affordability of quality sexual healthcare is the most obvious implication of this high poverty rate. A less evident barrier to accessing sexual health services is the cultural mistrust of the healthcare system due to the legacy of scientific and medical exploitation of Black patients, sexualized violence against Black women, and provider bias (Okoro, Hillman, and Cernasev 2020; Prather et al. 2016). Researchers have found that "cultural mistrust has been associated with low self-esteem, dissatisfaction with healthcare, and delayed medical treatment" (Prather et al. 2016, 666).

According to Beard and Hoytt (2012):

> Sexually transmitted diseases are infectious diseases spread through intimate contact—typically vaginal intercourse, oral sex, or anal sex. . . . They can sometimes be transmitted through skin-to-skin contact or a visible or microscopic sore, by sharing drug needles, during childbirth or breastfeeding, and even while using sex toys . . . chlamydia, gonorrhea, hepatitis, herpes, HIV/AIDS, human papillomavirus (HPV), syphilis, and trichomoniasis are among the most common STDs. (208)

Most STDs are preventable, and some are treatable, but all STDs have the potential to leave permanent, lifelong physical and emotional scars. There are other common infections of the reproductive system that should not be mistaken for STIs—bacterial vaginosis (BV), yeast infections, and urinary tract infections. These three infections are all treatable (CDC 2020). Sex can increase the risk of becoming infected, but it is not the sole cause. For example, BV and yeast can both be caused by a disruption in the vaginal pH caused by douching or scented feminine hygiene products, like tampons (CDC 2020). The vagina's pH can also be disrupted by the normal bacteria of the penis spread during vaginal intercourse. Tips for keeping the vaginal pH and urinary tract healthy include eating a healthy diet full of vegetables and fruit; drinking lots of water daily; getting regular exercise; cleaning the vulva before and after any sexual activity; urinating before and after sexual activity; using condoms; limiting sexual partners; and using nonscented feminine hygiene products that have natural, recognizable ingredients.

STDs can be prevented by practicing abstinence, always using condoms, limiting the number of sexual partners, getting tested and treated as often as needed, and getting vaccinated against viruses like human papilloma virus (HPV) and hepatitis. The CDC outlines the screening recommendations for each STD. In general, sexually active women should be screened for most STDs at least once per year, or more, depending on her number of sexual partners and if she is pregnant (CDC, 2015). In many instances, untreated and treated STDs can lead to more serious complications in women like infertility, ectopic pregnancy, pelvic inflammatory disease, infection of newborns, heart disease and brain malfunction (from syphilis), increased risk of HIV contraction, cancers of the reproductive system, and death from untreated syphilis and HIV (CDC, 2015).

Cancer is another taboo topic of discussion within Black communities. Mothers, grandmothers, and aunts often suffer in silence in an attempt to remain the strong, matriarchal glue of the family. This is dangerous for cancers that may be hereditary; it can leave women unknowingly at risk. Black women are dying at disproportionate rates from the following reproductive cancers: cervical, breast, uterine, and ovarian (American Cancer Society 2019). "Cancer is a disease in which abnormal cells grow, divide, and spread, often forming a mass called a tumor" (Bellenir 2010, 3). Factors that increase a woman's risk for developing cancer include age; tobacco use; genetic mutations; excessive alcohol intake; ultraviolet rays; some medications; substances in the home, workplace, and environment (like secondhand smoke and asbestos); family history; and infections like HPV (Bellenir 2010).

HPV is the most common STI in the United States and the main cause of most cervical cancer cases (American Cancer Society 2020; CDC 2020). HPV is transmitted easily because it is commonly asymptomatic and can be spread through skin-to-skin contact (CDC 2020). There are about 100 HPV virus types and more than 40 are sexually transmitted; in some cases, HPV will cause genital warts (Boston Women's Health Book Collective 2011). Cervical cancer usually affects women in midlife, between the ages of 35 and 50, but the good news is that it has high rates of successful treatment when it is detected early (CDC 2020). Condom use greatly decreases the risk of cervical cancer and regular screenings are imperative for early detection and treatment of the disease.

Breast cancer is the most common cancer diagnosis and the second most common cause of cancer death for Black women, according to the American Cancer Society (2019). It was estimated that 6,540 Black women would die from breast cancer in 2019. Research has shown that higher rates of obesity and stress, and less access to higher quality healthcare with advanced technology, like digital mammograms, can increase the number of diagnoses (Boston Women's Health Book Collective 2011). In addition to the risk factors for cancer mentioned above, breast cancer has also been linked to a personal history of breast cancer, having dense breasts, early onset of the menstrual period, never having children or having children after age 30, and hormone replacement therapy (Breastcancer.org 2018). Common symptoms of breast cancer include a lump in or near the breast; changes in the color, size, and shape of the breast; nipple discharge and orientation changes; and changes to breast skin (Breastcancer.org 2018). Mammograms, clinical breast exams, and breast self-exams can all aid in the early detection of breast cancer.

Uterine cancer is the most common reproductive cancer in the United States. It is estimated to be 65,620 new cases in 2020 (National Cancer Institute 2020). The most common type of uterine cancer is endometrial cancer, which starts in the lining of the uterus or endometrium. This is one of the cancers that has a lower rate among Black women than among White women (American Cancer Society 2019). The exact cause is unknown, but research has found a correlation to elevated levels of estrogen (Boston Women's Health Book Collective 2011). According to Beard and Hoytt (2012), "symptoms include bleeding between normal periods before menopause, vaginal bleeding or spotting after menopause, extremely long, heavy, or frequent episodes of vaginal bleeding after age 40, lower abdominal or pelvic cramping, and a thin white or clear vaginal discharge after menopause" (140).

Ovarian cancer starts in the ovaries and about half the women diagnosed are 63 years or older (American Cancer Society 2018). Black women's rates are among the lowest, but they have the second highest rate of death from ovarian cancer after White women (Beard and Hoytt 2012). Ovarian cancer commonly goes undiagnosed because the symptoms are similar to those of digestive and bladder problems (Boston Women's Health Book Collective 2011). The most common signs and symptoms of ovarian cancer include bloating, pelvic or abdominal pain, trouble eating or feeling full quickly, and urinary symptoms such as urgency or frequency (American Cancer Society 2018).

Contraction of STIs, unwanted pregnancy, and chronic stress are just a few risk factors for infertility and cancers of the reproductive system. Beard and Hoytt (2012) list the steps Black women can take to decrease the risk of developing cancers of the reproductive system. They include getting regular cancer screenings, mammograms, and pap smears; decreasing tobacco and alcohol use; and maintaining a healthy weight by consuming a healthy diet and getting regular exercise. Other noncancerous reproductive issues that affect Black women include fibroids, endometriosis, endometrial hyperplasia, uterine prolapse, ovarian cysts, polycystic ovary syndrome, and chronic pelvic pain (Bellenir 2010). It is crucial that Black women are fully informed and clear about their diagnoses, and all options they have for treatment, including natural and noninvasive choices.

Reproductive and sexual health is pertinent to the development and wellness of African American women at each stage of life. Researchers explain that racism and social determinants of health, including poverty, and limited access to education and employment, are chronic stressors that contribute to many of the reproductive health disparities seen in Black women across the life span (Prather et al. 2016). It is important to consider the social barriers encountered at each stage of a woman's life when developing interventions and programs that aim to improve reproductive and sexual health outcomes.

ADOLESCENTS

Adolescence (ages 10–19) plays a pivotal role in the healthy maturation and development of African American women. Typically, this is the time that girls experience many biological, social, and psychological changes, such as puberty and forming a sexual identity (Belgrave 2009). Black adolescents are extremely vulnerable to the media's hypersexualized, negative depictions of African American women and their promotion of unhealthy foods and substances (Belgrave 2009; Singleton 2003). Building healthy relationships with mentors, practicing positive affirmations, and promoting ethnic identity are ways to help negate harmful media messages and guide girls in becoming physically, emotionally, mentally, and spiritually healthy beings (Belgrave 2009; Singleton 2003). Adolescence is also a critical time to strengthen self-esteem, confidence, positive body image, and identity. Without proper guidance, in a society filled with "systemic racism, sexism, color bias and classism," Black girls risk basing their sense of self on the stereotypical, negative images of Black women portrayed through the media (Beard and Hoytt 2012, 23). Research shows that young Black girls who internalize negative stereotypes in the media are more likely to have multiple sexual partners (Prather et al. 2016). Researchers also note that these risky sex behaviors are impacted by self-esteem and increase the risk of HIV/STIs (Prather et al. 2016).

When adolescent girls reach puberty, they experience many physical changes, like getting taller, acne outbreaks, underarm and pubic hair growth, breast development, and starting their periods (Boston Women's Health Book Collective 2011). Unfortunately, this is also when societal taboos and cultural norms begin to conflict with girls' natural maturation. Black girls are often ridiculed for expressing sexuality in any form, and they commonly receive the intergenerational message to 'keep your legs closed' (Beard and Hoytt 2012, 28). In many instances, this message is the only type of sex talk that African American girls will receive from their caregivers, leaving them susceptible to inaccurate lessons about their growing bodies and sex from their peers and television. This also leaves Black girls vulnerable to many of the negative consequences of having sexual relationships, like unplanned pregnancy, STIs, "HIV, intimate partner violence, and potential emotional abandonment" (Beard and Hoytt 2012, 28; Prather et al. 2016).

According to the CDC (2019), young people ages 15–24 account for about half of the 19 million new cases of STIs every year (one in four will contract an STI, such as chlamydia or gonorrhea). In 2018, there were 6817.3 reported chlamydia cases among Black adolescent females age 15–19. This was 45 times the rate of white females in the same age range. Black adolescent females reported 1,756.4 gonorrhea cases. Black females reported a higher rate of 8.8 more than White adolescents. In addition to the former risk factors mentioned relating to lack of access to sexual health services, many young Black women are also burdened by lack of transportation, extended wait times, clinic hours that conflict with school, work and/or family obligations, shame in requesting STI services, and fear of the discomfort of testing (CDC 2019). The CDC also states that there is a biological factor that puts all sexually active adolescents at a higher risk for contracting STIs: They have "increased cervical ectopy. Cervical ectopy refers to columnar cells, which are typically found within the cervical canal, located on the outer surface of the cervix. Although this is a normal finding in adolescent and young women, these cells are more susceptible to infection" (CDC 2019). HIV/AIDS cases are astronomical in low-income African American communities. Although Black people make up 13% of the U.S. population, they accounted for about 42% of new HIV cases in 2013 (CDC 2020). In 2018, there were 37,832 new HIV diagnoses in the United States; 60% of cases were among Black adolescents aged 13–19 (CDC 2020).

YOUNG ADULTS

Young adulthood (ages 20–39) is an ideal time to make positive lifestyle changes that will promote happiness, health, and prosperity. Choices made during adolescence have the potential to impact a young woman's social environment and physical, mental, and spiritual health. For example, unprotected sex in high school could result in an energetic toddler in young adulthood, and school/career delays. Luckily, young Black women have many strengths that allow them to overcome sociocultural barriers and lead healthy, successful lives. Stanford scholar and workplace diversity expert, Katherine Phillips, explains that Black women are natural leaders who are viewed as competent, independent, and demanding of respect (Chandler 2011). Phillips relates the educational and entrepreneurial success of young Black women to these traits. Chandler (2011) writes, "Two-thirds of Black college undergrads are female." And, between 2002 and 2008, the number of businesses owned by Black women rose by 19%—twice as fast as all other firms and generating $29 billion in sales nationwide. Young African American women get their first feel for overt racism, sexism, and economic classism as they move out on their own and navigate life's challenges during their transition to adulthood, such as graduating from college, beginning full-time work, seeking long-term relationships, and considering forming families (Barr et al. 2018; Beard and Hoytt 2012). In addition, Black women are more intensely pressured to live up to "standards of beauty that are inconsistent with the normal phenotype of many African American women," which can contribute to lower self-esteem and unhealthy sexual behaviors (Norman 2012, 62). Young Black women can work toward achieving optimal reproductive health by adopting the following lifestyle changes: consuming a nutrient-rich diet, decreasing sugar and processed foods, staying hydrated by drinking adequate amounts of water, finding fun and creative ways to get regular physical activity, integrating stress-reducing techniques into their daily routines, becoming more intentional about using feminine hygiene products and other household products that are safe for reproductive health, and being informed about the sexual health status of current and potential sexual partners.

Researchers report that women have the right to sexual and reproductive health that is free from harm and discrimination (United Nations Human Rights, n.d.; Beard and Hoytt 2012). Reproductive and sexual health maintenance is multifaceted during young adulthood. Black women, like all women, have challenges managing their reproductive health due to how vastly different young adult lives are today from those generations ago. Researchers have suggested that young adults today, from late teens to late 20s, are in their "odyssey years"—a time of navigating the path to maturity (Boonstra 2009). Young women in this phase of life are taking longer to start careers, live independently and start families, which often leads to high rates of unplanned pregnancy and abortion (Boonstra, 2009). Black adolescent girls often do not get comprehensive sexual health education in school or basic discussions about reproductive health from caregivers, which Boonstra (2009) considers to be a risk factor for poorly managed sexual health and fertility.

The wellness of Black families and communities depends on the reproductive health of Black women of childbearing age. Family planning is key to ensuring favorable maternal and infant health outcomes, and improving sexual and reproductive health management in young adulthood. Black women have some of the highest rates of unintended pregnancies in the United States, which results in higher rates of unintended births and abortions (Dehlendorf et al. 2010). Researchers have found that disparities in family planning outcomes for minority women are related to disparities in contraceptive use. Dehlendorf et al. (2010) explain that Black women have fears about the safety and side effects of contraceptive methods, which is reasonable given the history of eugenics and reproductive genocide against African American women. The fears about contraceptive use and challenges with effective use can also be attributed to lack of knowledge about birth control and reproductive health that stems from "lower levels of education, culturally based health myths, and differences in familial communication about reproductive health" (Dehlendorf et al. 2010, 216). Healthier mothers produce healthier babies, which in turn creates healthier communities. Black women need better access to education on proper nutrition, safe physical activity, and access to mental health services before, during, and after childbirth. If women are experiencing chronic diseases like obesity, hypertension, and diabetes, they will also need better access to preventative healthcare services that can assist in disease management. Dehlendorf et al. (2010) outline additional recommendations for addressing family planning disparities: (1) universal healthcare coverage for contraceptives; (2) increased access to abortion and public funding of abortion; (3) increased access to culturally appropriate birth control education; and (4) increased access to culturally appropriate, patient-centered reproductive and sexual healthcare.

It is important for young Black women to remember that they are in control of their bodies and health and that they have the ability to shape a scope of care that is comfortable, pleasurable, and safe. Many women do not even know that they have options when it comes to childbirth providers and method and location of delivery. It is easy to get sucked into Hollywood's dramatic depiction of pregnancy and childbirth as a dreadful and painful process, filled with endless medical interventions that women have little control over. Most women in the United States choose to have an OB/GYN assist them in birthing their children, but many Black women are opting for midwives, in search of a "holistic care" experience that is free of unnecessary medical interventions and that will decrease the risk of pregnancy-related illness and death (Beard and Hoytt 2012, 53). Black women need increased access to and information on birthing centers and home birth options. Hospitals are typically the best option for women who have a high-risk pregnancy, but these two alternatives provide a more comfortable and less stressful environment for women to labor and deliver in, and for babies to be born into. Stress prevention of Black young adult perinatal women should be a top priority of researchers, interventions, and healthcare systems.

In 2018, Black women ages 20–24 accounted for about 7,087.7 reported chlamydia cases and 2,212.1 reported cases of gonorrhea per 100,000 women (CDC 2019). Interestingly, between 2016 and 2018, cases of chlamydia and gonorrhea decreased for Black adolescent girls but increased for Black young adult women (CDC 2019). This shows that there is a need for more effective sexual health interventions for young adults. When more young Black women gain the reproductive and sexual health knowledge needed to make positive informed decisions, there should be a downward shift in abortions, STIs, rape, and reproductive coercion. Molestation and rape are silent intergenerational occurrences within Black communities. Black girls are repeatedly molested by family members and family friends, while their caregivers keep it secret in fear of shaming the child and family. In the groundbreaking 1986 Putnam and Trickett study of the impact of childhood sexual abuse on female development, it was found that sexually abused girls experience cognitive deficits, depression, and challenges in sexual development such as early puberty (van der Kolk, 2014). According to van der Kolk, results from the study show that in comparison to nonabused girls, abused girls had 3–5 times more levels of testosterone and androstenedione, the hormones that fuel sexual desire. These results and the trend of sexual abuse within Black families may provide a deeper understanding as to why adolescent girls are engaging in early risky sexual behaviors, which have lasting impacts on early adulthood.

Unresolved sexual and reproductive traumas from childhood sexual abuse can cause psychological issues throughout adulthood that trickle down to future generations (which relates to the earlier discussion on epigenetics). Women are burdened with mental health and self-esteem issues as a result and are unprepared to teach their children on how to protect themselves and speak out against abuse in all forms. It is important to understand that intergenerational silence against sexual abuse can be traced back to American slavery. Slave owners would rape women and force sexual encounters between enslaved men and women in an attempt to increase reproduction for slave labor. Imagine how intense 400 years of sexual abuse had to have been during a time when Black women were not even considered to be human. Enslaved women were forced to keep their abuse a secret, or else risk losing their lives and the lives of their loved ones. Black women and families are still healing from this abuse and trauma (and symptoms of Post-Traumatic Slave Syndrome) over 150 years later.

MIDLIFE ADULTS

African American women deserve the opportunity to live happy and peaceful lives, with the confidence and freedom to authentically express themselves. Midlife adulthood (ages 40–64) is the perfect time for Black women to take total control of their health and heal from trauma endured during their younger years (Beard and Hoytt 2012). Women who practice good self-care habits in their young adult years typically look young, have high energy levels, and are filled with joy and happiness during midlife (Boston Women's Health Book Collective 2011). On the other hand, many Black women also struggle with obesity and other chronic diseases, like cardiovascular disease and diabetes (Khan et al. 2021). When good health habits are not established during the young adult years, it is harder to begin making behavioral pattern changes in midlife. In addition, if self-love and health knowledge are not strengthened during the younger years, midlife Black women will lack the confidence and drive to make vital lifestyle changes (Beard and Hoytt 2012). Many Black women focus more on their outer beauty and appearance than on being physically, mentally, and spiritually Healthy (Awad 2015; Beard and Hoytt 2012). Black women also tend to prioritize caring for their families over properly caring for themselves. Self-care is often viewed as a selfish act, as opposed to an act of self-preservation. This ideology of self-care needs to be reversed throughout Black communities to see an improvement in health and wellness. Research suggests that African American women in midlife, who have children transitioning into young adulthood experiencing unemployment, issues within romantic relationships, and challenges with the criminal justice system, are at risk for chronic diseases and decreased health from increased psychological distress (Barr et al. 2010). This research shows how vital it is for individuals, communities, researchers, and healthcare institutions to focus more on the physical, mental and emotional, social, and economic health needs of Black women. The lack of focus on self-preservation and holistic wellness are also patterns that have been carried forth from American slavery. Enslaved women were required to devote the majority of their time and energy to caring for their owners' families and lacked control and agency over their bodies African American women have also always encountered barriers to accessing safe and culturally appropriate healthcare services throughout history.

Black women in midlife are also having children. Attempting to reproduce in midlife can sometimes cause physical and emotional challenges, but success rates increase when women are healthy and free of chronic disease. Dr. O'Delle M. Owens, Cincinnati's first board-certified fertility specialist, states, "Unlike men, who produce sperm on a regular basis throughout most of their lives, women are born with a set number of eggs . . . the older you get, the fewer eggs you have" (Beard and Hoytt 2012, 77–76). Midlife women typically begin to experience perimenopause, the time when a woman's hormone levels begin to drop. By age 50, many women will actually transition into menopause, the time when her period stops (Santoro et al. 2021). Women experience menopause in many different ways, but Black women tend to have more "estrogen-related symptoms," like hot flashes, night sweats, vaginal dryness, and urine leakage than women of any other background (Beard and Hoytt 2012, 77). This is likely to be a result of poor health habits and chronic stress throughout life.

Contrary to popular belief, reproductive and sexual health is just as crucial during midlife as it is during young adult and adolescent years. Black women are less likely to marry during their midlife years, so they engage in more casual relationships during their sexual life (Beard and Hoytt 2012). It is vital that sexually active Black women at all life stages know that they are at risk for contracting any STI, especially when having unprotected sex with multiple partners. Like Black adolescent girls and young adults, midlife women need to seek and be knowledgeable about preventative reproductive and sexual health services. Regular breast exams, pelvic exams, and pap smears, and STI and HIV testing will contribute greatly to their overall wellness.

MATURE ADULTS

Self-care, or the lack thereof, is an important determinant of mature women's (ages 65 and up) wellness. Those who ate nutrient-rich diets were regularly physically active, and those who had effective routines for managing stress during their early and midyears enter their mature years with great health and a positive outlook on their evolving physical characteristics and social environments. Unfortunately, a disproportionate number of mature Black women struggle with chronic illness and lack a sense of fulfillment in their lives due to life circumstances and poor health choices (Beard and Hoytt 2012). It is important to remember that many of the women in this age group grew up in the civil rights era, amid the Black power and women's rights movements. In addition to being impacted by the dysfunction that slavery caused within Black families, mature Black women "were working to fulfil the dream of an integrated society, pursuing unprecedented job opportunities, raising families, tending to their husbands and homes, building and stabilizing our communities, and figuring out how to remain sane and available for all those who depended on them" (Beard and Hoytt 2012, 93).

This is the stage of life when women often begin to end their work lives, lose loved ones and spouses, notice extreme changes in their physical bodies and energy levels, and lose the culturally mythical status of the "Black superwoman" (Beard and Hoytt 2012, 93). There is a common theme of denial in this stage of life that is prominent within Black communities: Black women who struggle with diseases like hypertension and diabetes tend to describe themselves as having good health. This denial is caused by Black women's determination to be invincible caretakers, from poor health becoming a normal expectation, and by assigning a low value to health and wellness. Just as there is a need to educate young Black girls on the importance of self-care, it is also critical that it is reinforced for older adults. Elders in Black communities need to feel that they are valued and "respected for their struggles and sacrifices, achievements, the wisdom they gained, and the new generations they . . . birthed" (Beard and Hoytt 2012, 89).

There is a social stigma that mature adults do not have sexual desires and should not have sex (Boston Women's Health Book Collective 2011). Many Black women internalize this stigma and, as a result, have unsatisfying sex lives and lack awareness about their risk of contracting STIs. Some mature adult women are actively dating and have new sexual relationships, which can be challenging due to the small pool of available partners and chronic issues that affect Black men's sexual health (Beard and Hoytt 2012). Chronic diseases, such as obesity and cancer, can also affect sexual pleasure and performance in women (Boston Women's Health Book Collective 2011). The lack of conversations about sex and sexuality within Black communities does not only cause harm to adolescent girls, but it also puts sexually active Black women of all ages at risk. The reality is that too many mature women are avoiding engaging in healthy dialogue about sex.

CONCLUSION

The reproductive and sexual health of Black women is vital to healing the Black community because we carry, birth, and nourish each individual within the community. We must make a commitment to healing and living healthily to free our bodies from the damaging effects of trauma and chronic stress. Mark Wolynn, a leading expert in the field of inherited family trauma, describes how inherited family trauma impacts our development and provides simple tips for healing in his book, *It Didn't Start with You*. Wolynn (2016, 145) writes, "we're connected to people in our family history whose unresolved traumas have become our legacy. When the connection remains unconscious, we can live imprisoned in feelings and sensations that belong to the past."

It is time for Black women and communities to break free from the shackles of past trauma so that we can heal our bodies, minds, and spirits, and birth future generations who are healthy, whole, and thriving. DeGruy (2017, 158) urges that "any level of healing first requires an accurate assessment of the damage as it has impacted the individual, the family, the community and the society." She also outlines steps that African Americans can take toward healing in her book, *Post Traumatic Slave Syndrome*: (1) eating nutrient-rich, life-sustaining food and avoiding processed foods and fast food filled with unhealthy fat, sugar, and salt; (2) becoming more aware of the impacts of American institutions and systems, policy decisions of local and state governments, racial socialization, and learning to advocate for ourselves and communities to create the change needed to live well; (3) knowing ourselves and the strength and resilience we have shown throughout history, learning more about the positive contributions we have made through society, and debunking negative societal stereotypes and myths; (4) becoming more intentional about making healing a lifestyle by building on our strengths and drawing on our inner fortitude, resilience, endurance, creativity, spirituality, and ability to love; (5) building self-esteem and becoming more aware of the value we produce in society; (6) developing healthy coping skills for managing stress and anger; (7) modeling positive and healthy behaviors that we want our children to pass down to future generations; and (8) telling our stories confidently without fear or shame, and living authentically with pride for our cultural uniqueness.

IMPLICATIONS

The time has come to eradicate the taboos associated with conversations about sex and sexuality within Black families. We need to reverse the belief that natural occurrences like menstruation, normal vaginal discharge and odor, and hormonal changes due to pregnancy and menopause make women dysfunctional in some way. Sex and female physiology should be embraced as natural phenomena that allow human life on earth to continue evolving, not dirty or perverted circumstances. Black communities of the twenty-first century could benefit from increased access to accurate reproductive and sexual health education. This could come in the form of mandated reproductive and sexual wellness instruction in primary and secondary education; community centers that have regular sexual and reproductive educational workshops for youth and adults; and other interventions that advise and educate parents on how to have challenging conversations with their children about sexuality, hygiene, the functions of the reproductive system, and safe consensual sexual practices. In our "Digital Age," when media influences are at an all-time high, it would also be beneficial to incorporate sexual and reproductive health education into various media outlets. Researchers have found that new media platforms like social networking sites, microblogs, online video sites, and mobile phone applications are successful in shifting attitudes and increasing sexual health knowledge among African American adolescents and young adults (Teadt et al. 2020).

Music and television writers and producers should be more intentional about balancing sexualized images and ideas with self-care messages like eating healthily, drinking water, reducing stress, maintaining good hygiene, wearing condoms, knowing the STI status of all sexual partners, getting regular checkups by healthcare providers, and limiting the consumption of drugs and alcohol. When Black girls scroll through TikTok, Instagram, and Twitter, they should see overwhelming amounts of information on reproductive and sexual health and the importance of managing stress. When young girls walk to school or ride in the car with their caregivers, they should be bombarded with infographics on billboards that warn against the dangers of poor mental health, drug and alcohol abuse, and risky sexual behaviors. Young girls should also be encouraged to ask their caregivers, health professionals, teachers, and community leaders more questions about their bodies and what it means to have healthy and positive sexual experiences. Experts DeGruy (2017) and Wolynn (2016), both write about the importance of taking a multilayered and person-centered approach to healing from intergenerational trauma. Community and research efforts that aim to improve the reproductive and sexual health of women within Black communities should focus on the following:

- Education on anatomy and function, proper hygiene, and disease prevention of the reproductive system
- Prevention education on vaginal infections (not sexually transmitted)
- Prevention education on STIs, including HIV/AIDS
- Self-pleasure as a healthy alternative to delay sexual activity in adolescents, and for women of all ages to explore and become more comfortable with their bodies (debunk the myths about masturbation being unclean)
- Culturally appropriate family planning education and services to reduce the high rates of abortions, maternal and infant morbidity/mortality, and premature birth
- Holistic pregnancy and birth options, including information on the benefits of doula services
- Education on the benefits of vaginal births, avoiding C-section and other medical interventions during birth, breastfeeding, and skin-to-skin contact with infants immediately after birth
- Understanding that self-care is crucial for healthy development across the life span, and that it includes the body, mind, and spirit
- Realizing that chronic stress is an intergenerational disease that has manifested from the brutal, inhumane conditions of slavery and that it is a huge factor in the presence of many chronic diseases and illnesses
- Developing holistic strategies to cope with chronic stress across the life span, including exploring alternative medical services like reflexology, Reiki, acupuncture, chiropractic therapy, massage therapy, and so on
- Seeking culturally appropriate mental health services to heal from trauma
- Becoming self-informed about the side effects of common medications like birth control, and the dangers of toxic chemicals found in common feminine hygiene products
- Removing social and economic barriers to maintaining a healthy diet and committing to regular physical activity
- Empowering African Americans to advocate for themselves healthcare settings and other powerful systems

Society can learn a great deal from the resilience African American women and girls have shown over the past 550 years. We survived the debauching conditions of slavery, the inhumane conditions that sparked the civil rights movement, and we continue to prevail through the racist and sexist overtones of the Trump era. Black women have unbreakable strength, but the effects of historical trauma and everyday chronic stressors like discrimination and racism are undeniably contributing to debilitating reproductive and sexual health disparities. Researchers conclude that the effects of trauma and chronic stress are so detrimental to health because "they can be experienced across generations and negatively affect social relationships that are known to be health protective" (Prather et al. 2016, 666). Self-care, with a focus on healing from intergenerational trauma and mastering coping skills, is pivotal for improving the state of wellness within Black communities. Experts who identify as Black women are needed to assist in the development of culturally appropriate, strength-based prevention programs that can improve sexual health decision-making and demolish harmful reproductive conditions. These programs should strive to improve the self-esteem and self-efficacy of Black women and girls, increase reproductive and mental healthcare access, and decrease the incidence of pregnancy related illnesses and death. A study of 11,918 Black adolescents showed that sexual health interventions are "associated with improvements in abstinence, condom use, sexual health intentions, sexual health knowledge, and sexual health self-efficacy . . . which are [behavioral and] psychological outcomes associated with positive behavior change" (Evans et al. 2020, 683–684).

There is a critical need for more African American women in public health and preventative healthcare fields to accurately inform research and intervention efforts. Black women are also more likely to trust and comply with healthcare professionals that are relatable. Psychotherapy is one of the preventative health services that could aid Black women in healing from trauma and attaining the "clarity and balance" they need to be "effective and happy" in life (Singleton 2003, 2). Therapy is widely rejected throughout Black communities for a plethora of reasons that include the stigma that therapy is for 'crazy' people, a tragic history of Black people being unjustly disadvantaged for attempting to better their social situations, the perception that therapy is too expensive, and strong religious beliefs that God solves all human problems (Singleton 2003). Individual and group therapy can help African American women overcome the damaging effects that years of sexual and reproductive coercion have embedded into their psyche. It can provide a safe environment to discuss and process sexual abuse and other traumas that might be triggering. Group therapy is especially unique because it provides opportunities for women to feel like they are a part of a community and to realize that they are not alone on their healing journey. Psychotherapy can help to transform current generations and birth future generations that are reproductively, mentally, and spiritually well.

van der Kolk (2014) writes that:

> The training of competent trauma therapists involves learning about the impact of trauma, abuse, and neglect and mastering a variety of techniques that can help to (1) stabilize and calm patients down, (2) help to lay traumatic memories and reenactments to rest, and (3) reconnect patients with their fellow men and women. Ideally the therapist will also have been on the receiving end of whatever therapy he or she practices. (214)

It is important that Black women and communities have access to therapists who practice trauma-informed, culturally sensitive techniques. Mindfulness is one technique that comes highly recommended by researchers and clinicians. van der Kolk (2014) explains that self-awareness is a key component to healing from trauma, and that by noticing our annoyance, nervousness, and anxiety, we can immediately shift our perspectives and react in healthier ways. He writes, "Mindfulness puts us in touch with the transitory nature of our feelings and perceptions. When we pay focused attention to our bodily sensations, we can recognize the ebb and flow of our emotions and, with that, increase our control over them" (2014, 210). Wolynn (2016) suggests creating personal healing sentences to heal from inherited family trauma and release thoughts, emotions, feelings, behaviors, or symptoms that did not originate with us (Wolynn 2016, 149). Dr. Joy DeGruy (2017, 100) explains that, "It is from impacts of past assaults that we must heal, and it is from the threats of continuing assaults that we must learn to defend ourselves, our families, and our communities."

REFERENCES

Awad, Germine H., Carolette Norwood, Desire S. Taylor, Mercedes Martinez, Shannon McClain, Bianca Jones, Andrea Holman, and Collette Chapman-Hilliard. 2015. "Beauty and Body Image Concerns Among African American College Women". *Journal of Black Psychology 41*, no. 6: 540–564.

American Cancer Society. 2018. "Ovarian Cancer." Accessed January 4, 2021. https://www.cancer.org/cancer/ovarian-cancer.html.

American Cancer Society. 2019. "Cancer facts & figures for African Americans 2019–2021." Accessed December 30, 2020. https://www.cancer.org/content/dam/cancer-org/research/cancer-facts-and-statistics/cancer-facts-and-figures-for-african-americans/cancer-facts-and-figures-for-african-americans-2019-2021.pdf.

American Cancer Society. 2020. "HPV and cancer." Accessed December 30, 2020. https://www.cancer.org/cancer/cancer-causes/infectious-agents/hpv/hpv-and-cancer-info.html.

Barr, B. Ashley, Leslie Gordon Simons, Ronald L. Simons, Steven R. H. Beach, and Robert A. Philibert. 2018. "Sharing the Burden of the Transition to Adulthood: African American Young Adults' Transition Challenges and Their Mothers' Health Risk." *American Sociological Review 83*, no. 1 (February): 143–172. https://doi.org/10.1177/0003122417751442.

Beard, Hilary, and Eleanor Hinton Hoytt. 2012. *Health first! The Black Woman's Wellness Guide*. New York: SmileyBooks.

Belgrave, Faye. 2009. "Description and Demographics." In *African American Girls*: *Advancing Responsible Adolescent Development*, 3–9. New York: Springer. https ://doi.org/10.1007/978-1-4419-0090-6_1.

Belgrave, Z. Faye. 2009. "Self and Identity." In *African American Girls*: *Advancing Responsible Adolescent Development*, 11–29. New York: Springer. https://doi.org /10.1007/978-1-4419-0090-6_2.

Bellenir, Karen, ed. 2010. *Cancer Sourcebook for Women* (4th ed.). Detroit: Omnigraphics.

Boonstra, Heather D. 2009. "The Challenge in Helping Young Adults Better Manage Their Reproductive Lives." *The Free Library*. Accessed January, 4, 2021. https:// www.thefreelibrary.com/The challenge in helping young adults better manage their...-a0201946506.

Boston Women's Health Book Collective. 2011. *Our bodies, Ourselves*. New York: Simon & Schuster.

BreastCancer.org. 2018. "Symptoms and Diagnosis." Accessed December 30, 2020. https://www.breastcancer.org/symptoms.

Centers for Disease Control and Prevention. 2015. "2015 Sexually Transmitted Diseases Treatment Guidelines: Screening Recommendations and Considerations Referenced in Treatment Guidelines and Original Sources." Accessed March 26, 2018. https://www.cdc.gov/std/tg2015/screening-recommendations.htm.

Centers for Disease Control and Prevention. 2019. "Sexually Transmitted Disease Surveillance 2018: STDs in Adolescents and Young Adults." Accessed January 3, 2021. https://www.cdc.gov/std/stats18/adolescents.htm.

Centers for Disease Control and Prevention. 2019. "Sexually Transmitted Disease Surveillance 2018: STDs in Racial and Ethnic Minorities." Accessed January 3, 2021. https://www.cdc.gov/std/stats18/minorities.htm.

Centers for Disease Control and Prevention. 2020. "Genital HPV Infection - Fact Sheet." Accessed December 30, 2020. https://www.cdc.gov/std/hpv/stdfact-hpv. htm.

Centers for Disease Control and Prevention. 2020. "HIV: HIV and African Americans." Accessed January 3, 2021. https://www.cdc.gov/hiv/group/racialethn ic/africanamericans/index.html.

Centers for Disease Control and Prevention. 2020. "HIV Surveillance: Adolescents and Young Adults 2018." Accessed January 3, 2021. https://www.cdc.gov/hiv/pdf/ library/slidesets/cdc-hiv-surveillance-adolescents-young-adults-2018.pdf.

Centers for Disease Control and Prevention. (2020). "Maternal Mortality." Accessed December 30, 2020. https://www.cdc.gov/nchs/maternal-mortality/i ndex.htm.

Centers for Disease Control and Prevention. 2020. "Sexually Transmitted Diseases." Accessed January 4 2021. https://www.cdc.gov/std/default.htm.

DeGruy, Joy. 2013. "Post Traumatic Slave Syndrome." Accessed March 13, 2018. https://www.joyDeGruy.com/post-traumatic-slave-syndrome.

DeGruy, Joy. 2017. *Post Traumatic Slave Syndrome: America's Legacy of Enduring Injury and Healing.* Maryland: Uptown Press.

Dehlendorf, Christine, Maria Isabel Rodriguez, Kira Levy, Sonya Borrero, and Jody Steinauer. 2010. "Disparities in Family Planning." *American Journal of Obstetrics and Gynecology 202*, no. 3 (March): 214–220. 10.1016/j.ajog.2009.08.022.

Evans, Reina, Laura Widman, McKenzie N. Stokes, Hannah Javidi, Elan C. Hope, and Julia Brasileiro. 2020 "Association of Sexual Health Interventions with Sexual Health Outcomes in Black Adolescents: A Systematic Review and Meta-analysis." *JAMA Pediatr 174*, no. 7 (July): 676–689. doi:10.1001/jamapediatrics.2020.0382.

Flynn, Meagan. 2018. "Statue of 'Father of Gynecology,' Who Experimented on Enslaved Women, Removed from Central Park." *The Washington Post*, May 2, 2018. https://www.washingtonpost.com/news/morning-mix/wp/2018/04/18/statue -of-father-of-gynecology-who-experimented-on-enslaved-women-removed-from -central-park/.

Khan, Sadiya, Stephen Sidney, Donald M. Lloyd-Jones, and Jamal S. Rana. 2021. "National and Global Trends of Cardiovascular Disease Mortality, Morbidity, and Risk." In *ASPC Manual of Preventive Cardiology* (2nd ed.), edited by Nathan Wong, Ezra A. Amsterdam, and Peter P. Toth, 17–33. London: Springer, Cham. https://doi.org/10.1007/978-3-030-56279-3_2.

Mundt, Ingrid. 2017. "Margaret Sanger, Taking a stand for birth control." *The History Teacher 51*, no. 1 (November): 123–161. https://www.jstor.org/stable/44504545.

National Cancer Institute. 2020. "Trastuzumab May Improve Survival in Women with Rare Endometrial Cancer." Accessed December 30, 2020. https://www.cancer.gov/news-events/cancer-currents-blog/2020/endometrial-cancer-usc-her2-trastuzumab.

Norman, Gwendolyn Simpson. 2012. "Preterm Birth and the Perception of Risk Among African Americans." PhD diss., Wayne State University.

Owens, Deirdre Cooper. 2017. *Medical Bondage: Race, Gender, and The Origins of American Gynecology.* Athens: University of Georgia Press.

Prather, Cynthia, Taleria R. Fuller, Khiya J. Marshall, and William L. Jeffries IV. 2016. "The Impact of Racism on the Sexual and Reproductive Health of African American Women." *Journal of Women's Health 25*, no. 7 (July): 664–671. https://doi.org/10.1089/jwh.2015.5637.

Santoro, Nanette, Cassandra Roeca, Brandilyn A. Peters, and Genevieve Neal-Perry. 2021. "The Menopause Transition: Signs, Symptoms, and Management Options." *The Journal of Clinical Endocrinology & Metabolism 106*, no. 1 (January): 1–15. doi:10.1210/clinem/dgaa764.

Sherburne, Morgan. 2018. "The Weight of Racism: Daily Onslaught of 'Vigilance' Affects Health of Black Women." Michigan News. Accessed March 3, 2018. https://news.umich.edu/the-weight-of-racism-daily-onslaught-of-vigilance-affects-heal th-of-black-women/.

Singh, K. Gopal. (2010). "Maternal Mortality in the United States, 1935–2007: Substantial Racial/Ethnic, Socioeconomic, and Geographic Disparities Persist." *Health Resources and Services Administration, Maternal and Child Health Bureau.* Accessed December 30, 2020. https://www.hrsa.gov/sites/default/files/ourstories/mchb75th/mchb75maternalmortality.pdf.

Singleton, Dorothy Kim. 2003. *Broken silence: Opening Your Heart and Mind to Therapy- A Black Woman's Recovery Guide.* New York: The Random House Ballantine Publishing Group.

Teadt, Sierra, Jade C. Burns, Tiffany M. Montgomery, and Lynae Darbes. 2020. "African American Adolescents and Young Adults, New Media, and Sexual Health: Scoping Review." *JMIR mHealth uHealth* 8, no. 10 (October): e19459. https://mhealth.jmir.org/2020/10/e19459.

United Nations Human Rights, n.d. "Sexual and Reproductive Health and Rights." Accessed January 6, 2021. https://www.ohchr.org/en/issues/women/wrgs/pages/healthrights.aspx.

van der van der Kolk. 2014. *The Body Keeps The Score: Brain, Mind, and Body in the Healing of Trauma.* New York: Penguin Books.

Wolynn, Mark. 2016. *It Didn't Start With You: How Inherited Family Trauma Shapes Who We Are and How to End the Cycle.* New York: Penguin Books.

Chapter 7

Celebrating the Journey, an Extension Legacy

Past, Present, and Future
A Biography of Dr. Alma Hobbs

Alice F. Joyner

Cooperative extension has had a rich and broad history all over the United States. Authorized by the Morrill Act of 1862 followed by the 1890 organization of cooperative extension programs at historically Black colleges and universities, researchers, specialists, and extension agents led the charge with respect to community outreach. Dr. Alma Hobbs is one of the iconic legends who piloted cooperative extension to its pinnacle in the early years. Serving as an extension agent, Dr. Alma Hobbs began her career in 1970 as a clothing and textiles assistant at Tennessee State University, located in Nashville. Newly graduating with a bachelor's degree in home economics education from North Carolina Central University, Alma Hobbs set sail, accumulating several decades in public service.

Dr. Alma Hobbs grew up in Farmville, a small southern town in North Carolina. She attended segregated elementary and high schools. Even as a young girl growing up in a segregated south, Alma was always a visionary and dreamer. She states, "My personal and professional goals have always been to positively impact the lives of people through education to ensure they are empowered to reach their full potential." She boasts that her parents instilled in her a strong work ethic and a commitment to serve (Hobbs, Personal Communication, 2014).

From North Carolina to Washington, D.C., her career spans almost a half-century. Dr. Hobbs spent over 30 years working in the agriculture arena both locally and nationally. Putting down roots after graduating from North Carolina Central University, her first employment experience was as a 4-H and clothing and textile assistant. This inaugural introduction to cooperative extension began in Bertie County, North Carolina, working for North Carolina State Extension Service. This early experience launched a historical career stretching from 1970 to 2013, when she retired from the United States Department of Agriculture (USDA).

Chronologically, Dr. Hobbs served as an extension assistant in North Carolina, then moved to University of Tennessee in 1973, where she served as a 4-H agent in Davison County. Alma later returned to the North Carolina extension, where she subsequently attended North Carolina State University and received her master's degree in sociology with an emphasis in adult education in 1975. She then completed her doctorate, also in sociology/adult education, in 1981 (Hobbs, Personal Communication, 2014). Returning to Tennessee State University from 1981 to 1988, Dr. Hobbs continued her work as a clothing specialist with the cooperative extension system.

Dr. Hobbs's strong sense of vision and strategic mindset afforded her the opportunity through the newly forged Intergovernmental Personnel Act to work on-loan from the University of Tennessee for one year (1988–1989). Afterward, from 1989 to 1990, Dr. Hobbs moved to Tennessee State University, where she was the first woman in the nation to serve as an extension administrator (Hobbs, Personal Communication, 2014). Agriculture is typically a male-dominated profession; thus, the position was of historical significance. As the new extension administrator, Dr. Hobbs's major responsibilities in leading the extension and research units were to increase the prosperity, security, and sustainability of America's families, farms and ranches, business firms, and communities.

Dr. Hobbs's affinity for public service soon landed her a position with the USDA. She served as assistant deputy for 4H from 1990 to 1992, and later (1992–1993) she became deputy for 4-H, nutrition, and family and consumer sciences. Dr. Hobbs continued to aggressively expand outreach to numerous localities, states, and subsequently the nation. New programming and a drive to ensure that citizens all over the nation experienced the benefit of research-based information catapulted Dr. Hobbs to another position as deputy for economic and community development from 2000 to 2004.

Dr. Hobbs found herself at home at the USDA, where her tenure spanned two decades. From 2004 to 2006, Dr. Hobbs moved to another USDA position as special assistant to the assistant secretary of administration (USDA 2009). There, Alma led the charge, transforming USDA culture into a model organization positioned to meet the present and future needs of its employees and customers.

Breaking with her USDA employment trend in 2006, Dr. Hobbs was appointed dean of the School of Agriculture at Virginia State University, becoming the school's first female to serve in that position. Poised to make the School of Agriculture at Virginia State a premier unit, Dr. Hobbs created new programs, increased the research agenda, and launched more extension programs (Hobbs, Personal Communication, 2014). Dr. Hobbs held that position for three years, from 2005 to 2009.

In 2009, Dr. Hobbs returned to the Obama administration's USDA as deputy assistant secretary for administration, where she remained for approximately five years. In 2013, Dr. Hobbs retired from the USDA, but her public service-driven attitude soon afforded her the opportunity to serve on the board of visitors at Virginia State University. Dr. Hobbs was appointed by the governor of Virginia, Mr. Terry McAuliffe, in July 2014 (State of Virginia Office of Governor 2014).

Community development, impact, accountability, and sustainability were the central themes for Dr. Hobbs as she masterfully labored to transform the extension system into the superior organization it is today. Significant, renowned programs initiated by Dr. Hobbs include the 4H *Character Counts* and *Making the Grade* programs, the *Marriott* and *Farmers Project* programs, the *International Lobo* program, and the *Expanded Foods and Nutrition Education Program* (Hobbs, Personal Communication, 2014). Coupled with her tenure at the cooperative extension services, Dr. Hobbs served on numerous multifaceted professional organizations, committees, and boards. Dr. Alma C. Hobbs launched a herculean effort as she transformed communities in numerous corners of the globe, localities in the United States, and abroad.

REFERENCES

State of Virginia Office of the Governor. 2014. "Governor McAuliffe Announces Appointments to Virginia College and University Boards of Visitors". Accessed May 1, 2017. https://www.governor.virginia.gov/newsroom/news-releases/.

U.S. Department of Agriculture (USDA). 2009. "Agriculture Secretary Vilsack Names Dr. Alma Cobb Hobbs and Robin Heard Deputy Assistant Secretaries for Administration." Accessed May 1, 2017. https://usdasearch.usda.gov/search/docs? affiliate=usda&dc=166&query=Agriculture+Secretary+Vilsack+Alma+Cobb+Hobbs.

Part II

HISTORICALLY BLACK COLLEGES AND UNIVERSITIES

OPPORTUNITIES AND CHALLENGES

Once a beacon of hope for thousands of Black students denied access to higher education by predominantly White institutions, historically Black colleges and universities (HBCUs) have educated generations of Black scientists, doctors, lawyers, educators, and social activists. Today, these institutions face serious challenges. This section discusses the historical challenges and contributions of human sciences/family and consumer sciences to the education of students at HBCUs. The present state and future aspirations of cooperative extension and similar outreach programs will also be addressed.

Chapter 8 provides a historical perspective on the evolution of the human sciences/home economics/family and consumer sciences discipline at Virginia State University (VSU) and its contributions to the university, state, region, nation, and the globe. The chapter further portrays women leaders in the human sciences/home economics/family and consumer sciences at VSU who made significant contributions to the legacy of the program.

Chapter 9 offers a context for societal challenges and educating the next generation of family and consumer sciences (FCS) professionals. FCS, also known as home economics and the human sciences, has been a vital, long-standing component of the tripartite mission of 1890 land-grant universities. A discussion of the contributions of the FCS units at 1890s is offered. This chapter also provides commentary on future directions for FCS at 1890 institutions, including perspectives of 1890 administrators, educators, and researchers.

Chapter 10 discusses the perceived value of the American Association of Family and Consumer Sciences' accreditation among HBCUs, with primary focus on the 1890 universities. Traditionally, HBCUs have been the vehicle through which African American students have achieved higher education. Accreditation is viewed as a benchmark of quality within the HBCU community.

Chapter 8

Past, Present, and Future

An Exploratory of Transformation, Leadership, and Contributions of the Home Economics Department at Virginia State University

Alice F. Joyner and Dana D. Legette-Traylor

Virginia State University (VSU) is a historically Black land-grant university founded in 1882. VSU is one of the first institutions of higher education in Virginia to offer domestic sciences (home economics) programming for African American students. Early leaders understood the importance of the human sciences in providing a course of study to embrace both normal and industrial training. Capturing the importance of the second Morrill Act (1890) for land-grant institutions, in 1920 VSU became one of two land-grant institutions in Virginia and the only historically Black college or university (HBCU) in the state. Agriculture and human sciences/home economics were integral to course offerings to satisfy the demand throughout central and south Virginia. More importantly, with the first enrolled class of 117 students and enrollments growing to over 700 students, the program emerged as one of the largest in Virginia (Virginia State College undergraduate catalog 1954–1955, 31).

Growth in the student population led to changes in the certificate program to being named a school at the College during the early 1930s. The home economics program did more than provide accessibility and enhancement of opportunities for African Americans, it contributed significantly to the development of a well-skilled female workforce and female leaders in the discipline. Today, throughout the state and beyond, VSU's family and consumer sciences/human sciences alumni are among the most highly recognized teacher-educators, extension agents, early childhood providers, dietitians, textile scientists, apparel designers, and retail executives. The university's commitment to the human sciences/home economics discipline and the well-educated and well-trained graduates are as important today as they were in 1923.

This chapter aims to provide a historical perspective of the evolution of the human sciences/home economics/family and consumer sciences discipline at VSU and its contributions to the university, state, region, nation, and the globe. The chapter further portrays women leaders in the human sciences/home economics/family and consumer sciences at VSU who made significant contributions to the legacy of the program.

HISTORICAL BEGINNINGS

VSU was founded in 1882 when the legislature passed a bill to charter the Virginia Normal and Collegiate Institute. This bill was sponsored by Delegate Alfred W. Harris, who later became the institution's first president. Toppin (1992) relates:

> For the first twenty years, 1882 to 1902, Virginia State University existed under its original charter name of Virginia and Collegiate Institute. The State constitution was changed in 1902 to greatly reduce the number of African Americans allowed to vote. In this climate created by the state constitutional convention of 1901–1902, the General Assembly (the state legislature) changed the charter and mission of the institution. The collegiate designation was dropped, and the name was changed by state law to Virginia Normal and Industrial Institute. The new emphasis was to be manual training.

These turns of events redirected the emphasis of study for students enrolled in the domestic sciences program. When the school was changed to Virginia Normal and Industrial Institute, collegiate work was abandoned in 1902. President Gandy took the helm and under his leadership, college programs were restored (Toppin 1992). In 1920, the school was designated a land-grant college for Blacks in Virginia. This designation led to restoration of the institution, now known VSU, to the collegiate level. Virginia had a Black land-grant college (Hampton in 1872 and Virginia State in 1920). This occurred 18 years before the second Morrill Act of 1890, which created Black land-grant colleges (Toppin 1992). Emphasis was again placed on programs in home economics. Given this long history, the survival of programs in family and consumer sciences at VSU was inspired by an overview and vision of the many faculty members, chairpersons, and deans who led the battle to preserve institutions of higher education for African Americans.

VSU, a historically Black college and now university, is one of the first institutions of higher education in the state of Virginia to organize family and consumer sciences programs (formerly home economics) for African American students. The inception of the home economic program had its early beginnings in 1902. The initial goal of the program was to prepare individuals to teach homemaking in the public schools (Comprehensive Guide to Success 2000, 1). It was first entitled *Domestic Sciences*. Since 1921 the home economics department at VSU has experienced five name changes and several mergers and reorganizations. While the program survived, faculty and programs in the discipline were significantly reduced. The School of Home Economics faced another name change in 1976 to the Department of Human Ecology. Further, in the 1990s because of budget shortfalls, the department was merged with the Department of Agriculture and became the Department of Agriculture and Human Ecology. From the late 1990s to 2011, six new professors led the department. As the constant of change occurred (and despite restructuring, enrollment shifts, and program redirections), the department has continued to thrive as an integral component of VSU's past, present, and future.

THE TRANSFORMATIVE LEGACY OF HOME ECONOMICS AT VIRGINIA STATE UNIVERSITY

From the beginning, the Department of Family and Consumer Sciences (formerly home economics) had a purpose. In earlier years that purpose was to prepare individuals to teach homemaking, also referred to as domestic science, in the public schools. The home economics program was in the division of agriculture, where it was organized into an independent division. Ms. Cora Zuleme Jones, an instructor whose tenure has been recorded in the annals of the history of VSU, joined the staff in 1888 and served as an instructor in cooking and housekeeping (Toppin 1992). By 1921, the program was reorganized as a department. In the early years, the program focused on specialized training in home economics education and the domestic science trades such as cooking, housekeeping, and sewing. Additionally, normal two-year certificates were offered. In 1925, two years were added to the normal courses, enabling the department to offer a four-year college program leading to a bachelor's degree in 1926. The normal certificates were offered until 1931. Early graduates worked as home economics educators and in domestic services throughout the central and southeast Virginia regions. In addition, by 1930, ten faculty members were qualified and held master's degrees (Competitive Guide to Success 2000).

"The Department of Home Economics enrolled more students than the remainder of the Division of Agriculture; therefore, the Legislative Council voted that it become a Division of Home Economics in 1933" (Development of Home Economics 1928–1953, 3). Immediately, the programs were expanded and offerings were arranged in seven curricular areas: (1) applied art; (2) food and nutrition; (3) dietetics; (4) home and family life; (5) home economics education; (6) textiles and clothing; and (7) a trade course in cosmetology.

Enrollment continued to grow, launching the program in home economics into a College of Home Economics. Dr. M. E. V. Hunter, the first dean of the School of Home Economics, followed Motto Louise Sims as the department head (Toppin 1992). In 1931, Dr. Mary Hunter was appointed dean of the College of Home Economics. Under her leadership, the programs were expanded and offerings were arranged in eight curricula areas, including applied art, food and nutrition, dietetics, home and family life, home economics education, textiles and clothing, a trade course in cosmetology, as well as commercial foods (Comprehensive Guide to Success 2000). Careers specializing in these areas were key economic drivers and were often early employers of African American women. Graduate programs were established at the university in 1937 and the Master of Science degree program in home economics education was offered in 1940. The College of Home Economics was the first in the state of Virginia to offer a master's degree in home economics education. The college boasted strong enrollment from 1935 to 1955. Approximately 700 students graduated from the College of Home Economics during this period. Many students were highly honored by being selected to become members of honor societies, such as Alpha Kappa Mu, Iota Sigma Phi, Sigma Delta Epsilon, Beta Kappa Chi, and Delta Kappa Chi.

During this period, the graduates held positions as teachers in colleges, secondary and elementary schools, extension agents, assistant state supervisors of schools, USO supervisors, and buyers for clothing stores, nursery school supervisors, teachers, and designers. In 1952, the college was again reorganized into the School of Home Economics. Dr. Mildred Jordan was appointed dean in 1955 following the retirement of Dr. M. E. V. Hunter. These early program leaders were visionary, and their efforts reached beyond the university. Enrollment began to decrease, and emphasis on the domestic sciences declined significantly as additional program offerings were adopted by the university. Further, newer professional programs began to enroll female students.

From 1955 to 1972, the following major accomplishments were made when the School of Home Economics curricula were revised to increase general education and subject matter requirements; reorganize curricula concepts and generalizations; obtain approval from the American Dietetic Association (ADA), National Council for Accreditation of Teacher Education (NCATE), and the Southern Association of Secondary Schools, Colleges, and Universities; offer off-campus student teaching; establish the annual Home Economics Week and the crowning of Miss Home Economics; and offer scholarships for home economics/human ecology students in the names of M. E. V. Hunter, Eleanor Owens (home economics educator), Pauline C. Morton (VSU graduate and state coordinator), and Professor Armstrong (a clothing and textiles faculty member). Many students benefited from these scholarship funds.

To motivate students to acquire higher scholarship and leadership skills, and to develop a deeper appreciation of home economics as a profession, Kappa Omicron Phi national honor society (now Kappa Omicron Nu) was established in 1964 with the induction of 18 students, making this the first predominately Black institution to establish a chapter of this honor society. Students and advisors played a major role in establishing and expanding this organization at other HBCUs.

During this period (1955–1972), the school was concerned with the professional growth of its faculty and staff. All were encouraged to travel, enroll in doctoral programs, and to attend workshops and professional meetings. Many faculty members participated in family life seminars abroad through the International Federation of Home Economics (IFHE) in Scandinavian countries, the United Kingdom, Russia, the Orient, Africa, and the Near and Far East.

Through the reorganization of the college, the School of Home Economics became the Department of Home Economics in 1973 under the School of Education. It was during this time that teacher education became an option in each major except dietetics. Dr. Mildred Jordan, dean of the School of Economics for 18 years, retired and Dr. Mary Washington McCray, assistant professor, served as interim chairperson for the department from 1973 to 1974. This year experienced further preparation for wage earning occupations and education. With an emphasis on consumerism, programs were needed in home economics areas with a business orientation. Curricula were necessary to adequately prepare students to meet these changing needs. Harold West, an analyst with Corning Glass Works and Martha Easter, chairperson of the National HEIB (Home Economics in Business) worked diligently and closely with the chairperson, faculty, and students and the School of Business during 1973–1974 to immediately plan for the establishment of the HEIB program in the home economics department.

In 1974, upon completion of the PhD at the University of Maryland, College Park, Dr. Julia R. Miller, an instructor in the Colleges of Education and Human Ecology, was appointed associate professor and chairperson of the Department of Home Economics at VSU. Dr. Miller's leadership spanned from 1974 to 1986, creating impactful contributions during this pivotal period in both the discipline of home economics (later human ecology) and at the university. Dr. Miller served as chief administrator, associate, and professor, expanding undergraduate and graduate programs in education, family studies, human development, clothing and textiles/merchandising management, dietetics, and interior design. Moreover, in 1976, a need for change in the mission and scope of the profession of home economics precipitated the name of the Department of Home Economics to be changed to the Department of Human Ecology. This department was administered under the School of Education and later the College of Agriculture and Applied Sciences.

During the academic year 1975–1976, Dr. Miller, faculty, and students were committed to planning and establishing a HEIB program. This program included a core of business courses for all the content specialties except the home economics education program. Textiles and clothing/merchandising management; family, child, and community services; and nutrition and dietetics became concentrations under the HEIB program. Important to this focus on business was the inclusion of an ongoing internship program. During the summers, students were engaged with business and industry, working locally and nationally for six to eight weeks. These internships provided opportunities that led to employment after graduation. The department was the first unit in the state of Virginia to establish a HEIB program supported by the national HEIB organization.

Later in 1984, Dr. Miller negotiated with the dean of the School of Business to transfer the hotel and restaurant management program to the Department of Human Ecology. Initially, the program coordinator was Mr. Robert Ritz. When the program was transferred to the human ecology department, it was named hotel, restaurant and institutional management (HRIM). In Gandy Hall, the foods laboratories and a classroom were completely renovated into a beautifully decorated area, including a restaurant and up-to-date technological equipment such as a computer room. The restaurant seated approximately 54 persons and was operated by students enrolled in the HRIM program. During the existence of the program in the department, students and faculty could participate in an exchange program with a large out-of-state institution—the University of Wisconsin-Stout. Walt Disney World recruited yearly for students to gain the best service experience possible in the United States. Internships and scholarships were provided by Marriott International, Hyatt Hotels, the American Hotel and Lodging Association, the National Society for Minorities in Hospitality, and other local hospitality facilities.

In 1991, Dr. Cynthia R. Mayo, a registered dietitian, was named coordinator of the HRIM program. Hospitality support companies expanded to include Sheraton Hotels and the Virginia Hotel and Lodging Association. The hospitality program became accredited by the Accreditation Commission for Hospitality Administration (ACPHA) in 1995. At that time, it was the second HBCU hospitality program accredited, following Bethune-Cookman

University. A chapter of Eta Sigma Delta, a national hospitality society, was also chartered in the 1990s. On-campus student club representatives had the opportunity to work with state, national, and international students.

The Child Development Laboratory was a state-of-the-art programmatic thrust for the department and the university. Two directors, Dr. Jimmie Battle and later Ms. Sylvia Leftwich, along with a staff of two professional teachers, a food service employee, and foster grandparent employees, provided extraordinary leadership for this university-wide, community-based program. The program was a tuition-based, full-day program for preschoolers from the community, preschoolers of student parents enrolled at the university, and university faculty. The university also provided funding for implementation of the program to assist with providing excellent teaching resources, and with supplies and equipment. Innovative learning and teaching instructional models were implemented for preschoolers in the program and served as a model for undergraduate and graduate students within the department and across the university. Ultimately, the child development laboratory was designed for undergraduate and graduate students to become proficient in the learning and teaching process for preschoolers, and to provide community-based outreach and engagement.

For purposes of accreditation and to increase the university's rankings, a focus on research was expanded. Since VSU is a land-grant institution, federal funds were received for research, academics, and outreach/service. Across the university, chairpersons and faculty members were urged to become more actively involved in research. Since human ecology/home economics was considered as one of the initial land-grant areas, there were opportunities for the department to submit proposals and acquire federal funding through the land-grant programs of the university. Proposals were written and submitted. Dr. Miller, faculty, and staff acquired funding from a federal agency of the United States Department of Agriculture, the Science, Education, Agriculture Cooperative Research.

The funding supported research projects entitled *Effectiveness of a Homeowner's Counseling Model to Reduce Defaults of FmHA Loans*, *A Study of Food Habits and Nutritional Status of the Elderly in Southside Virginia*, and *Quality of Life of the Rural Elderly: Food, Clothing*. Dr. Miller served with faculty and staff hired for these projects as principal investigator or coprincipal investigator. The faculty continues to conduct research with its students and other colleges through surveys, thesis studies, experimentation, and poster sessions at state and national professional meetings. Additionally, Dr. Miller became associated with the international programs on campus under the auspices of the Bureau of Economic Research and Development and the Agency for International Development. She traveled to Africa with VSU faculty and faculty from collaborating universities to conduct research related to the home economics extension programs, and women in agriculture production in Ghana, Malawi, and Kenya. This research built an international component for the department.

Local funding was acquired by Dr. Miller and faculty from the Virginia State Department of Education to work with secondary home economics public school teachers to develop innovative curriculum designs. Some of these projects were a training model for teachers of handicapped and disadvantaged students, competency-based consumer education modules, competency-based teacher education in home economics, and curriculum designs for teaching various specialties in the profession.

During Dr. Miller's tenure with the Department of Human Ecology, she was dedicated to the land-grant mission of providing quality programmatic thrusts in teaching, research, and outreach/service. She and the faculty, staff, and students worked tenaciously and collaboratively within the department, across the university, within the community, nationally, and internationally to build a department that reflected the values of the land-grant mission. She was also active with alumni, representatives, and stakeholders who supported the department's programs and students.

In 1986, Dr. Miller resigned as chairperson of the department, while continuing to serve as a consultant to the Virginia State Department of Education. During this time, she also wrote curriculum for secondary home economics teachers, taught undergraduate and graduate courses, and conducted research in Malawi (south-central Africa). Dr. Mary McCray served as interim chairperson for one year. Also during July of that academic year, Michigan State University in East Lansing, Michigan, recruited Dr. Miller to become dean of human ecology.

In 1988, Dr. Mary Wyatt was named chairperson. Program standards were developed, and plans were started to develop a Vocational Technical Education Program jointly with agriculture and technology. The graduate program in home economics was dropped.

Dr. Mary Wyatt left in 1993 to take a dean's position. Dr. Cynthia Mayo was named interim chairman in 1995. She was also coordinator of the hotel restaurant and institutional management and dietetics programs. Dr. Cynthia Mayo, the new interim chairperson of the Department of Human Ecology, served for six years.

Ms. Della Bannister provided leadership for the dietetics program for more than 35 years. During that time, students engaged in summer internships in hospitals, restaurants, and other food establishments. The dietetics program was officially approved by the ADA. Later, a dietetics internship program officially began. The application for the program was written by Dr. Gloria Young and Dr. Mayo, who served as the interim chairperson of the human ecology department. The program was approved in 1994 and the first class of six started in January 1995. Four of the eight students stayed in the Home Management House, located near Gandy Hall. The house is currently the VSU Office of Planning and Institutional Effectiveness. In 2000, Dr. Mayo retired from the state of Virginia and became the director of the hospitality and tourism management program at Delaware State University.

In 2000, the university reorganized its academic programs. The Department of Human Ecology merged with the Department of Agriculture. Dr. Gloria Young became chairperson of the Department of Agriculture and Human Ecology. Dr. Young served in this position for four years, retiring in 2009. After her retirement, a chairperson was not immediately appointed. Since the department did not have an official chairperson in the position, Dr. Conrad Gilliam served as department chairperson from 2004 to 2008. In 2008, Dr. Robert Corley became chairperson of the Department of Agriculture and Human Ecology. Dr. Corley, a graduate of Tuskegee, led the department for three years until 2010. Dr. Odeh was appointed chairperson of the Department of Agriculture and Human Ecology in the fall of 2010. Dr. Odeh held this position until July 1, 2011, when the family and consumer sciences department again became independent.

During just three years, the hotel and restaurant management program was accredited by ACPHA (1995). The dietetic internship program was approved in 1994 and started in 1995 under the leadership of Dr. Gloria Young. The TAMM, FCCS, and education programs were consolidated into family and consumer sciences, the new name for home economics, which was approved in 1994 by the American Home Economics Association (now the American Association of Family and Consumer Sciences or AAFCS). All program curricula were reduced to a maximum of 120 hours.

In 2011, the university again reorganized its academic programs. The School of Agriculture became the College of Agriculture in 2012. The Department of Agriculture and Human Ecology was split a second time, forming two departments. Formerly the Department of Human Ecology, the Department of Family and Consumer Sciences (FCS) was established on July 1, 2011. Dr. Alice Joyner became chairperson of the newly formed Department of Family and Consumer Sciences. Dr. Joyner is a graduate of the program and holds a BS degree in HEIB with a concentration in foods and nutrition, as well as Master of Science degree in vocational and technical education with a concentration in family and consumer sciences from VSU and a doctorate in higher education leadership from Virginia Polytechnic Institute. Under her tenure, FCS, the education concentration, remains accredited by the Virginia Department of Education and NCATE Programs. Emphasis has been placed on addressing teacher shortages in Southside Virginia and beyond. Currently, students are awarded a baccalaureate degree in family and consumer sciences and may specialize in the following concentrations:

textiles; apparel; merchandising and management; family, child, and community service; and dietetics. They can also minor in education and receive a baccalaureate degree in hospitality management.

The department also houses a nationally recognized dietetic internship program. The didactic program in dietetics as well as the dietetic internship program was reaccredited in spring 2012. In 2012, the hospitality program became an independent department and the program was reaccredited by ACPHA in 2009. During the fall of 2014, Dr. Joyner provided leadership and support to the program modification of the textile, apparel, merchandising, and management curriculum. This program modification was designed to place emphasis on skills, practices, and technology usage compliant with current and future industry standards. Further, this program modification led to a modification of the family and consumer sciences core. This implementation ensures that programs within family and consumer sciences are supported with the foundation to meet accreditation standards.

AN OVERVIEW OF THE HOME
ECONOMICS FACILITIES

With the overall increase in college revenues between 1922 and 1923, the physical plant expanded. At that time, the Department of Home Economics was housed in five rooms on the second floor of the annex of Virginia Hall. The program remained housed in this building until 1937 (Development of Home Economics 1928–1953). Improper ventilation and structural problems with this location forced leadership to move the program to a temporary building constructed of lumber and tar paper. This building included only one classroom, one food laboratory, one clothing laboratory, and one laboratory for applied arts. The Department of Home Economics was temporarily housed in this building from 1937 to 1940.

In 1931, a brick, two-story early colonial home management house was built to serve as a laboratory for students majoring in home economics education. Its main thrust was to provide students with opportunities to develop managerial skills necessary for teaching high school students on how to maintain a home and carry out related activities in the community (Development of Home Economics 1928–1953, 2).

The Department of Home Economics moved from Virginia Hall to Vawter Hall where it was housed on the first floor of the building from 1940 to 1952. This facility encompassed two small food laboratories, one clothing and one applied art laboratory, one classroom, and one office, in addition to two small rooms that were used for nursery school education. In the 1950s, student and faculty enrollment increased significantly. To support the growth and expansion of programs, the physical plant expanded from five rooms to a freestanding building, known as Gandy Hall, which was named after the university's second president. Thus from 1952 to present, the home economics program, now family and consumer sciences, continues to be housed in Gandy Hall. The building includes 32 rooms, a central lecture room with 235 seats, three classrooms, one lounge/reading room, and 26 laboratories. These laboratories included household mechanics, applied art, food laboratories, nursery, and beauty culture. Further, there were four clothing studios, one of which was equipped with treadle machines and preparation tables. The clothing labs in the 1950s were equipped with sewing machines imported from Italy. In the late 1960s, the home economics workroom was established and used by areas of home economics. It included educational media, materials, research reports, thesis charts, graphs, journals, and abstracts useful to students and faculty.

Since the late 1990s, the department has been losing ground. Programs have been discontinued, resulting in a loss of valuable space once used by programs. Current facilities include one floor with a total of three classrooms, two clothing laboratories, two dietetic laboratories, and eight offices that house the faculty and administration.

THE IMPACT OF FAMILY AND CONSUMER SCIENCES ALUMNI

The Family and Consumer Sciences (FCS) program at VSU, through various name changes and reorganizations, has prepared a wealth of leaders in FCS including teacher educators, extension, textile and apparel and merchandising management specialists, dieticians, early childhood educators, and public servants (Comprehensive Guide to Student Success 2000). Their contributions are marked beyond southeast Virginia and have global reach. The essence of the program has prepared students with transferable skills and has instilled the importance of lifelong education and professional skill development. It is this emphasis that is carried by the department which serves as a legacy at VSU and the surrounding geographical area, across the state, nationally, and internationally.

In addition, the VSU family and consumer sciences faculty and program administrators have made significant contributions to the profession. These efforts include conducting research serving as principal investigators of federal grants, providing state-of-the-art academic programs, teaching, writing professional and community publications, and providing leadership for outreach/community service initiatives. Throughout the four major school districts in the Richmond/Petersburg area, VSU alumni maintain family and consumer science education positions. Moreover, many of these educators serve the Virginia FCS association, the AAFCS, and other professional organizations with their active memberships and leadership roles. Their voices have led to major advances and improved sustainability of the profession at the local, state, and national levels.

Throughout the history of home economics at VSU, alumni have provided ongoing support to the department by assisting with recruiting students, serving on the department's advisory board, and contributing financial donations for designated scholarships to encourage growth of the VSU family and consumer sciences legacy.

SUMMARY

The transition of the discipline from home economics to human ecology to family and consumer sciences has been met with many successes, as well as challenges across the country. Most of what the profession has experienced is mirrored throughout the nation's colleges and universities. This has especially been an issue at VSU. The program has seen periods of growth and displacement as an integral discipline. In the early periods (1952), the Department of Home Economics became a school with a student population of over 700, offering both undergraduate and graduate degrees. Through the years, the perception of home economics education and the evolution of the discipline have triggered realignment and redirection. As a result, today, VSU offers family and consumer sciences as a department within the College of Agriculture. The department offers the concentrations of family and consumer science; dietetics; and textile, apparel, and merchandising management. As each of these programs has increased importance to human development and offers significant economic value, program leaders are often required to provide justification to university leadership for continued support and promotion of the department's needs. Further, the department continues to position itself to avoid program elimination as university leadership devalues and underrecognizes the valuable contributions of family and consumer sciences. VSU, since its inception, has been an economic driver for southeast Virginia. The university is also currently the only institution of higher education in the southern region of Virginia that has continued its family and consumer sciences programs.

REFERENCES

Comprehensive Guide to Student Success. 2000. "Student Orientation Guide." Virginia State University. https://www.vsu.edu/admissions/index.php.

Development of Home Economics from 1928–1953 at Virginia State College. n.d. Petersburg, Virginia: Special Collections/Archives, Johnston Memorial Library.

Hunter, Mary E. V. 1955. "Development of the School of Home Economics 1931–1953 at Virginia State College." Special Collections/Archives, Johnston Memorial Library.

Toppin, Edgar. 1992. *Loyal Sons and Daughters: Virginia State University 1882-1992.* Pectoral Heritage, Co.

Virginia State College undergraduate catalog 1954–1955. 1954. Petersburg, VA: Virginia State University.

Chapter 9

Responding to Twenty-First-Century Opportunities and Challenges

Family and Consumer Sciences Achievements and Impact at 1890 Land-Grant Institutions

Ahlishia J. Shipley, William H. Whitaker Jr.,
and Brenda A. Martin

INTRODUCTION

Providing access and expanding educational opportunities to rural black audiences have been the historical, overarching objectives of the 1890 land-grant universities. This group of higher education institutions was created or formally designated as land-grant universities under the Morrill Act of 1890, which required states to show that race was not an admissions criterion, or to designate a separate land-grant institution for persons of color. These 1890 institutions, similar to their 1862 counterparts, uphold the land-grant mission of (1) educating the next generation of scientists, educators, producers, and citizens; (2) conducting research to solve complex food and agricultural issues facing the nation and world; and (3) offering research-based educational programs and resources to the public through cooperative extension. Family and consumer sciences (FCS), also known as home economics, has been a vital, long-standing component of the tripartite mission of 1890 land-grant universities. The FCS field draws from a broad range of disciplines to guide individuals, families, and communities in achieving an optimal and sustainable quality of life (AAFCS 2011).

As the 125th anniversary of the second Morrill Act establishing 1890 land-grant universities was recently celebrated, it is an opportune time to explore and elevate the role and contributions of FCS at 1890s from a contemporary frame. Collectively, these institutions have trained thousands of minority students in the various fields of FCS to educate families and communities, to advance science to solve societal challenges, and to become professionally engaged in our field. A discussion of these educational and research contributions of FCS units at 1890s will be offered, primarily highlighting investments administered through the federal partner of the land-grant university system, the USDA National Institute of Food and Agriculture (NIFA). This chapter also provides commentary on what is on the horizon for FCS at 1890 institutions, including perspectives of 1890 administrators.

A BRIEF HISTORY OF THE LAND-GRANT UNIVERSITY SYSTEM

The creation of the land-grant university system is inherently rooted in social justice, as these universities were intended to democratize higher education. In the 1800s, higher education was primarily reserved for the elite, wealthy class. Academic training at these institutions focused on the classics and professional education. To advance agriculture in the United States and spur innovation in production, agricultural information for people of common means was necessary (National Research Council 1995). As the possibility of expanding education and scientific pursuit became a part of the dialogue of the people at the time, the U.S. Congress took action to develop a higher educational system that would extend to broad sectors of the country's population (National Research Council 1995). In July 1862, President Abraham Lincoln signed into law a bill, introduced by Congressman Justin Morrill of Vermont, to establish land-grant institutions in each state. The Morrill Act of 1862 granted states public lands to be used for the establishment of at least one college that would teach agriculture, mechanical arts, home economics, and various applied professions. Over time, the tripartite land-grant mission of education, research, and extension would evolve into a dynamic, transformational model of learning wherein the issues and challenges of the public drive educational programs and research initiatives, which serve as the foundation for effective, meaningful outreach at the local level.

In the mid to late 1800s, society was characterized by millions of newly freed slaves due to the Emancipation Proclamation. This population also found themselves in need of education to fully participate in the economy. Booker T. Washington, a black educator, author, and orator, was an avid proponent of black people earning a practical education, especially learning those skills meaningful to his or her community. He wrote that

> the whole future of the Negro rested largely upon the question as to whether or not he should make himself, through his skill, intelligence and character, of such

undeniable value to the community in which he lived that the community could not dispense with his presence. (Washington 1901, 202)

Despite the intent of the Morrill Act of 1862 to provide necessary skills education to this proletariat class, the 1862 institutions in the southern states and a few neighboring states would not allow blacks to enroll. The Morrill Act of 1890 was passed to remedy this discrimination by forbidding racial discrimination in admissions policies for colleges receiving federal funds. A state could avoid adhering to this provision, however, if the state created or designated a separate institution and divided the funds in a "just," but not necessarily equal, manner (National Research Council 1995). Several states, located primarily in the southeastern United States, chose this option (Comer et al. 2006). In sum, these states designated 12 previously existing black institutions and, over time, established five new institutions under the second Morrill Act. Tuskegee University, although not an official land-grant university, is considered part of the 1890 institutions, as the U.S. Congress granted the Tuskegee Institute 25,000 acres of land and annual appropriations for a similar mission in 1899.

CONNECTION BETWEEN USDA AND THE 1890S

The link between USDA and the 1890 institutions dates back to the legislation that formalized their creation. NIFA (formerly the Cooperative State Research, Education and Extension Service) is USDA's extramural funding agency and the federal partner to the land-grant university system. Through federal funding, administration, and national program leadership, NIFA focuses on investing in education, research, and outreach in the context of food, agriculture, natural resources, and human sciences to solve critical issues impacting families, farms, communities, and the economy. NIFA's education portfolio supports learning and engagement, workforce development programs, and minority-serving institutions because solving societal challenges requires building and nurturing the human capital of diverse, competent learners and professionals to solve global challenges. NIFA administers several congressionally funded programs dedicated to the growth and success of 1890 institutions in the food and agricultural context. The 1890 Institution Teaching, Research and Extension Capacity Building grant program strengthens all three land-grant functions, supporting projects focused on curriculum design, faculty development, experimentation, extension program development and implementation, and student recruitment and retention. The Evans-Allen 1890 Research Formula program supports basic and applied research in food and agricultural sciences at 1890 institutions.

This funding has supported the science for breakthroughs in aquaculture efficiencies, sweet potato production, and obesity reduction. The 1890 extension formula program supports extension education that responds to the changing needs of limited-resource clientele. Through extension, these institutions continue to make meaningful impacts in rural communities and on the small farmer population, particularly socially and historically disadvantaged farmers. The 1890 facilities grant program provides funds to acquire and improve agricultural and food science facilities and equipment (e.g., child development centers and smart classrooms), so institutions can build human capital and maximize potential in the food, agriculture, natural resources, and human sciences workforce. Additionally, 1890 institutions are eligible and encouraged to apply to other NIFA funding opportunities, such as the Agricultural Food and Research Initiative (the agency's flagship research program), the Beginning Farmer and Rancher Development program, and the National Needs graduate and postgraduate fellowship grants.

Educational and outreach programs at 1890 institutions have historically responded to the learning needs of the black population, particularly in the context of their social locations (Neyland 1990). Around the time legislation was passed to create these institutions, there were approximately four million recently freed slaves in the United States in need of basic care and unequipped with the skills and training needed to enter the labor force or engage in entrepreneurship (Neyland 1990; Whitaker et al. 2009). Notwithstanding, despite emancipation, most black people were still confronted with unceasing racism, inequality, and injustice under the law. These institutions answered the call to uplift their race and worked to enhance the occupational skills of the black population with classes and training leading to gainful and honorable employment (Allen et al. 2007).

Educational offerings in FCS have evolved from industrial training courses rooted in domestic science to specialized degree programs preparing students for promising careers in research, leadership, policy, and education (Neyland 1990). Historically, the home economics, now FCS, disciplines have been responsive to the prevailing human and social conditions throughout the twentieth century.

At the beginning of the twenty-first century, Black people found themselves still confronting neoteric issues often rooted in past social conditions. The consequences of poverty and inequality among Black populations are apparent when outcomes, such as incarceration, health, family stability, and educational attainment, are considered. Between 1995 and 2015, the percentage of degree attainment among Blacks increased; however, the gap between Whites and Blacks in the rate of attaining a bachelor's or higher degree widened from 13 to 22 percentage points (National Center for Education Statistics 2016a). Education can, however, be the great equalizer in our society, granting individuals the opportunity to develop their potential and hope for a great future. The 1890 institutions still play a major role in educating students, especially in food and agricultural sciences. In the fall of 2014, this group of institutions enrolled approximately 87,000 students, with Black students comprising the majority among campus populations (National Center for Education Statistics 2016b). Through research, education, and outreach programs, 1890 institutions have worked to address the educational aspirations of the Black population, as well as underserved, limited-resource audiences.

APPLYING A CONTEMPORARY VIEW: FAMILY AND CONSUMER SCIENCES AT 1890S TODAY

All 1890 universities have offered degree programs in various areas of FCS over the course of their history. These programs were traditionally situated in agriculture units at their respective institutions—a relationship still prevalent on many of these campuses. Today, 15 (out of 19) of the 1890 land-grant universities offer academic programs in FCS or the human sciences. Given the demographic trends showing increasing diversity in the United States, 1890 universities have made significant contributions to preparing and producing a diverse pool of graduates who have joined the FCS professions. Since several of these institutions offer FCS education programs, their impact on the profession is particularly relevant given the call to fill the FCS educator pipeline across secondary, higher education, and cooperative extension settings. The shortage of highly qualified FCS secondary teachers is reported to be a concern in 50% of states reporting workforce projections (Werhan 2013).

INSTITUTIONAL PROFILES

The following institutional profiles offer an overview of the units that offer academic programs in FCS or human sciences at the 1890 universities. The profiles highlight current degree programs, student engagement activities, notable research projects, and plans for sustained growth and success. The profiles are intended to provide the reader with a contemporary look at these departments, rather than an exhaustive summary of all achievements since the turn of the century.

Alcorn State University

Alcorn State University has been preparing future professionals in FCS fields since 1916, when the focus was teacher training in vocational home economics. Today, these emerging leaders receive their training from the Department of Human Sciences in the School of Agriculture, Research, Extension, and Applied Sciences. The mission of the department is to prepare emerging leaders to address critical needs of individuals, families, and communities, empowering culturally competent, multidisciplinary, focused professionals through quality education, research, and service opportunities that enhance the health and well-being of families and communities. It also strives to promote professionalism, scholarship, and lifelong learning. The department aligns with the land-grant mission of Alcorn State to prepare and empower students through effective teaching, intensive training, rigorous research, and expansive public service. Alumni from this unit have been represented in fields including elected public office, early care and education, and FCS education.

The department offers undergraduate degrees in child development and the newly expanded food, nutrition, and community health sciences. The child development program equips students with a multidisciplinary lens to understand children and families, and opportunities to apply learning in the department's Child Development Laboratory Center, cooperative extension, and other community settings. This curriculum also includes family health courses to promote and improve health outcomes over the life span. Students enrolled in the FNCHS major are provided with the coursework required to enter into postbaccalaureate internship programs leading to eligibility to become registered dietitians (RDs). Students are engaged in Kappa Omicron Nu, Active Minds, and the department's Human Sciences Club. The average departmental enrollment is nearly 200 students with an average graduation rate of 25–28 students annually. The department is currently accredited by American Association of Family and Consumer Sciences (AAFCS). Future instructional plans are to increase enrollment and expand program offerings so that students may gain additional training in specialty areas. Plans to launch a fully online undergraduate program are underway. Eventually, the plans are to also launch master's degrees in both disciplines of nutrition and child development.

Recognizing the alarmingly high rates of childhood obesity in Mississippi, coupled with the importance of learning healthy habits early, department researchers successfully designed and launched a comprehensive program targeting preschool children encompassing nutrition, physical activity, and family engagement components. These are vital to effective obesity prevention initiatives. The *My Body Matters* program, supported through the Evans-Allen 1890 research program, engaged more than 500 preschoolers in forming healthy eating habits and gave an opportunity for undergraduate students to gain experience implementing community programs. Other significant research focuses on improving mental health outcomes for college students to improve retention and academic achievement through grants received from Substance Abuse and Mental Health Services Administration, and with the long-standing partnership with the Morehouse College School of Medicine HBCU Center for Excellence.

Kentucky State University

Kentucky State University's (KYSU) offerings and engagement in FCS have evolved in each of the land-grant functions. For many years, KYSU trained students in child development and family relations, fashion merchandising, and home economics education. As student enrollment declined in the mid-1990s, the FCS academic program was discontinued and the child development and family relations degree moved to the School of Education. This unit also offers an undergraduate teacher preparation program in interdisciplinary early childhood education.

In the fall of 2011, KYSU's food and agricultural units were restructured into the College of Agriculture, Food Science, and Sustainable Systems (CAFSSS) with the vision "to be an innovative college developing and facilitating experiential learning opportunities for students, individuals and families to make local, national and global communities more sustainable." A division of FCS was organized within CAFSSS with the mission to provide excellence in learning, discovery, and engagement to students and professionals to solve the complex problems faced by families and communities. KYSU has proposed reestablishing an academic degree program in FCS education with an option in FCS/business. Classes for two certificate programs are underway in FCS, and elements of fashion and home décor.

KYSU was awarded funding through an 1890 Capacity Building Program grant to further develop this new FCS program. Desired outcomes are to increase undergraduate extension knowledge and educational opportunities in the field, expand collaborative efforts between extension and academic programs, and contribute well-trained graduates to today's workforce to improve the well-being of individuals and families.

CAFSSS operates the long-standing Rosenwald Center, originally a child development center with a laboratory for students, which was the first of its kind to be accredited among institutions in Kentucky. With funding from the 1890 Facilities Grant program, this center is now the Rosenwald Center for Children and Families, a state of-the-art facility that incorporates education, research, and extension into its innovative model of learning for children, families, students, and KYSU professionals. In 2017, the mission shifted to focus on quality after-school 4-H youth programming for children and youth in kindergarten through grade eight and the facility became the Rosenwald 4-H Center.

Lincoln University

At Lincoln University of Missouri, the agriculture unit is the College of Agriculture, Environmental, and Human Sciences. The college does offer an academic program in FCS. The cooperative research program engages in related research areas, including food safety, health, and food security.

Prairie View Agricultural and Mechanical University

Prairie View A&M University's College of Agriculture and Human Sciences (CAHS) advocates for underserved student populations and limited-resource clientele in Texas. The unit is dedicated to fostering academic excellence, increasing health and well-being, and enhancing economic opportunities through research, education, and outreach in agriculture and the human sciences. The Department of Agriculture, Nutrition, and Human Ecology in CAHS (initially Girls' Industrial Development) has been delivering FCS programming since 1908. The original focus on refining women's ability to perform household chores has evolved to prepare all students for successful careers. Current human sciences offerings include a Bachelor of Science in dietetics with three options: (1) dietetics, (2) wellness, and (3) food service management; and a master's degree in human sciences focusing on marriage and family dynamics, providing a foundation for careers such as marriage and family therapy. The dietetics option is accredited by ACEND and prepares students to take the exam leading to RD credentials.

Department chair Dr. Kwaku Addo notes growing enrollment in the graduate program is a major strength and an ideal segue for dietetics or wellness students to enter advanced study in human sciences. There are plans to expand this program as the Bachelor of Science in family and community services is being phased out due to low enrollment. In 2015, the department received 1890 capacity building grant (CBG) funding to develop a Master of Science program in human nutrition. The department is also working to develop and engage multidisciplinary research teams focused on various ecological systems, taking into consideration the human and social dimensions of the food and agricultural system. The ultimate goal is to improve quality of life for Texas limited-resource audiences by utilizing research to effectively address food insecurity, obesity, food deserts, and overall health.

Southern University and Agricultural and Mechanical College

Southern University is the first known 1890 institution to offer home economics courses, which initially focused on building domestic skills in girls and women (Neyland 1990). By 1916, the program expanded to prepare home economics teachers and extension home demonstration agents. Today, the Department of Family and Consumer Sciences at Southern University offers a bachelor's degree in FCS with concentrations in apparel merchandising and textiles, child development, nutrition and dietetics, food science, and management.

Health promotion has been one area of department research. Since 2000, Louisiana's obesity rate has steadily risen to an all-time high of 36.2% of adults in 2015 (State of Obesity 2016). The prevalence of obesity in the state contributes to high incidences of chronic diseases like diabetes and hypertension. With support from Evans-Allen research funding, faculty have successfully completed projects designed to reduce adult and childhood obesity. This was accomplished by engaging caregivers and families in nutrition education while working with local organizations and programs that included Head Start, the Boys and Girls Club, and the East Baton Rouge Parish School System. Student involvement has been a feature of this research. Moving forward, the department will focus on efforts to strengthen early care and education training for students through curriculum refinement and development, establishing a childcare facility, creating experiential learning opportunities, and utilizing evaluation for program improvement. Once completed, these efforts will enhance access to quality childcare for Baton Rouge residents into the future.

Alabama Agricultural and Mechanical University

The mission of the FCS program at Alabama Agricultural and Mechanical University (AAMU) is the preparation of professionals, equipped to enhance the general well-being of individuals, families, and communities, within the context of the environments of which they are a part, through teaching, research, demonstration, and economic development activities. Under the leadership of Dr. Cynthia M. Smith (chair), the FCS unit operates within the total mission of the university's land-grant function of research, service, and instruction. More specifically, the main thrust of the department's program is individual and family well-being as impacted by various environmental settings and factor. The knowledge base includes basic concepts and principles regarding individual family structures, functions, and systems.

The Department of Family and Consumer Sciences is one of four departments within the College of Agricultural, Life, and Natural Sciences at AAMU. The FCS unit offers one major/degree in FCS at both baccalaureate and master's levels, with five concentrations housed in three program areas: apparel, merchandising, and design (fashion design and fashion merchandising concentrations); human development and family studies (human development and family studies, and FCS education concentrations); and nutrition and hospitality management (general dietetics and hospitality management concentrations). FCS education is offered in collaboration with the College of Education, Humanities, and Behavioral Sciences. The unit also participates with the 1890 Family and Consumer Sciences Distance Instructional Alliance (1890 FCS-DIA) to offer a concentration in family financial planning. The unit has an average enrollment of 236 students and a viable graduation rate of 18–20 students per year.

All undergraduate programs within the unit are accredited by the AAFCS Council for Accreditation. The unit received reaffirmation of accreditation in 2015. The unit has one additional accreditation for the nutrition and hospitality management area's dietetic concentration, which is fully accredited by the Academy of Nutrition and Dietetics' (AND) Accreditation Council for Education in Nutrition and Dietetics, as reaffirmed in April 2016.

The unit operates with a diverse and qualified group of faculty members within an up-to-date facility. Future plans for FCS involve an aggressive program of recruitment and retention, increased engagement in research and community service, and further development of the teaching/learning environment to include a third smart classroom, an obesity center, a screen-printing laboratory, and incorporation of livestreaming within the unit's public areas.

Delaware State University

At Delaware State University, preparation in FCS is offered through the Department of Human Ecology. The department's mission is to provide students with a high-quality undergraduate education for entry-level positions in food and nutritional sciences or textiles and apparel studies. At the undergraduate level, students can pursue degrees in both areas. For graduate study, a master's degree is offered in FCS education. This degree provides advanced preparation to students with backgrounds in the human sciences for professional positions in various sectors, and for entering a doctoral program in FCS or a related discipline. The program also provides coursework and training required for FCS education teacher certification. In response to the diminishing workforce and funding in the FCS education field, a department faculty member was awarded an 1890 CBG to focus on strengthening local FCS programs and attracting students to the profession. In this exciting, threefold project, faculty will develop experiential learning for college FCS students, learning workshops for local FCS teachers, and summer camps designed to expose students to the wide array of careers in FCS.

The department also offers a master's in food science, preparing students for careers in the high-tech food industry. Food science careers have been identified as high-demand careers through 2020 (Goecker, Smith, Fernandez, Ali, and Theller 2015). Through an 1890 CBP grant, the department is actively recruiting to increase enrollment in the food and nutritional science program from underrepresented and underserved populations. The department has established an articulation agreement with Delaware Technical Community College in Georgetown, Delaware, wherein students who have completed an associate's degree in food safety are able to transfer to the food and nutritional science program at DSU to complete their baccalaureate degree within two years. Additionally, the project team has planned outreach events and developed materials for high school students and teachers to increase awareness of career opportunities in food and nutritional sciences and dispel negative stereotypes about careers in agriculture.

Student learning is enriched through state-of-the-art facilities in the department. The Early Child Laboratory School provides quality childcare for toddler, preschool, and kindergarten ages. Undergraduate and graduate students are able to apply their knowledge from the classroom through observations and interactions with children in the lab school. Similarly, the department's food microbiology and microbial omics offers student scholars exposure and experience conducting cutting edge research that addresses major societal challenges, such as food spoilage, water quality, and food safety.

Florida Agricultural and Mechanical University

Florida Agricultural and Mechanical University (FAMU) currently does not have a formal FCS academic program. FAMU began its bachelor's degree program in home economics in 1912, but due to issues such as intermittent low enrollment, the cost of operating these programs, and a federal mandate to avoid duplicative programs, the home economics program officially ended in 1978 (Neyland 1990). The FAMU cooperative extension program continues to offer a family resource management program that includes an expanded food and nutrition education program (EFNEP), along with other outreach programs that focus on food safety, financial literacy, and gardening.

North Carolina Agricultural and Technical State University

North Carolina Agricultural and Technical State University's (NCAT) Department of Family and Consumer Sciences is located in the School of Agriculture and Environmental Science. The foundation for the department's approach to instruction, research, and outreach is rooted in the FCS body of knowledge. It reflects an understanding of individual, family, and community needs, while ecosystems and life course development underpin the dynamic, holistic, and integrative nature of FCS (Nickols et al. 2009). Through each facet of the land-grant mission, department faculty and students address twenty-first-century global challenges that include obesity, disruptive population trends, social inequality, health disparities, financial literacy, food safety, sustainability, and food security.

The department consistently has one of the highest enrollment figures across the school with an annual average of more than 400 students. The department offers Bachelor of Science degrees in child development and family studies, FCS with a concentration in consumer sciences, FCS with a concentration in fashion merchandising and design, food and nutritional sciences with a concentration in premedicine nutrition, and food and nutritional sciences with a concentration in food science. An advanced certificate in FCS, a certificate in family financial planning, and a Master of Arts in Teaching (MAT) in FCS education are offered through distance education and have been supported in part through an 1890 CBG. Additional graduate programs include a Master of Science in food and nutritional sciences nutrition, and a MAT in teaching in child development, early education, and family studies with a focus on birth kindergarten. Students are highly engaged in public service and professional development, with all students completing 50 hours of service learning through community outreach. Many students are also involved in academic conferences and professional organizations.

The NCAT FCS program is one of only three programs in North Carolina accredited by the AAFCS. Additionally, the department offers programs that have been approved by the National Council on Family Relations (NCFR) for the Certified Family Life Educator credential, notably making NCAT the only 1890 institution and historically black university to hold this designation. One of the department's goals is to rebuild its FCS education program leading to teacher certification at the undergraduate level, as secondary FCS teachers are in high demand to provide instruction for the state's 150,000 FCS students.

West Virginia State University

West Virginia State University (WVSU) does not currently offer an academic program in FCS. There are, however, courses related to family dynamics across several majors at the institution. WVSU extension includes an FCS program that delivers the EFNEP and educational outreach programs to promote healthy literacy and healthy lifestyles. Since West Virginia ranks fourth in the nation for grandparents raising grandchildren, WVSU extension, in partnership with the Department of Social Work, developed the Healthy Grand families Project. Funded through an 1890 CBG, grandparents attend workshops equipping them with knowledge and skills that empower them to make healthy choices and navigate through the complex challenges they face.

University of Arkansas at Pine Bluff

The mission of the Department of Human Sciences at the University of Arkansas at Pine Bluff is to provide educational research and outreach programs that prepare individuals, families, and communities to live an optimal and sustaining quality of life. The department also prepares graduates for competitive careers in FCS. In keeping with the mission of the department, the goals of the Department of Human Sciences are (1) to offer relevant and exemplary academic programs to respond to existing and emerging careers; (2) to engage faculty/staff and students in mission-oriented research and creative activities to solve problems and enhance the quality of life; (3) to develop research programs that create new knowledge based on emerging research trends; and (4) to review and update the departmental assessment plan for teaching, research, and outreach programs. Programs are accredited by the AAFCS.

The department currently offers one Bachelor of Science degree with four options: nutrition and dietetics; merchandising, textiles, and design; human development and family studies; and food service and restaurant management. Student engagement within the department has been proven to enhance student retention. Students are encouraged to get involved with Kappa Omicron Nu honor society, The Fashion Network Club, Human Sciences Club, and Human Development and Family Studies Club. The 4-H chapter is housed in the department and operates a food pantry to serve all university students.

The department's Child Development Center allows children from birth to pre-K to develop their cognitive, social, and physical skills for a successful transition into kindergarten. The Child Development Center received a $1.6 million Early Head Start-Child Care Partnership Grant in 2015. The award is renewable for four years and provides full-day, full-year service for infant and toddler classrooms to 13 partner childcare centers across the Arkansas Delta region.

Plans for the future include adding a nutrition and food science option, which is in the final stages of approval. "We are excited to begin research related to nutrition and food science," says Dr. Brenda Martin, chair of the Department of Human Sciences, "the newly hired faculty is ready to identify funding sources to begin food science research" (B. Martin, personal communication, August 15, 2017).

Fact-finding activities are forthcoming to add a Master of Science program in human sciences. Plans to move the FCS education program from the School of Education to the Department of Human Sciences should be finalized in the fall of 2017.

South Carolina State University

Training in home economics at South Carolina State University (SCSU) has roots dating back to 1917. Today, the Department of Family and Consumer

Sciences is focused on equipping students with the knowledge and skills they will need to compete in their chosen professions. The ultimate mission of the department is to provide resident instruction, conduct research, and provide community service. Housed within the College of Graduate and Professional Studies at SCSU, the department currently offers undergraduate degrees in two program areas: nutrition and food management and FCS business, which has three options namely child development, fashion merchandising, and multidisciplinary study. At the graduate level, students can earn a Master of Science degree in nutritional sciences or individual and family development.

To prepare students in child development and also offer quality early care and learning to the local community, the department manages the Child Development Learning Center, which is accredited by the National Association for the Education of Young Children. Also of note: This department is the only FCS academic unit in South Carolina with accreditation from the AAFCS. The department prepares students to be actively engaged in the field, and FCS students have a strong presence in student organizations that include the AAFCS student affiliate, the Fashion Merchandising Association, the NCFR, and Kappa Omicron Nu national human sciences honor society.

Over the past decade, the department has engaged in research, supported in part by Evans-Allen funding, that is relevant to the needs of residents and responsive to the challenges they face. South Carolina ranks 42nd in overall health, and 31% of the population is obese (United Health Foundation 2016). Faculty research projects have focused on preventing obesity and chronic disease across the life span. Examples include assessing the use of technology to promote good nutrition and adequate physical activity among elementary students, exploring the health behaviors and concerns of college students and how health influences educational outcomes, and determining the impact of weight training on elderly diabetes patients. Another ongoing research project focuses on enhancing entrepreneurial and financial literacy skills among Low country youth, who have limited access to such information and skills. With an eye on the future, Dr. William H. Whitaker Jr., department chair and lead for the project, is hopeful the work will result in expanding opportunities for rural youth to create a brighter economic future for both themselves and their families as they explore more global options for success.

Langston University

The Department of Family and Consumer Sciences is located in the School of Agriculture and Applied Sciences. The mission of the department is to (1) educate students for a dual role, including balancing successful family living and preparation for the professional world; (2) to improve rural and urban life so that it will be rewarding and satisfying by extending service through

FCS; and (3) to develop interest in the important scope and needs of research in FCS.

Program offerings focus on early childhood education and child development. The Department of Family and Consumer Sciences offers a Bachelor of Science degree in FCS with an option in early childhood education leading to teacher certification in early childhood education in collaboration with the School of Education and Behavioral Sciences. To enrich student learning and provide practical experiences, the department operates a demonstration teaching laboratory and an early childhood laboratory for children birth to 12 years. The department also offers an associate degree in child development.

Tuskegee University

Human sciences training at Tuskegee University is centered on nutrition and health. The Department of Nutritional Sciences is located in the College of Agriculture, Environment, and Nutrition Sciences. Reflecting the mission of the land-grant university, the mission of the department is to train students in acquiring adequate knowledge, skills, and competencies in food and nutritional sciences during integrated classroom instruction, hands-on research, and extramural experiential learning opportunities in preparation to be professionals in the global economy. The department offers Bachelor of Science degrees in food science and nutritional science, a didactic program in dietetics and public health, and dual degrees in food science and biology or in nutritional science and biology. It also offers thesis and nonthesis Master of Science degrees in food science or nutritional sciences and is part of the Doctor of Philosophy program in integrative biosciences. From this unit, as a top-ranked historically Black university, Tuskegee University has produced a significant number of Black dietitians and nutrition professionals.

Students are actively engaged in professional development through organizations such as the Institute of Food Technologists. The department also hosts an advisory board with members who represent government agencies and corporations. The board offers meaningful guidance related to funding and learning opportunities that spur research, instruction, innovation, and student career preparation. The department also benefits from internship, mentorship, and scholarship opportunities provided through the board.

Research conducted is responsive to issues among residents in Alabama's Black Belt region, an area burdened with social, economic, and health disparities. A major emphasis of the ongoing research has been to understand and combat obesity across the life span through dynamic, community-based models designed to empower individuals to make healthier eating choices, and to assist food retailers in contributing to a culture of health at the community level.

University of Maryland Eastern Shore

University of Maryland Eastern Shore's (UMES) Department of Human Ecology is located in the School of Agriculture, Food, and Resource Sciences. The department's mission is to prepare students for careers, graduate study, and leadership roles in fashion merchandising, child development, FCS, and food and nutrition. The department's strategic focus reflects the 1890 land-grant university mission and mandate. Dr. Grace Namwamba became department chair in 2015.

The department offers training responsive to diverse workforce needs across the state. Students have the opportunity to earn undergraduate degrees in FCS, FCS education, fashion merchandising, and nutrition and dietetics, with an internship in child development. The dietetics internship is a performance-based program with a diabetes education and counseling concentration, designed to bridge the gap between didactic education and entry-level dietetic practice. Graduates from the internship program will be equipped to address the prediabetes and diabetes rates in Maryland, particularly among minority populations. This intern program is accredited through ACEND. Additionally, UMES currently offers the only FCS education teacher certification program in the state of Maryland.

Through the support of CBGs focused on recruitment and retention, and by broadening the student experience through undergraduate research and service learning program, the faculty have been successful in engaging students in professional practice and enhancing academic programs. Student scholars have published and presented research projects in several forums, including the Historically Black College and University Research Symposium, KON Conclave and ScholarCon, the AAFCS Annual Conference, and the *Undergraduate Research Journal for the Human Sciences*. Research topics have spanned innovation in costume preservation, sustainable clothing design, and childhood obesity. Several students committed to service in the campus child and family development center. Areas of research included bullying and childhood obesity. The department is also vitalizing the fashion merchandising major through the establishment of a computer-aided design laboratory, which will enable the unit to enhance the curriculum and provide students with a competitive edge in the global apparel and textiles workforce.

Virginia State University

Virginia State University's Department of Family and Consumer Science equips students with twenty-first-century skills to effectively address global challenges. The FCS unit at Virginia State has a long history of producing graduates who make meaningful contributions to the profession. The department has several programmatic areas leading to a Bachelor of Science in family and consumer science, including dietetics; family, child, and community services; FCS teacher education; and textiles, apparel, merchandising, and management. The dietetic internship is a postbaccalaureate nondegree, noncredit, ACEND-accredited program that provides eligibility to take the national RD examination. A teacher education endorsement meets the requirements of the Virginia Department of Education. The curriculum focuses on preparing students for careers as teachers and for a variety of other professional settings in the public and private sectors.

Promoting student engagement, research, and experiential learning as strategies to extend learning outside the bounds of classroom walls is notable. Required field internships prepare students to understand the workplace and the content area, and to have a competitive edge in the job market. The department has forged fruitful collaborations and partnerships with local organizations and retailers, and there are plans to expand field experiences in the future. The FCS students are highly engaged in professional organizations and meetings, such as the Virginia State Association for the AND and the AAFCS. One of our previous interns shared:

> My education at Virginia State University prepared me with the knowledge needed to be successful in my chosen career. The professors and advisers ensured that students received needed resources by creating a really rich learning environment. Having access to professionals who were passionate allowed learning to be both fun and informative. Learning an array of topics ensured that I also left with new skills that I am able to use in my personal and professional life. (Personal communication, April 14, 2016)

Future efforts will focus on building a robust study abroad program, further integrating instruction, extension, and research into the overall student experience, and developing a Master of Science program in foods and nutrition sciences.

Fort Valley State University

The family and consumer sciences department at Fort Valley State University (FVSU) is located in the College of Agriculture, Family Sciences, and Technology. Since the FCS unit was established in 1939, home economics offerings have been popular at the institution. Leadership for this unit was solidified in 2014 when Dr. Vivian Fluellen, interim head for the Department of Family and Consumer Sciences, was permanently appointed to this position. Another event anchoring the department's bright future arrived in 2015 with the news of AAFCS reaccreditation for the Bachelor of Science degrees in infant and child development, and in food and nutrition. To build on this accomplishment, in 2016 the FVSU College of Agriculture hosted a ribbon-cutting ceremony for a new Family Development Center and Quality Child Care Complex, supported through the 1890 Facilities Grant Program. Dr. Fluellen shared:

> The new center has a research laboratory for scientists to explore family health issues, nutritious methods for food product development, food safety and sanitation issues related to healthy growth, and the development of infants and children. This new facility will enhance the teaching, research, and extension components, and also provide quality services to the students and the citizens of Georgia.

From 2004 to 2013, 984 students were enrolled across the baccalaureate programs. The department is a member of the FCS-DIA that offers courses for the Certified Financial Planner (CFP) certificate. The faculty is committed to student preparation and works to ensure students have meaningful experiential learning activities that propel them to success in their chosen fields. Under Dr. Fluellen's leadership, the department will continue to focus on strategic recruitment and retention efforts to ensure a critical mass of students is enrolled and that they graduate with the technical and scientific knowledge and skills necessary to thrive in today's global workforce.

Tennessee State University

The Department of Family and Consumer Sciences in the College of Agriculture, Human, and Natural Sciences at Tennessee State University's (TSU) mission is to provide a multidisciplinary approach in child development and family relationships, fashion merchandising, and foods and nutrition/dietetics through synergetic application of high-quality education of undergraduate students, innovative research, and relevant extension outreach and community engagement. The department is committed to the discovery, design, and dissemination of solutions for Tennessee, the region, and the global community that will empower individuals, strengthen families, and promote community vitality and well-being.

Over the past five years, the department has had an average enrollment of nearly 130 students across majors, with the numbers rising each year. Students can earn a bachelor's degree in FCS with a concentration in one of the following areas: child development and family studies, foods and nutrition/dietetics, fashion merchandising, and food service management. Although the current FCS education teacher certification program will be moving to the College of Education in the fall of 2017, student majors will still complete several courses in the FCS department.

Students work on various research and extension projects in consumer food safety education, childhood obesity, healthy eating behavior for families, and innovative methods of teaching young children STEM through agriculture. Students also have internship opportunities with industry, federal, state, and local partners within each concentration area. With a focus on equity, students in the department are expanding their reach to work on projects that address the area of food security, sustainability, and family dynamics as they relate to underserved populations. This will assist faculty and students in putting theory and application knowledge to work to meet the needs of TSU stakeholders.

Dr. Chiquita Briley, permanently appointed department chair in 2016, is committed to promoting a strong, diverse, competent FCS workforce. She will continue working to cultivate educational opportunities that meaningfully speak to future students in a way that compels them to train in FCS programs in order to effectively address complex issues among today's families and communities. Under Dr. Briley's leadership, future efforts include forging partnerships with other academic institutions to expand research and extension opportunities and provide students with professional development opportunities. Recognizing the importance of engagement between students and faculty, more deliberate, structured initiatives will be developed to foster cohesiveness, open communication, innovation, and mentorship. Dr. Briley's plans also include developing a master's degree program in FCS to further train the pipeline of FCS professionals.

Central State University

Central State University (CSU) located in Wilberforce, Ohio, was given land-grant status under the 2014 Farm Bill. Since 2014, CSU has been working to firmly establish the three land-grant functions—research, education, and extension.

CONTINUING THE LEGACY OF LEADERSHIP AND SERVICE TO FAMILY AND CONSUMER SCIENCES

As the twenty-first century forges on, the future of FCS at 1890 institutions holds much promise for continued impact and innovation across the land-grant mission areas. Human sciences units at these universities have made tremendous strides in the discovery, development, and dissemination of ideas and knowledge, and in programs that improve the well-being of families and communities (particularly those that are consistently underserved or never served). Faculty members at 1890 institutions continually work to create an

environment where students will become passionate inquirers, critical thinkers, and active contributors to the body of knowledge in FCS. The future and
the influence of the FCS workforce rest solely upon nurturing the intellectual
and creative capital of emerging professionals representing the kaleidoscope
of today's families and communities.

Collectively, the 1890 schools have contributed to a diverse workforce
through the training offered for many professions in the field, such as FCS
educators, dieticians, researchers, and financial planners. Although figures
have not been officially determined for diversity among FCS teachers,
students of color make up approximately 45% of the pre-K–12 population,
whereas teachers of color comprise about 18% of the educator workforce
(U.S. Department of Education 2016). Given the documented shortage
of FCS educators, it will be increasingly important for teacher education
programs at these institutions to remain viable and thriving. Currently,
8 of the 19 universities offer FCS or ECE teacher preparation programs.
Opportunities to support recruitment and retention, as well as innovations in curriculum development and instruction in the human sciences,
are available through NIFA funding programs such as Higher Education
Challenge, Multicultural Scholars, and Research and Extension Experiences
for Undergraduates.

In a similar vein, recognizing the demand for financial planners, but the
lack of diversity in the profession needed to serve minority communities,
eight of these universities created the 1890 FCS-DIA family financial planning program. Developed in 2004, FCS-DIA is a web-based instructional
program designed to prepare students to successfully complete the CFP
board's educational requirements and pass the CFP certification examination.
This ongoing collaborative effort, supported in part through an 1890 CBG,
represents the first online collaboration of its kind for HBCUs. The program
is approved by the CFP's Board of Standards.

The National Coalition of Black Development in Family and Consumer
Sciences, founded in 1980, also works to ensure a diverse, well-trained workforce for the field. The coalition has engaged in strategic efforts to promote
professional development among FCS units at HBCUs, including those of the
1890s, through student scholarships, mentorships, and recognition opportunities. Additionally, the coalition nominates members for awards and leadership positions within the AAFCS. Dr. Julia Miller, former coalition president
and former department chair at Virginia State University, asserts:

> The need for the coalition still remains evident as a light to guide our pathways
> to a sustained, enduring place in the profession. Rightfully, it is incumbent upon
> African American family and consumer scientists and colleagues from other
> ethnic groups to remain vigilant. A watchful network with diverse interests will

be required in perpetuity to continue active involvement in the profession's mainstream. (Miller 2010)

Students, faculty, and administrators at 1890 institutions have made meaningful contributions to the profession with respect to leadership and service. Many of these institutions strongly support the engagement of faculty and administration in the boards of organizations and associations that support FCS, lending their strengths to promote the represented professions.

There have been Distinguished Service Awards, the highest recognition given in the profession, to FCS professionals who have worked or are working at 1890 or other institutions and Organizations. These awardees were affiliated and strongly supported the National Coalition for Black Development in Family and Consumer Sciences. These individuals include:

1. Dr. Leola Adams (South Carolina State University)
2. Dr. Flossie M. Byrd (Prairie View Agricultural and Mechanical University)
3. Dr. Virginia N. Caples (Alabama Agricultural and Mechanical University)
4. Dr. Elizabeth W. Crandall (University of Rhode Island)
5. Dr. Clinita A. Ford (Florida Agricultural and Mechanical University)
6. Dr. Valerie I. Giddings (Hampton University, North Carolina Central University, Winston-Salem State University, Virginia Tech and North Carolina Agricultural and Technical State University)
7. Dr. Lillie B. Glover (South Carolina State University)
8. Dr. Kinsey B. Green (University of Maryland and Oregon State University)
9. Dr. Mildred B. Griggs (University of Illinois, Champaign)
10. Dr. Shirley Hymon-Parker (University of Maryland Eastern Shore and North Carolina Agricultural and Technical State University)
11. Dr. Gearldean Johnson (Tennessee State University)
12. Dr. Ethel G. Jones (South Carolina State University and Louisiana Tech)
13. Dr. Angela Radford-Lewis (Eastern Tennessee State University)
14. Dr. Julia R. Miller Arline (University of Maryland, Virginia State University, and Michigan State University)
15. Dr. Dorothy I. Mitstifer (Kappa Omicron Nu National Honor Society)
16. Dr. Gwendolyn A. Newkirk (North Carolina Central University and University of Nebraska Lincoln)
17. Dr. Raygene Paige (Mississippi Cooperative Extension Service)
18. Dr. Rosa Purcell (North Carolina Agricultural and Technical State University)
19. Dr. Penny A. Ralston (University of Massachusetts Amherst and Florida State University

20. Dr. Bernice C. Richardson (Alabama Agricultural and Mechanical University)
21. Dr. Cynthia Smith (Alabama Agricultural and Mechanical University)
22. Dr. Gladys G. Vaughn (North Carolina Central University and University of Maryland)
23. Dr. Virginia B. Vincenti (University of Massachusetts Amherst, University of Wyoming and Iowa State University)
24. Dr. Retia S. Walker (University of Maryland Eastern Shore, University of Kentucky, Coppin State University, and Southern University Agricultural and Mechanical University).
25. Shirley Hymon-Parker (University of Maryland Eastern Shore, North Carolina Agricultural & Technical State University)
26. Gearldean Johnson, CFCS (Tennessee State University)
27. Raygene Paige, CFCS (Mississippi State University)
28. Rosa Purcell, CFCS (University of Illinois, North Carolina Agricultural & Technical State University)
29. Bernice Carter Richardson (Alabama Agricultural and Mechanical University)
30. Cynthia Smith (Alabama Agricultural and Mechanical University)
31. Angela Radford Lewis, CFCS (East Tennessee State University)
32. Ethel Jones, CFCS (Louisiana Tech University, South Carolina State University)
33. Valerie Giddings (North Carolina Agricultural & Technical State University)
34. Jacqueline M. Holland, CFCS-HDFS (Morgan State University)
35. Joanne Bankston (Kentucky State University)

ADDRESSING THE FUTURE FOR FCS

Future opportunities, predicated on the strengths of FCS in 1890 land-grant institutions, have a strong foundation. In these institutions, proactive faculty nurture students by providing mentoring and individual assistance. This further builds upon the mission to educate successful graduates who are powerful contributors to society. More intense collaboration with agricultural departments is needed to reinforce the obvious corollary of healthy food supplies leading to healthier populations who benefit from FCS skills and knowledge. This ideal's time has come, particularly with the current societal emphasis on nutrition and health across every demographic.

Defining, establishing, and fortifying such collaborations in 1890 institutions will continue to generate a high rate of graduates: graduates who represent and embrace the needs of diverse communities, who influence the economic development of these communities in positive ways, and who achieve success by using new technologies and applying innovative concepts to the ever-growing need for effective FCS professionals.

REFERENCES

Allen, Walter R., Joseph O. Jewell, Kimberly A. Griffin, and De'Sha S. Wolf. 2007. "Historically Black Colleges and Universities: Honoring the Past, Engaging the Present, Touching the Future." *Journal of Negro Education 76*, no. 3: 263–280. https://www.jstor.org/stable/40034570.

American Association of Family and Consumer Sciences. 2011. "The AAFCS/FCS Co-Branding Toolkit." Accessed December, 2020. https://www.aafcs.org/about/about-us/family-consumer-brand.

Briggs-Dubose, Shaniqua D. 2016. Personal interview.

Comer, Marcus., Thasya Campbell, Kelvin Edwards, and John Hillison. 2006. "Cooperative Extension and the 1890 Land-Grant Institution: The Real Story." *Journal of Extension 44*, no. 3: 1–3. https://www.joe.org/joe/2006june/a4.php.

Goecker, Allan D., Ella Smith, J. Marcos Fernandez, Ray Ali, and Rebecca Theller. 2015. "Employment Opportunities for College Graduates in Food, Agriculture, Renewable Natural Resources, and the Environment. United States: 2015–2020." Accessed December, 2020. https://www.purdue.edu/usda/employment/.

National Center for Education Statistics. 2016a. "College Navigator." Accessed December, 2020. https://nces.ed.gov/collegenavigator/.

National Center for Education Statistics. 2016b. "The Condition of Education 2016 (NCES 2016–144)." Accessed December, 2020. https://nces.ed.gov/pubs2016/2016144.pdf.

National Research Council. 1995. *Colleges of Agriculture at the Land Grant Universities: A Profile.* Washington, DC: National Academy of Sciences.

Neyland, Leedell W. 1990. *Historically Black Land-Grant Institutions and The Development of Agriculture and Home Economics 1890–1990.* Tallahassee: Florida A and M University Foundation, Inc.

Nickols, Sharon Y., Penney A. Ralston, Carol. L. Anderson, Lorna Browne, Genevieve Schroeder, Sabrina Thomas, and Peggy Wild. 2009. "The Family and Consumer Sciences Body of Knowledge and The Cultural Kaleidoscope: Research Opportunities and Challenges." *Family and Consumer Sciences Research Journal 37*, no. 3: 266–283.

State of Obesity. 2016. "*State briefs.*" Accessed December, 2020. https://stateofchildhoodobesity.org/states/.

United Health Foundation. 2016. "America's Health Rankings Annual Report." Accessed May 1, 2017. https://www.americashealthrankings.org/learn/reports/2016-annual-report.

United States Department of Education. 2016. "The State of Racial Diversity in the Educator Workforce." Accessed May 1, 2017. https://www.ed.gov/news/press-releases/report-state-racial-diversity-educator-workforce.

Washington, Booker T. 1901. *Up from Slavery: An Autobiography.* New York: Doubleday.

Werhan, Carol R. 2013. "Family and Consumer Sciences Secondary School Programs: National Survey Shows Continued Demand for FCS Teachers." *Journal of Family and Consumer Sciences 105*, no. 4: 41–45.

Whitaker, William H., M. Virlyn Williams, M. Evelyn, Fields, Dannie L. Keepler, Bonita Y. Manson, and Sheila M. Littlejohn. 2009. "Historically black colleges and universities: The Development of Family and Consumer Sciences in HBCUs." In *African American Women's Contributions to the Human Sciences*, edited by Julia R. Miller, Dorothy I. Mitstifer, and Gladys G. Vaughn, 21–22. East Lansing, MI: Kappa Omicron Nu.

Chapter 10

The Value of AAFCS Accreditation at Historically Black Colleges and Universities

LaTonya J. Dixon and Cynthia M. Smith

INTRODUCTION

Most authorities agree that accreditation brings to mind such phrases as quality assurance, program review, outcome assessment, stamp of approval, and best practices—all concepts that convey standards of excellence. According to Eaton (2015), accreditation is "a process of external quality review created and used by higher education to scrutinize colleges, universities, and programs for quality assurance and quality improvement." Utz (2012) further describes accreditation as a process that offers assurance that an institution or program provides a quality education, in which the rigor and process differ based on the type of higher education accreditation.

Accreditation by the American Association of Family and Consumer Sciences (AAFCS) "assures the public that accredited undergraduate family and consumer sciences (FCS) programs provide the highest quality educational experiences and prepare students for professional roles to improve the quality of life for individuals, families, and communities" (Accreditation 2018). Since its inception, the AAFCS Council for Accreditation (CFA) has served as the premiere credentialing body for undergraduate programs in FCS that successfully complete the accreditation process and meet or exceed stated standards and criteria of educational quality (Pucciarelli et al. 2016). Traditionally, historically Black colleges and universities (HBCUs) have been the means through which African American students have achieved higher education. Accreditation is viewed as a benchmark of quality within the HBCU community. The purpose of this chapter is to discuss the perceived value of the AAFCS accreditation among HBCUs, with primary focus on 1890 universities.

As outlined in the 2010 edition of the Accreditation Documents, the three basic purposes of accreditation are to advance academic quality; demonstrate accountability; and encourage, where appropriate, planning and implementation for needed improvement (17). Driven by these purposes, AAFCS accreditation provides numerous benefits (Benefits of Accreditation 2018) to qualifying institutions:

1. Provides formal recognition by peers, both within the institution and across the country.
2. Encourages planning, identifies areas for change, and provides substantial information that can be used to support resource decisions.
3. Is extremely influential in recruiting outstanding faculty and students.
4. Contributes to the assurance that graduates of these programs have formal preparation that meets nationally accepted standards and quality.
5. Enhances credibility.
6. Helps position programs to accommodate the changes in the restructuring academic world.
7. Self-study and site visit processes provide opportunities to help faculty members, unit personnel, and institution leadership to better understand the FCS program.
8. Helps ensure that the institution is a leader in the development of FCS professionals.
9. May affect the amount of state monies that the unit or institution receives.
10. Promotes program improvement.
11. Helps FCS units in discussions about resource allocations with university administrators.
12. Can be a very strong factor in program retention discussions.
13. Offers a competitive advantage for programs, students, and careers.

FCS ACCREDITATION AT HBCUS

Are these benefits valued by FCS programs at HBCUs? HBCUs with programs in the FCS profession are primarily the 1890 land-grant universities. These universities include Alabama Agricultural and Mechanical University (AAMU), Alcorn State University (ASU), Delaware State University, Fort Valley State University (FVSU), Kentucky State University, Lincoln University, North Carolina A&T State University (NCAT), Prairie View A&M University (PVAMU), South Carolina State University (SCSU), Southern University and A&M, Tennessee State University (TSU), University of Arkansas at Pine Bluff (UAPB), University of Maryland Eastern Shore (UMES), Virginia State University, and Tuskegee University. Morgan State University (MSU) is one of the few HBCUs external to the 1890 universities with a viable human sciences program.

Currently, there are 36 AAFCS accredited institutions of higher education accessible on the AAFCS website (aafcs.org/credentialing-center/accreditation/accredited units; Carol Anderson 2020). Of these institutions, five are 1890 HBCUs (AAMU, FVSU, NCAT, TSU, and UMES), and one MSU which is not an 1890. Two programs (ASU and SU A&M) are working toward reaccreditation. All place immense value upon AAFCS accreditation. To determine the value of AAFCS accreditation to programs, department chairpersons and faculty at HBCUs offering a baccalaureate degree in the area of FCS were contacted (via email) and asked to provide a brief description of their accreditation status. Responses were received in 2016/2017 from AAMU, ASU, FVSU, MSU, NCAT, SCSU, SU A&M, TSU, UAPB, and UMES and needed updates were completed in the fall of 2020. The provided accreditation statements follow.

ALABAMA A&M UNIVERSITY DEPARTMENT OF FAMILY AND CONSUMER SCIENCES

The Department of FCS at Alabama A&M University in Normal (Huntsville), Alabama, received notification of its reaffirmation of accreditation by the CFA of the AAFCS in May of 2015. The efforts leading to this action occurred under the leadership of the current chair of the department, Dr. Cynthia M. Smith. Accreditation is granted for a 10-year period. Therefore, the current accreditation will expire in the spring of 2024, with the next self-study report due in February 2023.

The department received initial accreditation in 1983 and has maintained accreditation status through subsequent reviews leading to the current reaffirmation. The department is among 36 programs nationwide with AAFCS accreditation. It is one of three accredited FCS programs in Alabama and the only one at an Alabama HBCU. The department offers one Bachelor of Science and one master's degree in FCS each with concentrations in three areas: apparel merchandising and design (fashion design and fashion merchandising), human development and family studies and nutrition and hospitality management (general dietetics and hospitality management). Degrees in FCS education (BS, Med, and EdS) are offered in cooperation with the College of Education.

Alcorn State University Department of Human Sciences

The Department of Human Sciences at ASU in Lorman, Mississippi, received its most recent reaffirmation of accreditation by the CFA of the AAFCS in spring 2008. The efforts leading to this action occurred under the able leadership of the then chair of the Department, Dr. Wanda Newell. Accreditation status was granted for a period of 10 years, with an expiration date of 2018. Due to extenuating conditions. the department had to request an extension to allow for submission of the self-study report in 2023. The department is currently in the process of seeking reaccreditation.

The Department of Human Sciences, earlier known as child development and family studies and much earlier as home economics, received initial accreditation from AAFCS in 1983. Currently, the department has two programs, the child development program and the food, nutrition, and community health sciences program. The Department of Human Sciences is housed in the School of Agriculture and Applied Sciences.

Fort Valley State University Department of Family and Consumer Sciences

The Department of FCS at FVSU in Fort Valley, Georgia, received notification of reaffirmation of accreditation by the CFA of the AAFCS in May 2015 under the leadership of Dr. Vivian M. Fluellen, CFCS. Accreditation is granted for a 10-year period. The current accreditation will expire in the spring of 2021, with a due date of the self-study report of February 2020.

The department received initial accreditation in 1982 and has successfully maintained accreditation status through subsequent reviews leading to the current reaffirmation. The department is among 36 programs nationwide with AAFCS accreditation. It is one of two accredited FCS programs in the state of Georgia and the only one at a Georgia HBCU. The department offers one Bachelor of Science degree in FCS with concentrations in two areas: infant and child development, and food and nutrition.

Morgan State University Department of Family and Consumer Sciences

The Department of FCS, formerly the Department of Home Economics, at MSU offers the Bachelor of Science degree in FCS with two comprehensive tracts: Fashion Merchandising and General Family and Consumer Studies. An application for accreditation was submitted in September 2017 to the director of accreditation of the AAFCS. The CFA reviewed the initial report and requested additional information which was completed and submitted in December 2019. Accreditation was granted to the Morgan State Department of FCS on April 24, 2020.

North Carolina A&T State University Department of Family and Consumer Sciences

NCAT's Department of FCS in Greensboro, North Carolina, received reaffirmation of accreditation by the AAFCS in 2014 under the leadership of Dr.

Valerie L. Giddings. The next full review will be held in 2024. The department is the largest of four academic units in the School of Agriculture and Environmental Sciences with an enrollment of over 400 students and has been a unit within the school since its inception in the 1932–1933 academic year. The department was first accredited by AAFCS in 1984 and has successfully maintained its accreditation for over 30 years. The department is among 36 programs nationwide with AAFCS accreditation. It is currently one of three accredited programs in the state of North Carolina and the only one at an HBCU in North Carolina. The department offers three Bachelor of Science degrees with concentrations in child development and family relations, child development early education and family studies (B-K licensure), fashion merchandising and design, consumer studies, nutrition, food science, and premedicine in nutrition.

South Carolina State University Department of Family and Consumer Sciences

The Department of FCS at SCSU in Orangeburg received notification of its reaffirmation of accreditation by the CFA of the AAFCS in April of 2009. The efforts leading to this action occurred under the leadership of Dr. Ethel G. Jones. Accreditation is granted by the CFA for a 10-year period. Therefore, the current accreditation expired in the spring of 2019, and the program received full reaffirmation in 2020.

The department received its initial accreditation in 1979 and has successfully maintained accreditation status through subsequent reviews leading up to the current reaffirmation. The department is among 36 programs nationwide currently with AAFCS accreditation. It is the only accredited FCS program in the state of South Carolina. The department currently offers two Bachelor of Science and two master's degrees. The two BS degrees are in nutrition and food management with concentrations in dietetics and the food management; and FCS business with concentrations in child development, fashion merchandising, and multidisciplinary. The two MS degrees are in nutritional sciences and individual and family development.

SOUTHERN UNIVERSITY AND A&M COLLEGE DEPARTMENT OF FAMILY AND CONSUMER SCIENCES

The Department of Family of Consumer Sciences at Southern University and A&M College in Baton Rouge, Louisiana, was first accredited by the forerunner of the AAFCS in 1983. The late Dr. Eula Davis Masingale led efforts that resulted in what was then known as the College of Home Economics being among the first—if not the first—programs on the campus of Southern University to be accredited nationally.

Currently, accreditation in the Department of Family and Consumer Sciences at Southern University has lapsed. Reasons for the lapse include the departure of the former FCS chair in the midst of completing the self-study, the hiring of an interim chair with competing responsibilities, and the lack of a critical mass of faculty to assume completion of the self-study. Unfortunately, a new permanent chair has not yet been appointed to lead the self-study process. The Department of Family and Consumer Sciences at Southern University offers a Bachelor of Science degree in FCS in three program areas: apparel merchandising and textiles, child development, and human nutrition and food. Additionally, human nutrition and food has concentrations in (1) nutrition health and wellness and (2) food management. FCS at Southern University consistently ranks as the fifth or sixth largest producer of graduates at the baccalaureate level at the university.

Tennessee State University Department of Family and Consumer Sciences

The Department of Family and Consumer Sciences at TSU in Nashville received reaffirmation of accreditation by the CFA of the AAFCS in January 2014 under the leadership of Dr. Gearldean Johnson. The departmental programs have been accredited by the CFA for over 40 years. The administration and faculty conducted the self-study in 1972 and received accreditation in 1973. This made Tennessee State one of the first group of programs that sought and received accreditation by the council. Maintaining accreditation has been a priority for the Department of Family and Consumer Sciences throughout the years. In the past, the university received points from the state of Tennessee for having programs accredited by their professional accreditation councils. The Department of Family and Consumer Sciences offers a Bachelor of Science degree with concentrations in child development and family relations, foods and nutrition (accredited by ACEND), food service management, fashion merchandising, and FCS education (on hiatus). Also on hiatus is a certificate program in family financial planning, an online instructional program with the 1890 FCS—Distance Instructional Alliance.

University of Arkansas at Pine Bluff Department of Human Sciences

The Department of Human Sciences at the UAPB received accreditation reaffirmation by the CFA of the AAFCS in the fall of 2012. Accreditation is granted for a 10-year period. Therefore, the 2012 accreditation will expire in the September of 2022 with a due date of the next self-study report of September 2021. The human sciences program is one of two accredited FCS programs in the state of Arkansas and the only accredited program at an HBCU in Arkansas. The department offers one Bachelor of Science degree with concentrations in four areas: merchandising, textiles and design; human development and family studies; food service and restaurant management; and nutrition and food science.

University of Maryland Eastern Shore
Department of Human Ecology

The Department of Human Ecology at the UMES attained a historical milestone when it was granted full accreditation by the AAFCS for the first time in June 2020. The accreditation was granted under the leadership of the current department chair, Dr. Grace Namwamba, and Dr. Lombuso S. Khoza, who served as chair of the accreditation committee. The human ecology program has concentrations in child development, dietetics and nutrition, fashion merchandising, FCS, and FCS education.

CONCLUSION

Accreditation has been—and continues to be—a pivotal process at HBCUs, particularly the 1890 land-grant universities, whose missions traditionally remain fertile soil for the development and nurturing of quality programs in the area formerly regarded as home economics. The highlighted programs discussed in this chapter all attest to the value placed on accreditation among these unique institutions, which constitute only about 3% of higher education institutions in the United States. Nonetheless, often limited-resource HBCUs have manifested the value of accreditation through valiant investments of both time and financial support. The result has been a tangible mark of excellence through accreditation.

The process for accreditation from the former American Home Economics Association (AHEA, now AAFCS) began in 1969, with the very first accreditation granted in 1971. Even in the formative years of accreditation, HBCUs were not only attuned to the process but were preparing their campuses for full engagement. Indeed, the forerunner for AAFCS accreditation of the HBCU programs presented herein was TSU, which acquired accreditation in 1973. Six years later, SCSU achieved accreditation. These two early programs were followed by programs at the UAPB and FVSU in 1982, with Alabama A&M, Alcorn, and Southern joining the accredited institutions in 1983, and North

166 LaTonya J. Dixon and Cynthia M. Smith

Carolina A&T in 1984. Although undocumented, it is a widely held view that the PVAMU home economics department, under the direction of Dr. Flossie Byrd, received accreditation during the early years as well. The most recent two HBCUs to achieve accreditation in 2020 are the UMES and MSU.

As relatively small institutions with often small AAFCS affiliated programs, HBCUs depend on their substantial investments in the accreditation process to not only provide sanctioning from the accrediting body but also to assure their public and prospective students of the quality inherent in their programs. In a market where institutions with large endowments and big state coffers attract students with myriad extras, accreditation supplies a competitive edge to smaller institutions that appeals to a certain group of students as well.

It should not be lost on any accrediting agency that the largest impediment to full accreditation has often been fiscal resources and financial integrity. Yet, the lion's share of HBCUs were founded in an era when they were expected to succeed without or with only minimal financial support. State HBCUs were monitored in terms of the curricula they could provide. Thus, many turned out graduates that—while still productive to society—were not able to give back dollars substantially to alma maters. As states devote significantly less of their budgets to higher education, public HBCUs are hit from all angles—especially as, even today, so many African American youths are first-generation college students whose parents are unable to afford educational costs. Even with these and numerous other barriers to their existence, HBCUs still regard accreditation as an equalizer among those factors that actually make a difference in the futures of individuals.

REFERENCES

AAFCS Council for Accreditation (Ed.). (2010). *Accreditation documents for undergraduate programs in FCS*. Retrieved from higherlogicdownload.s3.amazonaws.com/AAFCS/1c95de14-d78f-40b8a6ef-a1fb628c68fe/UploadedImages/CredentialingCenter/AAFCS_ Accreditation_Standards.pdf.

Accreditation Status Report. Alabama A&M University, Dr. Cynthia M. Smith, 2016 and 2020.

Accreditation Status Report. Alcorn State University, Dr. Martha Ravola, 2017 and 2020.

Accreditation Status Report. Fort Valley State University, Dr. Vivian Fluellen, 2017.

Accreditation Status Report. Morgan State University, Dr. Lurline Whittaker, 2017 *and 2020*.

Accreditation Status Report. North Carolina A&T State University, Dr. Valerie Giddings, 2015.

Accreditation Status Report. South Caroline State University, Dr. Ethel Jones, 2017.

Accreditation Status Report. Southern University and A&M College, Dr. Doze Butler, 2017.

Accreditation Status Report. Tennessee State University, Dr. Gearldean Johnson, 2017.

Accreditation Status Report. University of Arkansas at Pine Bluff, Dr. Brenda Martin, 2017.

Accreditation Status Report. University of Maryland Eastern Shore, Dr. Grace Namwamba, 2017 and 2020.

American Association of FCS. (2018).

Accreditation. Retrieved from aafcs.org/credentialing-center/accreditation.

American Association of FCS. (2018). *Accredited Units.* Retrieved from aafcs.org/credentialing-center/accreditation/accredited-units.

American Association of FCS. (2018). *Benefits of*

Accreditation. Retrieved from aafcs.org/credentialingcenter/accreditation/benefits-of-accreditation.

American Association of FCS, Council for Accreditation (2020), Dr. Carol Anderson, CFA Director.

Eaton, Judith. S. 2015. "An Overview of U.S. Accreditation." Last revised November 2015. https://files.eric.ed.gov/fulltext/ED569225.pdf.

Pucciarelli, Deanna L., Scott Hall, and Amy Harden. 2016. "A National Survey of the Perceived Value of American Association of Family and Consumer Science Accreditation." *FCS Research Journal 44,* no. 4: 375–393. https://doi.org/10.1111/fcsr.12170.

Utz, Deborah Gay. 2012. "Accreditation Measures Value." *Radiologic Technology 83,* no. 6: 639–640.

Part III

INTERNATIONALIZATION AND THE HUMAN SCIENCES

Human sciences in other countries have contributed significantly to strengthening programs aimed at women, families, and children. The human sciences integrate science while being practical in nature, centering on family life. The human sciences extend into culturally different societies to bring awareness to differences and similarities among interactions between human beings and their environments. This section promotes research regarding family well-being in different settings and with different population groups. The results are used as the basis for improving the living conditions of individuals, families, and communities abroad as well as for promoting family welfare internationally.

Chapter 11 examines the variety of past and present international programs involving family and consumer sciences (FCS) professionals (also known as home economists), both in collegiate-level international study and service opportunities, and in secondary school internationally focused experiences. This chapter also describes FCS organizations that provide international connections and addresses historically Black colleges and universities that offer international opportunities to their faculty and students.

Chapter 12 brings to the attention of the world that although there has been some progress toward the empowerment of women, it is miniscule compared to the need for a universal mindset that does not question women and girls' roles in social, economic, political, civil, and cultural development.

Chapter 13 describes the intercultural learning outcomes gained by students in an Interdisciplinary Ghana Study Abroad Program.

Chapter 11

Global Contributions of the Human Sciences

Jacqueline M. Holland, Juanita Mendenhall, and Joanne Pearson

INTRODUCTION

Professionals trained in the human sciences have been sharing their skills around the world in response to a vast array of human needs for more than 100 years. In more recent years, international travel and experiences have enabled these professionals and preprofessionals (students) to have a greater global awareness and cross-cultural sensitivity for work with people from a broad spectrum of ethnicities and cultures. The first portion of the chapter looks at the variety of programs where family and consumer sciences (FCS) professionals, also known as home economists, have been and are involved internationally, at collegiate-level international study and service opportunities, and in secondary school internationally focused experiences. The second portion describes the organizations within the field of home economics that provide international connections, and the final section addresses historically Black colleges and universities (HBCUs) that have international opportunities for their faculty and students.

The terminology used throughout this chapter will switch back and forth between home economist and FCS professional. The names of people mentioned in the chapter do not represent the entirety of the population of FCS professionals involved in international endeavors. They are but examples of the many people who have shared their skills internationally.

FCS PROFESSIONALS AND THEIR
INTERNATIONAL EXPERIENCES

FCS professionals from the United States have been working internationally since the end of the nineteenth century when the Civil Service Commission began recruiting home economists to teach in newly acquired U.S. territories such as the Philippines and Puerto Rico (Hanson 1965). In 1915, Helen Kinne of Teachers College, New York used her sabbatical year to introduce home economics to missionary schools in China and to lecture at Canton Christian College where they were interested in organizing a home economics department (Schroeder, unpublished manuscript). At the end of World War I, there were 84 dietitians assigned to military hospitals serving overseas (Stage and Virginia 1997, 136).

In 1922, Ava Milam Clark, dean of the School of Home Economics at Oregon State College, went to China to help establish a home economics department at Yenching University in Peking (Beijing) and during the following 30 years she periodically had assignments as consultant in home economics in various universities in the Far East. From 1950 to 1952 she worked for the United Nations Food and Agriculture Organization (FAO) as a home economics advisor in Syria and Iraq (Oregon State University Libraries. n.d.).

In the decades following the 1920s, home economics departments were established internationally, extension programs were expanded, and many home economists shared their knowledge and skills with World War II ravaged countries in Europe and Asia. Some of the many professionals involved in this work included Helen Strow, who served in England and Germany with the Red Cross from 1944 to 1948 and then went to Germany to expand extension programs (Schroeder, unpublished manuscript); Opal Stech, who spent 1947–1949 in Warsaw, Poland, assisting in the development of the home economics program at Central Agriculture College (Grandstaff-Hentgen Funeral Service, Inc. n.d.); Geraldine Fenn, who originated the International Farm Youth Exchange (IFYE) in 1948 and was a visiting youth specialist in Germany in 1950 (Geraldine G. Fenn. n.d.); Kathleen Flom, who served as regional program leader for Europe and the Far East for IFYE beginning in 1954 and served as a home economist with the British government in Uganda from 1960 to 1962 (National 4-H History Preservation Program. n.d.); Cecile Hoover Edwards, who taught in India for two years in the 1960s; and Flossie M. Byrd, who spent two weeks in the Philippines teaching and consulting in the 1970s (Schroeder, unpublished manuscript).

Legislation signed in 1946 authorized the Fulbright Program, the premier international exchange program sponsored by the U.S. government. The first female Fulbright Scholar was Mary Jane Sharp, a 1948 home economics graduate from the University of Tennessee (Mary Jane Sharp 2015). Some home economists who received Fulbright grants in the 1950s were Hazel Hauck to Thailand in 1952–1953, Margaret Justin to Norway in 1954, and Wanda Montgomery to Burma in 1957–1958 (O'Toole 1988). Flemmie Kittrell went to Baroda, India (1950–1951) on a Fulbright award as a technical specialist to help organize the College of Home Science and to develop a research program in human nutrition. She returned several years later to continue this work and later conducted nutrition surveys in India, Thailand, Kenya, and Uganda (O'Toole 1988). She returned to India for the last time in 1977 to lecture on another Fulbright grant (Ware and Braukman 2004). Gwendolyn Newkirk was a Fulbright lecturer at Winneba Training College in Ghana and also provided assistance to the University of Ghana in Legon in the development of a home economics degree program in 1966.

Many FCS professionals have received Fulbright Scholar grants in the intervening years, including Sharon Nickols to Malawi in 1983–1984; Frances Magrabi to India in 1985; Richard Ahrens to Kenya in 1987–1988; Kristi Lekies to Potsdam, Germany, in 1995–1996; Deborah Wooldridge to Bahrain in 1999–2000; Joanne Pearson to Moldova in 2001; Elizabeth Goldsmith to Trinidad and Tobago in 2006; Susan Reichelt to Slovenia in 2007; Stephan Wilson to Kenya in 2007; and Lucy Delgadillo to Costa Rica in 2010. Stephan Wilson is an example of a person who had been a Peace Corps volunteer and then returned to the country some 22 years later as a Fulbright Scholar (University of Nevada 2007). Lucy Delgadillo is a native Costa Rican who returned to her homeland and taught in Spanish during her Fulbright experience (USU professor received Fulbright to Costa Rica). Several FCS professionals have had more than one Fulbright grant, and others have become a part of the Fulbright Specialist program, including Elizabeth Goldsmith who went to Malta in 2011 as a Fulbright Specialist. In 1996–1997, Herma Williams was a Fulbright Scholar at the University of the Western Cape and the University of Cape Town in South Africa. She is now a member of the Fulbright national board of directors (Fulbright 2015). With the advent of the Peace Corps in 1961, greater numbers of FCS professionals volunteered to serve in a variety of roles internationally. In 1962, the director of the Peace Corps requested help from the American Home Economics Association (AHEA) in recruiting 500 home economists within a year (Pundt 1980, 315). The first several classes of Peace Corps volunteers each included multiple home economists including Wanda Montgomery (Thailand) and Mary Andrews (India). Each of these women maintained contact with their respective countries throughout their years of employment and for many years into retirement. In the first 50 years of the Peace Corps, more than 100 FCS professionals served as Peace Corps volunteers. Many of these professionals continued to be involved in international work including Wanda Montgomery (Thailand), who worked for FAO in Nigeria, in Southern Africa, and in

Malawi and on numerous other projects in Africa (Obituary Note—Wanda Lucille Montgomery 2015); Mary Crave (Morocco), who provided technical assistance to African 4-H programs as part of a Global 4-H Partnership; and Nancy Granovsky (Paraguay), who served as a Peace Corps technical trainer and consultant, visiting volunteers in Columbia and Ecuador. She also served as the president of the International Federation for Home Economics (IFHE) from 1996 to 2000 (Andrews 2011).

The first female and first African American to be a Peace Corps director was Carolyn R. Payton. She was appointed to the post in 1977 and served in that role for about a year. Carolyn, who majored in home economics and graduated in 1945, completed graduate work in clinical psychology and worked in that field throughout her professional career. She began her work with the Peace Corps in 1964, helping to prepare trainees for assignments in West Africa. Later she worked as country director for the Caribbean region (Estrada 2001).

The People-to-People Citizen Ambassador Program, established in 1956 by President Dwight D. Eisenhower, offered students and professionals the unique opportunity to meet and interact with colleagues around the world (The Eisenhower. n.d.). Some of the FCS professionals who have been involved in the program have included Katherine Buckley, who participated in a three-week study tour to Russia and Czechoslovakia (Quinn-McGowen Funeral Home. n.d.); Juanita Mendenhall, who led programs for FCS professionals to China and to South Africa; and Jacqueline Holland, who was a delegate to China.

Many FCS professionals have conducted research or taught internationally, funded through their institution of employment, federal government grants, United Nations programs, Fulbright grants, philanthropic organizations, religious organizations, and many other entities. Flemmie Kittrell conducted some of the earliest international research in 1947 in Liberia, where she carried out a nutritional survey sponsored by the U.S. government. Her results focused on "hidden hunger," which affected some 90% of the country's population. As a result of her research, the government in Liberia made changes in the agricultural and fishing industries (Ware and Braukman 2004, 346).

More recently, a number of FCS professionals have taught and served as consultants overseas. In the 1970s, Julia Miller worked with the home economics extension program in training extension agents to teach basic nutrition to women in Ghana. She returned to Ghana, Kenya, and Malawi many times through the late 2000s, working on projects related to women in development (Jackson, Wolf, Vincenti, and Browne 2009). With the breakup of the Soviet Union, a series of home economics training conferences for teachers was held in Eastern Europe between 1994 and 2000. Leaders of these conferences included Sally Williams from the United States.

In 1980, Gwendolyn Newkirk served as home economics curriculum consultant in Yambio, Sudan, and in 1982 Barbara Clawson served as a consultant at Oyo State College of Education in Nigeria. In 1992, Leola Adams, Virginia Caples, and Bernice Carter Richardson traveled to South Africa to provide consulting services in a number of content areas across the region. Harriette Pipes McAdoo received a faculty grant from Howard University to travel to Nairobi, Kenya, focusing on an examination of migration of women and families over generations as they moved from rural to urban areas. In the 1990s, she conducted research on HIV/AIDS in Zimbabwe for two summers and then went to Ghana to study stress and HIV/AIDS among women in marketplaces (McAdoo and Miller 2009).

Not all research has been conducted in developing countries. Retia Scott Walker conducted a project in Europe in 1989 entitled *Comparative Study of Long-Term Care of Elders in the United States and Three Western European Countries: Sweden, Denmark, and the Netherlands.* There she worked closely with colleagues in those countries to carry out the project (Hymon-Parker 2009). Joanne Pearson spent the 1994–1995 academic year at Wageningen University in the Netherlands conducting further analysis of data from the Survey in Europe on Nutrition and the Elderly, a Concerted Action study (Pearson, Schlettwein-Gsell, Staveren, and Groot 1998).

COLLEGIATE-LEVEL INTERNATIONAL EXPERIENCES

Many FCS programs in the United States offer study abroad courses and international study tours led by FCS faculty. Some are special topics courses and tours and others are taught on a regular basis. Institutions offering these courses include University of Georgia in multiple departments including housing and household economics, dietetics, and fashion merchandising; Iowa State University (ISU) in the foods and nutrition department for graduate dietetic interns; and the University of Kentucky.

Another variant of international study is that of international service learning. In some institutions this is offered as a structured course in an international setting and in other colleges and universities it is an alternative spring break or postterm experience. Examples of international service learning are those offered at ISU and the University of South Florida (USF). At ISU the experience is a five-week program in Kenya (Cowan et al. 2003), while at USF the experience is a one-week program in Belize (Wright and Lundy 2015).

INTERNATIONAL EXPERIENCES FOR SECONDARY
TEACHERS AND THEIR STUDENTS

When the Peace Corps was first started, the call for volunteers went out to professionals in many fields including home economics teachers. Today, the number of teachers who leave the profession for 27 months in an international Peace Corps setting is smaller than it was 50 years ago, with proportionally more of the new recruits coming directly from college. Some of the people who had been teachers and then joined the Peace Corps or had become teachers following service in the Peace Corps include Wanda Montgomery (Thailand 1961–1963) and Marie Olson-Badeau (St. Lucia 1977–1979) (Andrews 2011).

The Fulbright-Hays program provides grants for teachers that result in a greater global perspective in U.S. classrooms. The programs are of several types including short-term seminars, four to six weeks in length, which help to integrate international studies into an institution's curriculum, and group research or study projects, 2–12 months in length, for a group of faculty from institutions of higher education or graduate students to conduct research or study in a foreign country. In 2003, Caryl Johnson led a group of 18 New Mexico classroom teachers on a Fulbright-Hays Group Projects Abroad grant to Ghana, West Africa. The teachers lived for three weeks in a small rural village. While there, they learned what daily life is like and interacted with students and teachers at various levels in rural Ghana, and with faculty at the University of Ghana. The teachers began planning teaching units while in Ghana and then carried them out when they returned to their classrooms (Johnson 2006).

Teachers can also receive grants to work overseas during the summer. Gretchen Ann Speerstra, a FCS teacher from Wisconsin, received a National Education Association/US Agency for International Development (USAID) summer grant to work with home economics teachers in Ethiopia (Speerstra 2010).

THE HISTORY AND ROLE OF INTERNATIONAL
ORGANIZATIONS FOR THE HOME
ECONOMICS PROFESSION

Antecedents to the formation of a home economics organization had an international component, as documented by Genevieve Schroeder in her American Association of Family and Consumer Sciences (AAFCS) 100th Anniversary Convention presentation in June 2009: "Probably the first American women engaging in teaching domestic subjects were missionary wives in the early

1800s" (Schroeder, unpublished manuscript). Throughout the decade of 1900–1910, interest in promoting and organizing home economics as a field gained momentum throughout the world. Many were already practicing what was to become the profession of home economics (Schroeder, unpublished manuscript).

The First Home Economics Organization, IFHE

The first worldwide organization for home economics professionals is IFHE. IFHE traces its beginning to an international conference on home economics education. Its first Congress was held for three days in September 1908 in Fribourg, Switzerland, with around 750 persons attending. It was "a platform for international exchange with other home economists" practicing various forms of domestic science, as it was commonly called. IFHE was established at that meeting and elected the first president, M. Georges Python, the conference organizer (Schroeder, unpublished manuscript).

Over more than a century, IFHE has become a professional organization with these aims: to provide opportunities for global networking among professionals; promote the recognition of home economics in everyday lives; promote continuing education in home economics; provide opportunities for professionals through practice, research, and professional development; and improve the quality of everyday life for individuals, families, and societies. Additionally, IFHE provides international information and exchange through publications, Congresses, conferences, and workshops (International Federation for Home Economics 2008).

IFHE headquarters have been located in Fribourg, Switzerland (1908–1954); Paris, France (1955–2000); and Bonn, Germany (2001–present). Originally, records were kept in French. IFHE became trilingual when English and German were added as official languages of the Federation. In 1994, the official language became English (International Federation for Home Economics 2008).

World Congresses of the Federation are now held every four years, rotating around the globe. They are the major convention events of the organization. Congresses have been held in Gent, Belgium; Paris, France; Copenhagen, Denmark; Rome, Italy; College Park, Maryland; Manila, Philippines; Accra, Ghana; Minneapolis, Minnesota; Kyoto, Japan; Bangkok, Thailand; Lucerne, Switzerland; and Melbourne, Australia (Arcus 2008, 427–430). Congress 2016 was in Daejeon, South Korea.

IFHE has worked with the United Nations and is an International Non-Governmental Organization with consultative status at the UN since

1952. IFHE appoints volunteer representatives to the Economic and Social Council, FAO, United Nations Economic and Social Council, United Nations International Children's Emergency Fund, and the Council of Europe. Representatives are the pipeline between IFHE and the UN, keeping members informed, presenting workshops, attending conferences, and involving members with the UN.

An accomplishment initiated by the IFHE with the UN was the International Year of the Family (IYF) that was celebrated in 1994 and was followed with special anniversary celebrations around the world of the 10th and 20th IYF anniversaries. Margaret Fitch, the first IFHE president from the United States, initiated IFHE program committees in 1981. They provide increased opportunities for members to work in areas of interest and to advance the federation's program of work.

The elected executive committee includes the president, four-year term; president-elect, two years; past president, two years; secretary, four years; and treasurer, four years. Five regional vice presidents and five regional representatives are elected in their own region, each serving four years. The five regions are Africa, Asia, Europe, the Pacific, and the Americas. IFHE is a membership-driven, dues-supported organization.

The American Home Economics/Family and Consumer Sciences Association's International Organizations and Influence

Only three months separate the founding of IFHE in Fribourg, Switzerland, and the founding of AHEA in Washington, D.C., in 1909 as the worldwide movement was blossoming (Baldwin 1949). In 1915, AHEA authorized membership in IFHE for the first time. In 1922, AHEA members went to the third IFHE Congress in Paris. During World War I (1914–1919), "focus was on selection and food preservation, improved health and well-being, teaching meatless and wheatless meals . . . and to remind every citizen to save on coal and to grow victory gardens" (Pundt 1980, 21–22). In 1920, the AHEA international committee raised funds to establish a chair of home economics at the Constantinople College for Girls. Alice P. Norton, then editor of the *AHEA Journal,* was selected to direct the project, serving from 1921 to 1923. The first AHEA international scholarship was awarded in the 1930s to an English home economist teaching in India. In 1934–1935, grants were given to two Chinese students for study at Yenching University, China. Scholarships and fellowships have also been awarded to students from foreign countries to study home economics-related programs in the U.S. colleges and universities. From 1930 to 2007, AHEA/AAFCS awarded more than 375 fellowships to international students representing over 65 countries who were enrolled in more than 80 U.S. institutions (Schroeder, unpublished manuscript). In 1956, AHEA increased its support of IFHE by sponsoring 30 memberships, which were distributed among the AHEA-affiliated state associations.

Recognizing the importance of family development and family planning, the AHEA population education committee secured a contract in 1971 with the USAID to assist with family planning training for home economists in developing countries. Under the direction of Helen Strow, the Working with Villagers project was carried out through 1981. In 1977, the Inter-American Commission of Women sponsored an AHEA workshop on nutrition in Honduras for delegates from 21 Latin American countries. Also in 1977, the association approved the international division of AHEA (Schroeder, unpublished manuscript) which coordinated the first regional IFHE Conference for the Americas, held in Guatemala later that year (Schroeder, unpublished manuscript). Wanda Montgomery initiated the AHEA/USAID-funded Global Connections Curriculum project. Training workshops were held across the United States to implement the materials (Schroeder, unpublished manuscript).

AHEA changed its name to the AAFCS in 1994. The international division became the Global Perspectives (GP) community. Today, GP is a vibrant community with elected officers and a program of work. They authored an AAFCS resolution in 2014 entitled *Unaccompanied Children Who Enter the United States* to raise awareness and increase action related to illegal immigration of children and youth into the United States that had reached epidemic proportions (American Association of Family and Consumer Sciences 2015).

The International Federation for Home Economics-United States, Inc. (IFHE-US)

In 2000, IFHE-US, Inc. was established as a separate 501(c)(3) organization. IFHE members were expected to organize according to the 1996 changes in the IFHE Constitution. Juanita Mendenhall was asked to chair the committee to develop the IFHE-US organization. The AAFCS and IFHE-US boards accepted a Memorandum of Understanding in 1999, and IFHE-US was officially launched at the 2000 Annual Convention of AAFCS. Mendenhall served the first four-year term as president followed by Mary Andrews, Mary Warnock, Carol Anderson, and Roxie Godfrey. IFHE-US selects its own delegates and participates directly in the work of the federation. *IFHE-US Connections* is the e-newsletter and ifhe-us.org is the website. Board and business meetings are held at the AAFCS annual conference and other meetings may be held. IFHE-US is part of the IFHE, Region of the Americas.

In 2005, the IFHE-US Development Fund was initiated as a not-for-profit fund within IFHE-US. The fund is the United States' affiliate of the

IFHE Development Fund, initiated by Nancy B. Leidenfrost in 1996. These funds support educational programs and projects in developing countries. The most recent example is the grant given to the Disaster Assistance Partnerships (DAP) Honduras Initiative. DAP is a committee of IFHE council (International Federation for Home Economics 2018).

An example of joint cooperation between IFHE and IFHE-US was a 30-month school gardens project in Moldova, beginning in 2006. This was funded by a grant from the Monsanto Fund, the philanthropic arm of the Monsanto Company. Joanne Pearson, a member of both IFHE-US and the Outreach to Central and Eastern Europe Countries Committee of IFHE, managed the project. Results of the project were presented at IFHE Congress in Switzerland in 2008 (Pearson 2008).

The International Home Economics Services, Inc. 1974–Present

The International Home Economics Services, Inc. (IHES) is a 501(c) (3) not-for-profit organization, incorporated in 1974 in Washington, D.C., that carries out home economics efforts in developing countries. For more than 45 years IHES has strengthened and supported home economics programs of various kinds in many developing countries. Materials, funds, and expertise are donated by supporters to accomplish the IHES mission, which is to develop and strengthen formal and nonformal home economics programs and projects in less developed countries; utilize the expertise of U.S. home economists to assist and disseminate knowledge and skills in home economics to enhance the social, economic, cognitive, emotional, and physical well-being of individuals and families; and to enable women to fully participate in the development processes of their countries and their professional associations.

A 15-member elected board of trustees governs IHES. A donation request letter and newsletter are sent to selected donors each year. There is no paid membership fee. Written proposals are reviewed, evaluated, and selected by trustees and are monitored and evaluated during and after completion of the project. Projects of all sizes have been carried out in Africa, Eastern Europe, Russia, Samoa, the Philippines, the Caribbean, Asia, and South and Central America.

Disaster Assistance Partnerships for Home Economics Programs in Developing Countries

A new international organization for home economics collaboration is the Disaster Assistance Partnership (DAP). IHES initiated the organization in 2010 to address increasing requests for disaster assistance. DAP is not a "relief" organization, it is an assistance program cooperatively designed to receive requests from home economics-related programs. Worldwide, DAP partners are professionals and nonprofessionals, working together as needed. IFHE regions, countries, states, professional and corporate organizations, and individuals can all become partners by agreeing to assist. Since 2015, DAP has worked with the Madina Village School in Sierra Leone, sending school supplies and assisting the women of the village in income generation. The new Honduras Initiative is addressing the AAFCS immigration resolution (American Association of Family and Consumer Sciences 2015) by establishing home economics programs in Honduras (International Federation for Home Economics 2018).

Participation of Historically Black Colleges and Universities

Within the international contributions of human sciences/FCS, many professionals and students from historical black colleges and universities (HBCUs) have made significant contributions. Such support has included international projects sponsored by AAFCS; student internships and study abroad programs (SAPs); and faculty collaboration, training, and professional presentations at international conferences. Following is an overview of global activities at several HBCU institutions.

University of Maryland Eastern Shore, Princess Anne, Maryland; North Carolina A&T, Greensboro, North Carolina; Southern University and A&M College, Baton Rouge, Louisiana

In 2005, Shirley Hymon-Parker, chairperson at the University of Maryland Eastern Shore (UMES), initiated a proposal to support a joint SAP initiative including North Carolina A&T (NCAT) in Greensboro, North Carolina, and Southern University and A&M College (SUBR) in Baton Rouge, Louisiana. The project, entitled *Globalizing the Fashion Curriculum at 1890 Institutions*, provided students with a global perspective of the fashion curricula at the universities. With funding from the United States Department of Agriculture this project assisted students to be successful in future career endeavors and exposed them to the diversity of culture beyond the United States (Walker 2009). Between 2006 and 2009, 24 students participated. A relationship established with the London College of Fashion (LCF) in London, England, exposed students to fashion, marketing, advertising, and manufacturing industries in European countries. Business representatives, including Liz Claiborne, were identified by LCF, and a two-week winter study tour ensued in which students earned three transferable academic credits. In addition, they were able to apply for a summer/semester SAP at LCF, earning 15 academic credits that transferred to their home institution to be utilized in the undergraduate degree program. The funding provided teaching and research opportunities for faculty and staff, and enabled students to learn a foreign language, become knowledgeable of international politics and economics, and develop an understanding of the influence of globalization on nations (S. Hymon-Parker, personal communication, January 15, 2016).

University of Arkansas Pine Bluff, Pine Bluff, Arkansas

Kaye Crippen, an associate professor at the University of Arkansas at Pine Bluff, has conducted significant research related to textiles in Asian countries. Before joining the university in 2009, Crippen managed extensive research related to textiles following her tenure at DuPont USA. Since that time, Crippen has continued to share her research on various topics such as traditional textiles in Tenganan, Bali and Indonesia; sustainability within international textiles and apparel; and textile tourism (K. Crippen, personal communication, January 19, 2016). Assistant Professor Janette Wheat teaches a course entitled "Families Across Cultures," in which students often complete an internship in another country. One student interned at the Rhema Christian Center Philippines, Inc. in Tarlac City, Philippines, during the summer of 2008. As a teacher's assistant, the intern participated in a variety of assignments, including helping children with personal hygiene, monitoring and guiding the children's behavior, and assisting teachers with instruction. Another student volunteered with the West Africa AIDS Foundation in Accra, Ghana, where she created a management information database based upon a comprehensive assessment of nutrition intervention with mothers and their children. International concepts are incorporated in many of the classes taught in the department (J. Wheat, personal communication, January 20, 2016). Students have also traveled to Brussels and Paris to explore the fashion industry (K. Crippen, personal communication, January 19, 2016).

Alabama Agricultural and Mechanical University, Huntsville, Alabama

Alabama Agricultural and Mechanical University (AAMU) faculty and students have made a significant contribution on the international level. Jerry Blackmon Sr., associate professor, participated in the Ethiopian Call for Action Aid program in 2005–2006. Through the faith-based Foundation of Faith International organization, he provided opportunities for churches to become partners in addressing some of the pressing family needs of that country.

Virginia Caples, professor and administrator of 1890 extension, participated in several global projects through research and on-site teaching. This included representation to the Southeastern Consortium for International Development/ Women in International Development for AAMU, consulting for Kellogg International and South African Christian Association in Johannesburg, South Africa, in the summer 1992. In this capacity, she provided workshops and other presentations to home economics teachers and administrators in the country (Vincenti, Browne, Dolby-Plunkett, and Smith 2009). Caples, along with Bernice Richardson, also conducted three-week workshops for home economics supervisors, part of AHEA's "Project Rural Reach" Dar es Salaam, Tanzania. These workshops ran between 1986 and 1989. The professors collaborated with other human sciences professionals to author the abstract, *Project Rural Reach: An Experiment in Self-Reliance, Families in Transition* published at the IFHE Congress in Hanover, the Federal Republic of Germany in 1992. Caples also participated in several international conferences, including agriculture production conferences sponsored by the Phelps Stokes Fund and the American University of the Caribbean's linkage program in St. Kitts and Nevis, British West Indies, and in St. Croix, U.S. Virgin Islands, 1981 (Vincenti, Browne, Dolby-Plunkett, and Smith 2009).

AAMU faculty members Patricia Young, Maria Wilkie, and Cynthia Smith have conducted fashion apparel tours with students in Canada and England. Smith also served as a member of the South-East Consortium for International Development/USAID. Johnson Kamalu, Ann Warren, Jannie Carter, Donnie Cook, and Adraine Langham represented the university at the Food and Nutrition Summer Institute, held in Accra, Ghana, 2001. At this event, nutrition and health educators from each region in Africa shared the status of food security, food safety, and health in their area. Participants visited Accra's public health clinic, the Food Research Institute, and the University of Ghana. The team presented *The Modification of Peanut-Based Foods Commonly Consumed in Africa to increase Their Vitamin A Content as a Vehicle to Reduce Night Blindness in the Region.* Dorothy Brandon has extensive international experience in Botswana. Since joining the faculty at AAMU, she has reviewed the Bachelor of Science degree program in FCS at the University of Botswana and has served as a presenter and facilitator at several national professional meetings in the country (C. Smith and B. Richardson, personal communication, January 16, 2016).

Morgan State University, Baltimore, Maryland

The FCS department at Morgan State University (MSU) currently has two programs of study: general family and consumer studies and fashion merchandising. From 2014 to the present, fashion merchandising students have completed SAPs in Milan, Paris, and London. Jacqueline Holland participated in conferences of international organizations including the Caribbean

Association of Home Economics, 2011–2015, and presented at IFHE World Congresses in Switzerland, Ireland, and South Korea, 2010–2016. Holland also implemented campus service projects that supported IFHE's World Home Economics Day initiative. Cassandra Dickerson, a lecturer in the department, traveled with 12 other committee members representing several universities of the Knowledge Exchange Institute (KEI) to Milan, Italy; Paris, France; and London, England. The purpose of the trip was to visit the programs where FACS fashion merchandising students take classes while studying abroad through KEI, which offers fashion design and merchandising programs in Italy, Ireland, Scotland, and France (C. Dickerson, personal communication, January 20, 2016).

North Carolina Agricultural and Technical State University

In addition to the partnership with the UMES and Southern University (SURB), NCAT students in fashion design and food and nutrition science traveled to Montreal, Canada, between 2006 and 2009. One preservice education student completed her student teaching in Germany as a result of a collaborative relationship between professors. The university provided partial funding for the student's living expenses and for professor visits. Also, students in the child development program, as part of the school of education at the university, traveled to Malawi for one semester. Monetary support for the trip was obtained through the students' financial aid. The International Programs office is very supportive of students in every subject area desiring to travel aboard; they provide extensive information and assistance for students interested in such an experience. In evaluating student requests, the office investigates personal, academic, and financial needs (North Carolina A&T State University 2016). Part of this takes place in tandem with the academic department. Many students have participated in SAPs. In some instances, professors have served as chaperones or instructors in a variety of countries. Faculty have also traveled abroad to give seminars related to food science and similar training for various businesses and institutions. The department currently has a memorandum of agreement with China Agriculture University to do collaborative research. Jordan, Qatar, and Saudi Arabia are other countries where the faculty has conducted professional development seminars (V. Giddings personal communication, November 2, 2015).

South Carolina State University, Orangeburg, South Carolina

In 1989, Leola Adams, representing the university president, traveled to Sierra Leone to establish a relationship between South Carolina State University (SCSU) and the University of Sierra Leone. This partnership established a faculty and student exchange program between the two universities. In 1992, Adams received funding from The Kellogg Foundation and the USAID to visit South Africa; she became part of a team of educators who visited several areas where preschool education was not available. With the support of the South African government, the team traveled to underserved regions and townships throughout the country. They met with parents, school officials, civic leaders, and corporate entities to facilitate discussions on the importance of educating their young children. This experience was reported by a guest appearance on the television program, *Good Morning South Africa* (L. Adams, personal communication, January 18, 2016).

Virginia State University

In the summer of 2012, Ghana, West Africa was the location in which five FCS students from Virginia State University participated in a two-week service-learning project, established to assist Ghanaian families in creating sustainable communities for children and families. Alice Joyner, the chairperson of the department, secured funding to support student participation. During their visit, students engaged in educational initiatives for children, learned the West African native craft of batik, and assisted in building a village school. As part of this experience, the students also enrolled in early childhood administration and global studies classes (AAFCS-Virginia Affiliate Newsletter 2012, 3).

CONCLUSION

U.S. FCS professionals have contributed on a global scale from the profession's earliest years. Numerous FCS professionals have taken the lead and participated in addressing human issues in diverse regions around the world. These professionals have engaged themselves in national initiatives, including the Civil Service Commission, Peace Corp, Fulbright program, and People to People. In times of world challenges, FCS professionals have assisted in establishing programs as well as consulting in developed and developing nations. FCS educators and students on all levels have and continue to participate in SAPs. International organizations such as IFHE, through partnership with the United Nations, serve as a conduit and platform from which FCS professionals can further tackle the universal needs of individuals, families, and communities to obtain a better quality of life. The IFHE-US has a global presence through established enterprises that address crucial needs in mostly developing nations. HBCUs also have a long history of various international activities. This historical perspective illuminates the foundations of the profession as FCS professionals and students continue to have a viable presence in the global work of the human sciences.

REFERENCES

American Association of Family and Consumer Sciences. 2015. "Unaccompanied Children Entering the United States. Resolutions of the American Association of Family and Consumer Sciences." Accessed December 10, 2015. https://higherl ogicdownload.s3.amazonaws.com/AAFCS/1c95de14-d78f-40b8-a6ef-a1fb628c68 fe/UploadedImages/advocacy/resolutions/Unaccompanied_Children_Entering _the_United_States_Resolution%20(1).pdf.

American Association of Family and Consumer Sciences-Virginia Affiliate Newsletter. 2012. "Making Connections". Accessed December 10, 2015. https:// www.vafcs-aafcs.org/uploads/5/7/3/4/57348791/2012_fall_newsletter.pdf.

Andrews, Mary. 2011. "Case Studies of Home Economists/Family Consumer Scientists in the Peace Corps." Unpublished report.

Arcus, Margaret E. 2008. "100 Years of the International Federation for Home Economics, 1908-2008." Food and Agriculture Organization of the United Nations. Accessed December 12, 2015. https://agris.fao.org/agris-search/search.do?recor dID=US201300139845.

Baldwin, Keturah E. 1949. *The AHEA saga: A Brief History of the Origin and Development of the American Home Economics Association and a Glimpse at the Grass Roots from Which it Grew*. Washington, DC: AHEA.

Cowan, Donna L., Leah Kagima, Margaret Torrie, Cheryl Hausafus, and Rachel Machacha. 2003. "Serving a New Community: A Sustaining Model of International Service Learning." *Journal of Family and Consumer Sciences 95,* no. 2: 54–55.

The Eisenhower. n.d. "People-to-People Program." Accessed November 17, 2015. https://www.eisenhowerlibrary.gov/research/online-documents/people-people-p rogram.

Estrada, Louie. 2001 "Peace Corps' Former Director Carolyn Payton Dies at Age 75." The Washington Post, July 14, 2001. https://libguides.wvu.edu/c.php?g=418946 &p=2855023.

Fulbright. 2015. "Meet Our Board of Directors." Accessed November 12, 2015 https ://fulbright.org/about/board-of-directors/.

Fenn, Geraldine G. n.d. "Montana State 4-H Staff." Accessed October 2, 2015 from http://www.4-h-hof.com/montana.pdf.

Grandstaff-Hentgen Funeral Service, Inc. n.d. "Opal D. Stech." Accessed November 16, 2015 https://www.grandstaff-hentgen.com/obituary/6325507.

Hanson, Doris E. 1965. "Pioneers in the Field of Home Economics Work Abroad." *Journal of Home Economics 57,* no. 4: 255–259.

Hymon-Parker, Shirley. 2009. "Retia Scott Walker: Leading by Example." In *African American Women: Contributions to the Human Sciences*, edited by Miller, Julia R.,

Dorothy I. Mitstifer, and Gladys Gary Vaughn. East Lansing, MI: Kappa Omicron Nu.

International Federation for Home Economics. 2008. *100 Years of the International Federation for Home Economics, 1908-2008.* Bonn, German: Commemorative History Publication, IFHE. Accessed October 8, 2015. https://www.ifhe.org/about -ifhe/who-we-are/history-book-100-years-ifhe/.

International Federation for Home Economics. 2018. "IFHE Special Newsletter, March 2018. DAP Disaster Assistance Partnerships for Home Economics/FCS Programs in Developing Countries." An IFHE Council Committee. Accessed October 8, 2015. https://www.ifhe.org/fileadmin/user_upload/IFHE_2019/Our _Work/IFHE_NL_Spezial_Issue_April_2018_DAP.pdf.

Jackson, Vanessa P., Elizabeth Wolf, Virginia B. Vincenti, and Lorna B. Browne, 2009. "Julia R. Miller: A Leadership Journey of Dreams and Fate." In *African American Women: Contributions to the Human Sciences*, edited by Miller, Julia R., Dorothy I. Mitstifer, and Gladys Gary Vaughn. East Lansing, MI: Kappa Omicron Nu.

Johnson, Caryl. 2006 "Global Experiences for FCS Professionals." *Journal of Family and Consumer Sciences 98,* no. 3: 17–19.

McAdoo, Harriet. P., and Julia R. Miller. 2009. "Harriette Pipes McAdoo: A Renowned Scholar of African American Studies." In *African American Women: Contributions to the Human Sciences*, edited by Miller, Julia R., Dorothy I. Mitstifer, and Gladys Gary Vaughn. East Lansing, MI: Kappa Omicron Nu.

National 4-H History Preservation Program. n.d. "4-H Memorials–Kathleen Flom." Accessed October 2, 2015. https://4-hhistorypreservation.com/In_Memoriam/Obit .asp?O=4.

North Carolina A&T State University. 2016. "International Programs: How to Choose a Study Abroad Program." Accessed October 8, 2015. https://ncat.abroado ffice.net/howtochoose.html.

Obituary Note–Wanda Lucille Montgomery. 2015. International Federation for Home Economics IFHE. Accessed September 24, 2015. https://www.ifhe.org/.

Oregon State University Libraries. n.d. "Ava Milam Clark Papers, 1856–1972." Accessed October 2, 2015 http://scarc.library.oregonstate.edu/findingaids/index. php?p=collections/findingaid&id=2459&q=Ava+Milam+Clark+.

O'Toole, Lela. 1988. ' Twenty-four Early Pioneers in International Service." In *The International Heritage of Home Economics in the United States*, edited by Lela. O'Toole, 37–10. Washington, DC: AHEA.

Pearson, Joanne M. 2008. "Improving Nutritional Health in Schools: Gardens in Moldova." *Journal of Family and Consumer Sciences 100,* no. 3: 42–43.

Pearson, Joanne M., Daniela Schlettwein-Gsell, Wija van Staveren, and Lisette de Groot. 1998. "Living Alone Does Not Adversely Affect Nutrient Intake and Nutritional Status of 70- to 75-Year-Old Men and Women in Small Towns Across Europe." *International Journal of Food Sciences and Nutrition 49*, no. 2: 131–139.

Pundt, Helen Marie. 1980. *AHEA: A History of Excellence.* Washington, DC: AHEA.

Quinn-McGowen Funeral Home. n.d. "Katherine Isabelle Buckley." Accessed November 20, 2015. https://www.quinnmcgowen.com/obituary/Katherine-Bu ckley.

Sharp, Mary Jane. 2015. YouTube. October 8, 2015. https://www.youtube.com/watch
    ?v=zbw_y-t8Ozy.
Speerstra, Gretchen A. 2010. *AAFCS Annual Conference and Expo Program Guide.*
    Washington, DC: AHEA. Accessed November 20, 2015. https://www.aafcs.org/
    home.
Stage, Sarah, and Virginia B. Vincenti. 1997. *Rethinking Home Economics: Women
    and the History of a Profession.* Ithaca, NY: Cornell University Press.
University of Nevada, Reno. "Prolific Family Studies Scholar Stephan Wilson
    Accepts Post at Oklahoma State." Nevada Today, November 1, 2007. https://www
    .unr.edu/nevada-today/news/2007/prolific-family-studies-scholar-stephan-wilson-
    accepts-post-at-oklahoma-state.
Utah State University. 2009. "USU Professor Receives Fulbright to Costa Rica."
    Accessed October 6, 2015. https://www.usu.edu/today/story/usu-professor-rece
    ives-fulbright-to-costa-rica
Vincenti, Virginia B., Lorna B. Browne, Michelle Dolby-Plunkett, and Cynthia M.
    Smith, 2009. "Virginia Caples: A Beacon for Excellence." In *African American
    Women: Contributions to the Human Sciences*, edited by Miller, Julia R., Dorothy
    I. Mitstifer, and Gladys Gary Vaughn, 127–152. East Lansing, Michigan: Kappa
    Omicron Nu.
Walker, Retia S. 2009. "Shirley Hymon Parker: Passionate and Courageous
    Administrator." In *African American women: Contributions to the human sciences*,
    edited by Miller, Julia R., Dorothy I. Mitstifer, and Gladys Gary Vaughn, 299–311.
    East Lansing, MI: Kappa Omicron Nu.
Ware, Susan, and Stacy Braukman. 2004. *Notable American Women: A Biographical
    Dictionary. Volume 5: Completing the Twentieth Century.* Boston: Harvard
    University Press.
Wright, Lauri, and Mary Lundy. 2015. "Perspectives of Cultural Competency from an
    International Service-Learning Project." *Journal of the Academy of Nutrition and
    Dietetics 115,* no. 5: S6–S9.

Chapter 12

Progress and the Endless Battle

Injustices against Women and Girls

Julia R. Miller Arline

INTRODUCTION

If one would reflect on women, empowerment, human rights, and social justice, there is an integrative thread that intertwines these issues which are intricately linked.[1] Actually, they form a web that should not be untwined until the complexities among global national agendas and cultures visibly recognize the role of women in creating a just humanity. Recognizing that the Beijing Platform for Action Turns 20 brings to the attention of the world that although there has been some progress toward the empowerment of women, it is miniscule compared to the need for a universal mindset that does not question women and girls' roles in social, economic, political, civil, and cultural development. A historical perspective on various social, political, economic, civil, and cultural movements reveals that the context of 20 years since the Beijing Platform for Action may not be considered by some for a long time. On the other hand, one has to look at what women and girls have endured and were subjected to in terms of humanity before the Beijing Platform for Action was formulated. In fact, there was and remains a need for global understanding that women's issues are the world's issues (Dunlop, MacDonald, and Kyte 1996). Today, because in many nations women are still discriminated against and marginalized, the need for this global understanding exists and remains a critical issue worldwide (Muscat 2014).

Context for the Beijing Platform for Action and the Home Economics Profession Goodness of Fit Model: Implications for the Relationship between the Beijing Platform for Action and the Home Economics Profession. In carefully analyzing the Beijing Platform for Action, Beijing + 5 outcome and its relationship to the home economics profession, a review of the Lerner, Richard M., Fred Rothbaum, Shireen Boulos, and Domini R. Castellino's

(2002) discussion of the implications of developmental contextualism and the parent–child relationship is useful. Lerner et al. (2002) emphasized that the relationship among the child, parent, and other levels of the organization within a developmental system (e.g., the neighborhood, political and economic policies, and cultural) is important in understanding the role of the ecology of human development on the child's developmental processes. Actually, this relational process of human development should be integrated across time as the actions of the child, parent, and broader context of the ecological environment are studied. In essence, the "Goodness of Fit" of these relations, with the interactions among the child, parent, and ecological system in an integrated manner, is invaluable to positive outcomes that are sought for both the developmental processes of the parent and child. Accordingly, creating a context in the family, school, and community that matches the developmental characteristics and needs of both children and their parents constitutes an effective means to create "fit" between people and their world that nurtures positive and healthy development (Lerner 2004). Miambo-Ngcka (2014) discussed in the Beijing Platform for Action, Beijing + 5 outcome, 12 critical areas of the document, namely: (1) poverty, (2) education and training, (3) health, (4) violence, (5) armed conflict, (6) economy, (7) power and decision-making, (8) institutional mechanisms, (9) human rights, (10) media, (11) environment, and (12) the girl child. This document further elaborates on the areas for which programs do not exist or have not advanced significantly. These areas stated with some modifications include: (1) access to decent work with global variations in this need; (2) differences in the gender wage gap, a worldwide phenomenon; (3) rebalancing of the employment workload and family responsibilities; (4) ending violence currently resurfacing in the forms of family violence, human trafficking, and kidnapping of women and children; (5) reducing maternal mortality, an increasing issue among ethnic groups of color; (6) women's control of sexual and reproductive health and rights; and (7) participation in power and decision-making at all levels—home, community, politics, workplace, civil, and other sectors (Miambo-Ngcka 2014, 5).

The home economics profession is one that uses an interdisciplinary, integrative, ecological and developmental perspective to address issues that promote a positive quality of life for individuals and families. Globally, some subspecialties of the profession include but are not limited to (1) human nutrition and food, (2) child development, (3) family and individual financial management, (4) retailing/the business economy, (5) human development and family studies, (6) housing and the internal and external environments, (7) clothing and textiles, and (8) marriage and family therapy. Within the context of these subspecialties, the 12 critical areas identified in the Beijing Platform for Action, Beijing +5 outcome, historically have been a "fit," addressed in formal and informal education and training worldwide. Accordingly, within a global perspective, the profession has formulated collaborative efforts through engagement with local, state, and federal governmental agencies and organizations; other related professional organizations outside of home economics; grassroots-level community groups; foundations and institutions. In concert, these collaborative efforts have continued to address the 12 critical areas of the Platform for Action. It must be emphasized that the successes of these efforts have been dependent upon the social, political, economic, cultural, and civil dynamics seen within an integrated, ecological and developmental perspective across nations.

A REEXAMINATION OF FUTURE PATHWAYS:
THE CONTEXT FOR HOME ECONOMICS

Home economics professionals and practitioners have seized the opportunity to cast widely our ideology related to the importance of recognizing disparities and disempowerment of women. Not only has the casting of our reach been within the spheres of our professional interactions, engagement in political advocacy with governments, institutions, policymakers, educators, and other stakeholders globally, but also to women and men, and girls and boys on "grassroots levels" in developed and developing countries. The literature consistently reveals that to eliminate gender disparities, both women and men must be collaboratively engaged in the process. One of the keys to empowerment of women is education. As stated earlier in this chapter, from the perspective of the home economics profession, engagement has been both within the context of informal and formal educational sectors for women and girls globally. In establishing the context for our work to reduce gender disparities, the thinking of Sharma and Varma (2008) establishes a framework for the motivation and actions that have transpired among professionals.

They stressed:

> It is unfortunate that because of centuries of inertia, ignorance and conservatism the actual potential role of women in society has been ignored, preventing them from making their rightful contributions to social progress. They are denied their status and access to developmental resources and services contributing to their marginalization. With regard to their multidimensional responsibilities, it is required to empower women socially, economically and technologically to enable them to stand in society on their own with confidence. (Sharma and Varma 2008, 46)

Although home economics professionals and practitioners have historically been engaged in uplifting women globally, we should not sit on our laurels. We should continue to examine critical areas set forth in the Beijing Platform for Action. The following questions must be examined and reexamined within the context of the Beijing Platform for Action, Beijing + 5 outcome (2014), and the Millennium Development Goals (Kabeer 2005):

- How are we using innovative strategies to reduce the persistent and increasingly greater burden of female poverty that is occurring globally?
- Are we educating and training both women and men, and girls and boys with knowledge that can transfer to issues related to critical issues pertinent to human survival?
- How are we addressing and advocating against violence and human trafficking of women, children, and men?
- How have we spoken out and taken actions against the kidnapping, murder, and sale of women and girls that is occurring globally?
- How have we kept visible the effects of armed conflicts and other kinds of conflict on women, including those living under foreign occupation?
- What research-based knowledge is being communicated through social media and other venues that addresses problems associated with negative stereotyping of women, inequality in economic structures and policies related to productive activities, and access to human and nonhuman resources?
- How have we promoted the sharing of power, equality, and decision-making in all spheres of global societies?
- What are the critical issues pertaining to inequalities of women in the management of environmental resources?
- Are we involved in initiatives to continue to promote women's reproductive rights?
- What is the range of other health and nutrition issues that impact women, girl children, and total family survival?
- How are we addressing the lack of respect and inadequate promotion and protection of women's human rights?
- What discriminatory practices still exist globally related to the negative impact on the rights of female children?

CONCLUSIONS

Although there has been some progress among some nations since the advent of the Beijing Platform for Action 20 years ago, this progress is not universal. Women are still being discriminated against and marginalized in many nations around the world. Home economics professionals have and must continue to educate and advocate for the global eradication of discrimination against women and girls worldwide. Not only should the voices of women be heard, but also the voices of men speaking collectively with women about the rights of women and girls for a just humanity must resonate loudly across the globe. Mlambo-Ngcuka, under secretary general, executive director of the United Nations stated (2014, 4):

> There is a new sense of real urgency, a recognition that we are at a turning point for women's rights, a recognition that realizing gender equality, the empowerment of women and the human rights of women and girls must be a pressing central task.

Carter (2014) in his book *A Call to Action: Women, Religion, Violence, and Power* eloquently stated the words of Ruth Messinger, president of the American Jewish World Service, which emphasized:

> If the [developing] world was a molecule put under a powerful microscope, we would see a complex web of barriers that keep women from fully realizing their inherent human rights and living in dignity. Strands of this web include barriers to securing property rights; pursuing an education and earning a decent living at fair wages; and making decisions about obtaining health care. We would also see the invisible DNA that keeps this web intact: a sense of powerlessness, violence by social coercion, rigid gender roles, homophobia, violence and rape. Finally, we would see that only the women who face these barriers can push them aside, change their own lives, and transform the societies in which they live. It is our obligation to support them.

It is the position of this author that this web of barriers exists in both the developing and the developed worlds. It is a web that must be untangled with the leadership and actions of both women and men working collectively for freedom that must be realized by all, regardless of gender.

Finally, women's rights and the rights of the girl child can be framed within the ideology of Megan Wilkes Karraker. It is Karraker's (2013) position that the sustainability of families and communities is dependent upon the accountability placed on the ethical infrastructure that is implemented for the well-being of all involved. In 1948, this ethical infrastructure was outlined in the Universal Declaration of Human Rights of the United Nations that was set forth by member states. Although there was universal acceptance of these human rights by member states, some reservations were also exhibited (Karraker 2013, 217).

Further, Karraker (2013, 217) stressed that the failure of some governments to entirely accept these standards of human rights that were established for the ethical infrastructure was an indication of the lack of political will, rather than a derogation of the standard that was established. Although it is important to note that without the standard, governments forcibly dealt freely, arbitrarily, and cruelly to undermine their citizens of material welfare without accountability to their citizens and the global community. Further, she emphasized that countries cannot be incarcerated, but they can be made to change by force of international public opinion, coupled with advocacy by domestic constituencies empowered by knowing their rights (Karraker 2013, 217). This is our opportunity, this is our challenge!

NOTE

1. Reprinted with permission from the International Federation for Home Economics' March 2015 Newsletter.

REFERENCES

Carter, Jimmy. 2014. *A Call to Action: Women, Religion, Violence and Power.* New York: Simon & Schuster.

Dunlop, Joan, Mia MacDonald, and Rachel Kyte. 1996. "Women Redrawing the Map: The World after the Beijing and Cairo Conferences." *SAIS Review* 16, no. 1 (Winter-Spring): 153–165.

Kabeer, Naila. 2005. "The Beijing Platform for Action and the Millennium Development Goals: Different Processes, Different Outcomes." Accessed December 23, 2020. http://nailakabeer.net/wp-content/uploads/2005/09/13552070512331332273.pdf.

Karraker, Meg Wilkes. 2013. *Global Families* (2nd ed.). New York: Sage.

Lerner, Richard M. 2004. *Liberty: Thriving and Civic Engagement Among America's Youth.* Thousand Oaks: Sage.

Lerner, Richard M., Fred Rothbaum, Shireen Boulos, and Domini R. Castellino. 2002. "Developmental Systems Perspective on Parenting." In *Handbook of Parenting: Biology and Ecology of Parenting*, edited by Marc H. Bornstein, 344–315. Mahwah: Lawrence Erlbaum Associate Publishers.

Miambo-Ngcka, Phumzile. 2014. "Introduction." *Beijing Declaration and Platform for Action: Beijing + 5 Political Declaration and Outcome.* New York: United Nations.

Muscat, Samer. 2014. "Women's Rights." Human Rights Watch. Accessed December 23, 2020 https://www.hrw.org/topic/womens-rights#.

Sharma, Preeti and Shashi K. Varma. 2008. "Women Empowerment Through Entrepreneurial Activities of Self-Groups." *Indian Research Journal of Extension Education* 8, no. 1: 46–51.

Women, U. N. 2014. *Beijing Declaration and Platform for Action: Beijing + 5 Political Declaration and Outcome.* New York: United Nations.

Chapter 13

Learning Outcomes in an Interdisciplinary Study Abroad Program

Developing a Global Perspective

Bettye P. Smith and Wenting Yang

The purpose of this study was to determine the intercultural learning outcomes (ILO) for students in the Interdisciplinary Ghana Study Abroad Program.[1] Data were collected from 28 students using the ILO questionnaire containing 29 statements and 5 content domains (functional knowledge, world geography knowledge, interpersonal accommodation knowledge, global interdependence knowledge, and cultural sensitivity knowledge). Data were collected before engaging in and after completing the short-term program. Overall mean ratings showed that 83% of the 29 statements increased from pretest to posttest, whereas none of the statements experienced a decrease in ratings. Paired t test revealed that a significant increase occurred in mean ratings for two content domains—functional knowledge and knowledge of global interdependence.

The demand for study abroad programs continues to emerge as a top trend in higher education. The number of students from the United States studying abroad increased by 5% in the 2013–2014 academic year, which is the highest rate of growth since before the 2008 economic downturn (Institute of International Education Network 2015). Students at the University of Georgia (UGA) in Athens are no exception. The university is among the top 20 nationally in study abroad participation. With more than 2,200 students studying abroad for academic credit in the 2013–2014 academic year, UGA was ranked 17th among all U.S. institutions in study abroad participation (Institute of International Education Network 2015). As part of the family and consumer sciences (FCS) body of knowledge, globalization was identified as an external influence and a cross-cutting thread central to the work of the profession (Baugher et al. 2000). The active participation of FCS students in study abroad programs underscores the development of a global perspective.

The Interdisciplinary Ghana Study Abroad Program at UGA is a faculty-led 21-day program. It was started in 2001 and is open to all undergraduate and graduate students at UGA and to any U.S. institution of higher education. The goal of this program is to involve students and faculty in an educational trip with a mutual exchange of knowledge and practical experiences while participating in a cultural and historical tour of the country. As an interdisciplinary program, the faculty participants are from the College of Education, the College of Family and Consumer Sciences, and the School of Social Work.

West African society, history, and culture is a required course that provides the link that connects all the disciplines, focusing on the interdisciplinary nature of the program. When planning an international or study abroad program, one should blend lecture and structured presentations with active participation to enhance the students' academic experience (Fabregas, Ricardo, and Rodrigo 2012; Koernig 2007; Patten and Peters 2001). This recommendation was of utmost importance in planning and implementing this interdisciplinary program. Learning activities in the program include daily journaling; course lectures and presentations by American and Ghanaian scholars; tours (cultural, educational, and historical); and service-learning projects. The required course was the foundation of learning outcomes for this study. Since the beginning of the program, more than 300 students have participated. Students return and present projects as a testament to the impact of the program on their lives. However, given that no empirical studies have been undertaken on this phenomenon, this study on ILO collected data from all students participating in the Interdisciplinary Ghana Study Abroad Program for three consecutive years.

REVIEW OF RELATED LITERATURE

Early in the twenty-first century, Sutton and Rubin (2004) recognized that limited attention had been given to knowledge and skills acquired abroad. Consequently, they secured funding for the University System of Georgia Learning Outcomes of Students Studying Abroad Research Initiative (GLOSSARI). This was a 10-year research project with a publication in 2004 and another in 2010. Sutton and Rubin compared learning outcomes between study abroad participants and nonparticipants based on the GLOSSARI project. Unlike other studies, they focused on five different content domains: (1) knowledge of strategies and skills for functioning in other cultures, (2) knowledge of intercultural interaction techniques, (3) global interdependence, (4) knowledge of comparative civics, and (5) knowledge of world geography. The research also compared effects among different majors. Sampled majors were education, business, journalism and media, and social science.

Results show that studying abroad had positive effects on participants' learning outcomes that were not due to preexisting differences in levels of academic achievement. Specifically, students who studied abroad showed a higher level of functional knowledge than those who did not study abroad. In addition, knowledge of global interdependence increased among participants. Studying abroad exerted great effect on knowledge of cultural relativism; business majors scored lower than other majors in this area. Finally, knowledge of verbal acuity, knowledge of interpersonal accommodation, and cultural sensitivity knowledge were not affected by studying abroad among any majors in the study.

To measure learning outcomes of studying abroad, Williams (2009) used the Reflective Model of Intercultural Competence as a framework. This model classifies learning outcomes into four dimensions: (1) increased understanding of international and cultural issues, (2) increased flexibility, (3) increased open-mindedness and curiosity, and (4) enhanced critical skills. In order to develop students' awareness of learning outcomes before they went abroad, the researcher required students to read the predeparture handbook, discuss expectations, and join orientation with suggestions for how to adapt, behave, react, and understand the situation. In addition, students were offered an introduction to cultural differences and they formally agreed to a student code of conduct.

After students studied abroad, the data were collected by open-ended questions and photo submissions. Williams (2009) included demographic questions about gender, academic major, previous travel, and program evaluation. Findings indicate that students gained cultural and global awareness as they became more familiar with the host country and culture. First, some students felt the experience increased their empathy. Second, many students initially had problematic issues, but they adjusted to different lifestyles, habits, language, and culture. They were proud of their maturity and awareness in adaptation to differences. Third, students showed more differences in open-mindedness and curiosity than they did in other dimensions. Some students were conservative and others showed more openness and introspection. Finally, students felt a sense of accomplishment and growth in studying abroad by solving problems independently. The responses and photos also showed their confidence and self-reliance.

McLeod and Wainwright's (2008) paradigm explored how study abroad experiences affect psychological constructs in addition to study abroad-related outcomes. By analyzing focus group comments, the researchers discovered four themes in the data. First, students who had positive expectations for their life abroad felt desperate when they had difficulty adjusting to academic and social life. Second, as students had some successful experiences, they gradually gained self-confidence. Third, with more confidence, students tended to gain more self-perception by taking risks, getting involved, and learning new personal and social skills. Last, those students who were confident experienced changes in their perceptions of the world.

During the GLOSSARI project, Sutton and Rubin (2010) developed an instrument to evaluate learning outcomes. They sought to assess student learning in study abroad programs and also to determine learning outcomes among study abroad participants and nonparticipants. First, for functional knowledge, there was a significant increase among study abroad students but not among those who did not study abroad. Second, self-reported knowledge of world geography decreased across time for study abroad and control group students alike (e.g., there was no significant difference between study abroad and domestic students—both reported a decline in knowledge of world geography). Third, there was no significant difference in knowledge of global interdependence between study abroad and control group students, either at pretest or posttest. Fourth, regardless of the time of testing, study abroad students exceeded the control group in knowledge of interpersonal accommodation. The greater knowledge of interpersonal accommodation by study abroad students was not attributable to studying abroad. Last, students who studied abroad grew in knowledge of cultural context; control group students were static.

According to the above studies, there are some benefits to studying abroad. A study abroad program can have a positive effect on students' experiences; students gain cultural and global awareness, and they feel a sense of accomplishment and growth. Because some U.S. institutions have requirements that include experiential learning experiences like study abroad, more research is likely to be conducted on learning outcomes.

THEORETICAL FRAMEWORK

The concept of experiential learning is not new in education. Educational theorists and prolific authors such as Dewey, Rogers, and Kolb established the framework and background decades ago for learning through experiences. Experiential learning is a philosophy and a method whereby educators purposefully engage students in direct experiences and focused reflection in order to increase knowledge, develop skills, and clarify values (Association for Experiential Education 2014). The theory is termed *experiential learning* to emphasize the central role that experience plays in the learning process (Kolb, Boyatzis, and Mainemelis 2000).

Experiential learning theory defines learning as the process whereby knowledge is created through the transformation of experience (Kolb 1984). The aforementioned descriptions of experiential learning capture the activities of the Interdisciplinary Ghana Study Abroad Program generally; more specifically they describe the required course, West African society, history, and culture. Therefore, experiential learning theory was deemed appropriate for this group of students in higher education. In Rogers's (1994) description of experiential learning theory, he visualized learning as two major types, *cognitive* and *experiential*. Cognitive learning was characterized as *academic knowledge*—the type of learning one engages in through memorization of vocabulary words, multiplication tables, and other types of rote practices. Rogers described this type of learning as meaningless. Conversely, he viewed experiential learning as *applied*—the application of knowledge—and thereby, significant.

Experiential learning is parallel to personal change and growth (Kolb 1984; Kolb, Boyatzis, and Mainemelis 2000; Rogers 1994). These concepts and explanations of experiential learning exemplify the goals of the Interdisciplinary Ghana Study Abroad Program. The purpose of this study was to determine the ILO for students participating in a short-term study abroad program in Ghana. The specific objectives were to determine and compare the ILO before beginning and after completing a study abroad program for the three consecutive years combined.

METHODS

Sample

The 28 participants of the 2012, 2013, and 2014 short-term Interdisciplinary Ghana Study Abroad Program held during "Maymester" were included in the sample. A list of students who had paid program fees and obtained a visa for Ghana was obtained from the School of Social Work, Office of International Education for three consecutive years (2012, 2013, and 2014). Before departure, students were sent an email invitation to participate in the study. Data were collected before and after the program. Students in this study were undergraduate, Caucasian, female, and from the School of Social Work and the College of Family and Consumer Sciences, with majors in textiles, merchandising, and interiors. A majority of the participants were from the College of Family and Consumer Sciences.

A longitudinal survey using a trend study design (Fraenkel, Wallen, and Hyun 2011) was used to conduct this study with students participating in the Interdisciplinary Ghana Study Abroad Program for three consecutive years.

In a trend study design, a different sample is taken from the same population at different times. The measurement is the same and the population changes somewhat, but the responses obtained each year are representative of the population. The researcher examines and compares responses from year to year to see if any trends are apparent.

Instrumentation

The ILO is a 29-item questionnaire using a five-point Likert-type scale with five dimensions/content domains of intercultural learning: functional knowledge, knowledge of world geography, knowledge of global interdependence, knowledge of interpersonal accommodation, and knowledge of cultural sensitivity. In the ILO, learning outcomes were measured in five different content domains: (1) knowledge of strategies and skills for functioning in other cultures, (2) knowledge of intercultural interaction techniques, (3) global interdependence, (4) knowledge of comparative civics, and (5) knowledge of world geography. Sutton and Rubin (2004) used the ILO in the GLOSSARI project released in 2010 (Sutton and Rubin 2010). The reported reliability for the ILO is .88.

The instrument asked participants to record their first impression by indicating the degree to which they agreed or disagreed with each statement. Each statement described a characteristic. A five-point Likert scale was used to rate each characteristic. For this study, the average of the ratings from 1 to 1.4 indicates *strongly disagree*, 1.5 to 2.4 *disagree*, 2.5 to 3.4 *neither agree nor disagree*, 3.5 to 4.4 *agree*, and 4.5 to 5 *strongly agree*. The instrument was developed by Sutton and Rubin (2004) with the objective of creating an instrument that would be specific to the kinds of learning outcomes that might be derived from studying abroad. It was also deemed sufficiently generic to work across a wide variety of programs in a diverse set of disciplines.

The questionnaire was intended to be generic so it would work across the curriculum; consequently, it was deemed appropriate for use in this study. The researchers were aware that all of the content domains were not specifically represented in the courses offered in the program. However, this absence does not preclude concomitant learning outcomes in some of the content domains. Descriptive and inferential analyses were used to analyze the data. Paired *t* tests were used to determine the differences in the pretest and posttest for the three years combined. Data were merged for the three years and presented by the 29 ILO statements and the five different content domains.

RESULTS

Table 13.1 includes the descriptive analysis (means and standard deviations) of the 29 statements for a three-year period (2012, 2013, and 2014). The mean scores for pretest range from a low of 2.40 (.92) for *giving directions* (within the functional knowledge dimension) to a high of 4.75 (.44) for *know names of seven continents* (within the knowledge of world geography dimension). The mean scores for the posttest range from a low of 2.57 (1.07) for *know names of three rivers in Asia* (within the knowledge of world geography dimension) to a high of 4.79 (42) for *know names of five countries in Africa* (within the knowledge of world geography dimension). Twenty-four (83%) of the 29 statements achieved an increase in the mean score from the pretest to the posttest.

The dimension of functional knowledge achieved the lowest mean score (M = 3.02, SD = .73) on the pretest and second to the lowest mean score (M = 3.84, SD = .46) on the posttest (see table 13.2). This indicates that participants were in the *neither agree nor disagree* category on the pretest and *agree* on the posttest for this dimension.

Further contrast was conducted by a paired-sample *t* test. Pretest and posttest for the functional knowledge dimension was significantly different. Participants had a higher mean score on the functional knowledge posttest (M = 3.84, SD = .46) than they did on the pretest (M = 3.02, SD = .73); $t(27)$ = −5.3, $p < .05$.

Of the five dimensions, knowledge of world geography obtained the second to lowest mean score of 3.54 (.73). However, it was also rated as the lowest dimension on the posttest (M = 3.66, SD = .53). Participants indicated *neither agree nor disagree* on the pretest and *agree* on the posttest. Among the five statements in this dimension, the greatest mean score increase from pretest to posttest was in *knows names of four countries in South America*, from 3.11 (1.52) to 3.50 (1.17). The knowledge of world geography dimension on the posttest (M = 3.94, SD = .62) did not significantly differ from that of the pretest (M = 3.54, SD = .73); $t(17)$ = −.70, $p > .05$.

The dimension of knowledge of global interdependence was rated as the third highest in pretest (M = 3 61, SD = .85) and the second highest in posttest (M = 3.94, SD = .62), signifying that participants were in agreement on both tests. The mean scores of the five statements were slightly increased from the pretest to the posttest. The greatest increase existed in *compare political and cultural freedom*, with a mean difference of .57. For this dimension, pretest (M = 3.62, SD = .85) and posttest (M = 3.94, SD = .62) were significantly different: $t(27)$ = −2.15, $p < .05$.

Knowledge of interpersonal accommodation received the highest mean score among the five dimensions on the pretest (M = 4.52, SD = .49) and the second highest on the posttest (M = 4.54, SD = .53). Study participants' rating for this dimension was *agree* for both pretest and posttest. The mean scores on the pretest for the knowledge of interpersonal accommodation dimension were approximately the same as that on the posttest. This indicated that there was no significant difference ($t(27) = -.17, p > .05$), in pretest and posttest.

Of the five dimensions, knowledge of cultural sensitivity achieved the second highest mean score on the pretest (M = 4.31, SD = .64) and the highest mean score on the posttest (M = 4.45, SD = .60), as shown in table 13.2. Among the three statements in this dimension, the general trend of mean scores increased slightly. Table 13.2 reflects that the difference between pretest (M = 4.31, SD = .64) and posttest (M = 4.45, SD = .60) in knowledge of cultural sensitivity was not significant ($t(27) = -1.03, p > .05$).

DISCUSSION AND CONCLUSIONS

There were four major findings from this study. The first finding revealed that an overwhelming majority (83%) of the 29 statements on the ILO questionnaire increased mean scores from the pretest to the posttest for the 28 students in this study. There were no statements that decreased in mean ratings from the pretest to the posttest. Although not specified as overall learning outcomes, this finding is similar to that of Williams (2009), whereby students gained cultural and global awareness.

Next, students' overall posttest mean ratings increased over pretest scores for four of the five content domains. Those content domains that experienced an overall mean increase were functional knowledge, knowledge of world geography, knowledge of global interdependence, and knowledge of cultural sensitivity. This finding is in contrast to that of Sutton and Rubin (2004), wherein the study abroad students did not score higher on content domains. However, this increase in overall mean scores from pretest to posttest in this study is a testament to the effect of the Interdisciplinary Ghana Study Abroad Program upon learning experiences established for the courses generally and specifically the required course, West African society, history, and culture.

Third, the mean score remained the same for knowledge of interpersonal accommodation, which was the highest rated area on both pretest and posttest. This dimension deals with interpersonal communication skills (Sutton and Rubin 2010). Similar to the Sutton and Rubin's (2004) finding, this dimension/content domain was not affected by studying abroad. Although not affected by studying abroad, it is noteworthy that this dimension/content domain achieved a rating of *agree*.

Finally, the largest mean score difference occurred in functional knowledge. This finding parallels that of Sutton and Rubin (2010), who found a significant increase among study abroad students on this dimension, which portrays the knowledge needed to effectively navigate daily routines in a new and different environment. Functional knowledge is regarded as especially useful in empowering individuals in their study abroad experiences. This finding is encouraging as faculty prepares students for the study abroad experience through guest speakers and topic discussions prior to departure. Additionally, once students arrive in Ghana, faculty further prepared through required readings and discussions, time to reflect on the variety of experiences through structured class activities, and spontaneous experiences.

This study is limited in several aspects. In particular, it is reliant on self-reported data. Although differences in learning outcomes were found, the causal effect of the study abroad experiences on those improvements has yet to be confirmed. Comparative methods or experimental design should be considered in future research to test the causality. In addition, the learning experiences covered in the required course (West African society, history, and culture) are not directly aligned with the 29 statements on the questionnaire. However, reflections and further research in preparation for submission of projects can lead to additional and unintended learning outcomes. The study is also limited in generalizability because of the sample size. Future studies using a larger sample size or in-depth interviews can shed more light on intercultural learning experiences.

In conclusion, students gain from study abroad experiences in a range of learning outcomes and personal experiences. For the four trends detected in these data, the experiential learning theory indicated that students grow and develop when an activity is of interest to them. Students participating in the 21-day Interdisciplinary Ghana Study Abroad Program showed knowledge gains among the five content domains of ILO (functional knowledge, world geography knowledge, interpersonal accommodation knowledge, global interdependence knowledge, and cultural sensitivity knowledge) after experiencing the study and tour of Ghana.

NOTE

1. *Learning Outcomes in an Interdisciplinary Study Abroad Program: Developing a Global Perspective*, JFCS, Volume 109(1) has been reproduced with the written permission of AAFCS. No republication or distribution of this material is permitted without AAFCS' consent.

REFERENCES

Association for Experiential Learning. 2014. *"What is Experiential Learning?"* Accessed May 1, 2019. https://www.aee.org.

Baugher, Shirley L., Carol L. Anderson, Kinsey B. Green, Sharon Y. Nickols, Jan Shane, Laura Jolly, and Joyce Miles. 2000. "Body of Knowledge of Family and Consumer Sciences." *Journal of Family & Consumer Sciences 92*, no. 3 (2000): 32–29.

Fabregas Janeiro, Maria G. Ricardo Lopez Fabre, and Rodrigo Tello Rosete. 2012. "Developing Successful International Faculty Led Program." *US-China Education Review* B *4*: 375–382.

Fraenkel, Jack R., Norman E. Wallen, and Helen H. Hyun. 2011. *How to Design and Evaluate Research in Education* (8th ed.). Boston: McGraw-Hill.

Institute of International Education Network. 2015. "Open Doors 2015 Data." Accessed December, 2020. https://www.iienetwork.org/.

Koernig, Stephen K. 2007. "Planning, Organizing, and Conducting a 2-week Study Abroad Trip for Undergraduate Students: Guidelines for First-time Faculty." *Journal of Marketing Education 29*, no. 3 (2007): 210–217. https://doi.org/10.1177 /0273475307306886.

Kolb, David A. 1984. *Experiential Learning: Experience as the Source of Learning and Development.* Upper Saddle River: Prentice-Hall.

Kolb, David A., Richard E. Boyatzis, and Charalampos Mainemelis. 2000. "Experiential Learning Theory. Previous Research and New Directions." In *Perspectives on Cognitive, Learning, and Thinking Styles*, edited by Sternberg, R. J., and L. F. Zhang, 35–10. Mahwah: Lawrence Erlbaum.

McLeod, Mark, and Philip Wainwright. 2009. "Researching the Study Abroad Experience." *Journal of Studies in International Education 13*, no. 1: 66–71. http:// doi.org/10.1177/1028315308317219.

Patten, Ronald J., and Robert Peters. 2001. *Whither Thou Goest: The Intrigue of an International Study Seminar.* Washington, DC: Office of Educational Research and Improvement.

Rogers, Carl R. 1994. *Freedom to Learn* (3rd ed.). New York: Merrill.

Sutton, Richard C., and Donald L. Rubin. 2004. "The GLOSSARI Project: Initial Findings from a System-wide Research Initiative on Study Abroad Learning Outcomes." *Frontiers: The Interdisciplinary Journal of Study Abroad 10*, no. 1: 65–82. https://doi.org/10.36366/frontiers.v10i1.133.

Sutton, Richard C., and Donald L. Rubin. 2010. "Documenting the Academic Impact of Study Abroad: Final Report of the GLOSSARI Project." In *Annual Conference of NAFSA: Association of International Educators*, Kansas City, MO. 2010. Accessed December, 2020. http://glossari.uga.edu/datasets/pdfs/FINAL.pdf.

Williams, Tracy Rundstrom. 2009. "The Reflective Model of Intercultural Competency: A Multidimensional, Qualitative Approach to Study Abroad Assessment." *Frontiers: The Interdisciplinary Journal of Study Abroad 18*, no. 1 (2009): 289–306. https://doi.org/10.36366/frontiers.v18i1.267.

Part IV

HUMAN SCIENCES FOUNDATIONS FOR NEW CAREER PATHS

Human sciences coursework supports and facilitates career exploration and professional development for all students. This section provides examples of research and experiential learning and explores programs and career transitions that provide a foundation for current and future professionals to explore new content directions and career paths.

Chapter 14 discusses some of the different communities children are members of, the importance of communities investing in children, why communities should begin investing in children during the early years of their development, and the benefits of serving young children in their communities. This chapter also provides recommendations for communities to engage with young children. along with a discussion of implications for practice.

Chapter 15 traces the career of an African American leader in the human sciences who, following a 20-year administrative career and service as a national leader, turned her attention to health equity. The focus on continuity and reinvention draws from theories related to life course development and successful aging. The human sciences body of knowledge posits that life course development is an important integrative element.

Chapter 16 explores middle school children's development toward career choices. This study addressed the effect FCS had on the self-efficacy and career development of eighth-grade middle school students. It further examined what FCS supports and resources contribute to the self-efficacy of students' needs to pursue career interests, and what human social factors influence students enrolled in FCS.

Chapter 17 provides a testament to a human sciences professional philosophy that was gained through countless experiences as the only African American, the only woman, or the only African American woman on a committee. The chapter inspires professionals who may feel isolated to persist and remain willing to lead initiatives, to speak out for fair and equal opportunities, and to support initiatives that benefit minority faculty and students, minority citizens, and minority institutions.

Chapter 14

Young Children and Community Engagement

An Ecological Approach

Amber N. Smith

Every adult individual has a part in developing well-rounded children. Collectively, children and adults form the communities that impact children's education, growth, and development. Children receive all their knowledge through various communities. The home community provides a set of values and traditions that shape children's perspectives on families. The school community provides knowledge for children and impacts their learning. The religious community, if a child is part of one, contributes a set of values relating to children's moral development, such as fairness. Many of these communities teach children the same lessons, and although they are separate communities, they can come together in collaborative efforts that benefit children.

This chapter discusses some of the different communities children are members of, the importance of communities investing in children, why communities should begin investing in children during the early years of their development, and the benefits of serving young children in their communities. Lastly, this chapter provides recommendations for communities to engage with young children, along with a discussion of implications for practice.

IMPORTANCE

Community involvement in early childhood education and care is important for various reasons. It allows children to reap the benefits of access to adults with specific training to nurture their development. Moreover, this access occurs during a critical time in child development. During the first five years of life, children experience major areas of development, such as motor skills and cognition (Rolnick and Grunewald 2003). Therefore, it is important for communities to invest early to ensure that children have healthy development.

Children do not develop on their own; they do so with the guidance of adults whose skills are already developed so they can effectively assist children to develop their own. It takes the help of the community to make this happen. This is demonstrated in an Australian study conducted by Kostadinov et al. (2016), examining the influence of perceived community leadership readiness (PCLR) on child obesity intervention programs. Results revealed that PCLR increases influenced the intervention populations and the length of exposure to the intervention.

While community members with specialized training in child development and education are helpful, that does not diminish the impact individuals without specialized training can have on children. Special qualifications are not required to invest in children, spend time with them, implement activities, or create community environments conducive to child development. Children benefit from people who are willing to make a positive difference in their lives, particularly when there is a collaborative effort between communities. Furthermore, everyone can be an advocate and can contribute to children's development, education, and lives (Osuchukwu and Edewor 2016). Children also learn through relationships, and communities serve as a way for them to develop healthy relationships (Marion 2011). There are several types of communities in which children can have meaningful relationships, including school, family, church, and government. Relationships serve in several capacities that are beneficial to children. They are investments of time, forms of communication, and ways for children to learn about others and themselves. Relationships consist of children and adults or children and peers; however, the help of the communities is needed to ensure that these relationships have a place in children's lives.

Finally, community involvement with young children is important because it solidifies their self-worth and value. According to Marion (2011), children should have high self-esteem, self-worth, and value. They obtain these traits when they are acknowledged in ways that indicate that they are worthy of respect. This applies to the way communities interact with children; not only in the ways community members talk to children, but also ways in which they invest their time and support children's development. Children must know that they are cared for, and it is the responsibility of communities to ensure and to implement this care, and to provide the compassion children are entitled to.

THEORETICAL FRAMEWORK

According to Bronfenbrenner (2009), children are influenced by the communities they live in or are a part of. These communities are referred to as ecological systems. This ecological systems theory is composed of five systems: microsystem, mesosystem, exosystem, macrosystem, and chronosystem. These five systems have direct and indirect effects on children, regardless of how much time a child spends in them.

Microsystem

The *microsystem* consists of the places children have direct contact with on a consistent or even daily basis (Bronfenbrenner 2009). Such places can be school, home, church, other religious institutions, childcare facilities, group homes, and neighborhoods. However, the microsystem is not limited to the inclusion of places, but individuals as well. Individuals can be parents, siblings, immediate relatives, extended relatives, teachers, childcare providers, pastors, religious leaders, church members, and peers. These individuals collectively represent several communities that children engage with, resulting in the creation of an environment that includes the child.

Mesosystem

The *mesosystem* consists of the relationships between child, family, and community (Bronfenbrenner 2009). In the mesosystem, various factors influence relationships, including personal beliefs, culture, attitudes, perceptions, and personal, individual, and community beliefs. These factors are in turn influential on children's information processing and relationships with others. Mesosystems link the community's children spend extensive time in, such as school and home. These communities often intersect, making it important to form collaborative partnerships between the communities. These partnerships are valuable due to their direct effect on children.

Exosystem

The *exosystem* consists of a relationship between a child and an environment the child may not have direct contact with but is still impacted by (Bronfenbrenner 2009). This environment usually intersects at a meeting point with an environment a child does have contact with. These external environments can cause changes to the environments children are in and be influential in their development and well-being (e.g., they may impact the amount of time being spent with the child). This further stress the importance of communities in ensuring that the necessary steps are taken to provide adequate time between children and the adults who make up the community, whether it is at school or home.

Macrosystem

The *macrosystem* consists of the cultural environment. Culture plays a critical role in the way communities are formed and engaged (Bronfenbrenner 2009). This includes the components that create cultures, such as traditions, beliefs, values, politics, religion, morals, ethics, and social class. These factors can vary among communities and can cause communities to differ from one another, affecting community engagement and making it important to take cultural contexts into consideration for community engagement with children. Cultural norms are influential in several areas, including but not limited to an individual's actions, perception, motivation, reasoning, and interactions with the community and environment.

Chronosystem

The *chronosystem* consists of the events within communities that impact the community's children or individuals (Paquette and Ryan 2001). Several events can directly influence a child's communities, such as moving to a new neighborhood or state, transferring schools, getting new teachers, entering new social settings, or a family member leaving the home. It is important for children to engage with their communities in environments conducive to their development. These environments should enable children to be resilient, despite the events, transitions, or challenges that may threaten their development and resiliency.

BENEFITS OF COMMUNITY ENGAGEMENT WITH YOUNG CHILDREN

Better Future Outcomes

The earlier communities begin investing in children and their development and care, the better later outcomes will be for both the children and the communities in which they live. Studies have shown that children with access to early education are less likely to commit a crime, be involved in criminal activity, become incarcerated, or drop out of school (Rolnick and Grunewald 2003). Additionally, school is just one community with a connection to children, and early investment can be applicable to other communities as well. For this reason, it is helpful to for these various communities to connect with families, as strong family rapport and community involvement have been shown to benefit children.

Positive Self-esteem and Awareness of Others

Early community involvement allows children to be more successful as they grow within the communities to which they are connected. For example, having access to high-quality early childhood care and attending preschool allows children to utilize and develop many skills they will need when they begin school and throughout their lives, such as fine motor skills, gross motor skills, peer relationships, positive behavior, listening skills, and the ability to coexist with others in their communities. Religious institutions can be a moral compass for young children, instilling in them early morals, ethics, values, and fairness, which lay the foundation for the way they will make decisions and solve problems in the future. A study conducted by Hou et al. (2015) examined an online community of children between the ages of 7 and 10 from Hungary, Mexico, and the United States and their interactions with one another. Findings showed that in this international community, children developed awareness of one another by learning about their countries, and they developed positive attitudes toward each other through full disclosure of their identities.

In the home, families can reinforce the skills their children are developing in other communities by creating opportunities for them to use those skills. Families can nurture children's development of skills through their own values and even their culture. This process is enhanced through access to programs created to help families develop these skills and through individuals who have the training to nurture these skills in young children. The earlier children begin to gain experiences utilizing these skills, the better they will be at using them throughout their development.

Communication

It is important for communities to communicate and be involved with children. Moreover, the importance of communication among a child's communities cannot be overemphasized. Communication helps to bridge any gaps that may exist between communities, and to develop strong partnerships. Each community with a connection to children is separate from the others, but all should act cohesively in being productive and conducive to children's growth, development, and well-being. A study conducted by Xu (2011) examined the relationship between caregivers' and children's communication styles and development, and found that children's communication and development are influenced by the communication styles of their caregivers and other early childhood professionals. Communication in communities should build upon children's self-esteem, provide age and developmentally appropriate guidance, discipline appropriately and accordingly, and enable children to reach their full social, emotional, physical, and academic potential in a safe environment.

Developmental Outcomes

Community involvement is also important for children when they encounter weaknesses and need further help to develop in a certain area. Furthermore, communities can join in a collaborative effort to help children struggling with weaknesses by creating and implementing plans, observing and monitoring plan effectiveness, and providing feedback for improvement. There are also negative predictors associated with weaknesses in early childhood, such as the likelihood of being diagnosed with attention and behavioral disorders. A collaborative effort can help to counteract these negative effects on children or address them by having actions in place that prevent hindrances to a child's future developmental, behavioral, or academic performance.

Relationships and Coexisting in the Environment

The children live within their communities and they depend on them for their development, well-being, health, and safety. Children can only thrive in their communities if the environments are created with the intention for them to thrive. This happens when there are strong relationships between children and communities that are comprised of individuals who are willing to make the necessary investments in children. Children learn through relationships, and according to Marion (2011), children need strong, positive relationships with the adults who guide them.

Adult Involvement Is Key

Marion (2011) also states that the relationship is the adult's responsibility. The adults in a child's communities must take the necessary steps to ensure not only strong relationships, but also the child's safety, well-being, security, and ability to function within these communities. It is up to the adult members of these communities to provide children with the tools they need to be successful. This includes families, educators, school administrators, caregivers, religious leaders, those who are in training to guide children, and those who aspire to one day lead children.

COMMUNITY ROLES IN AN
ECOLOGICAL PERSPECTIVE

As we have seen, the ecological systems theory's five *systems* or *environments* are, in fact, synonymous with *communities* because they describe communities that are connected to the child. There are several ways communities can serve young children, both as individual communities and in collaboration with other communities. The following discussion assesses implications for practice by making connections between each system in the ecological systems theory and the system's corresponding communities.

Microsystem: Home and School

Home and school are two examples of microsystems whose environments children have direct contact with. Home consists of the family, and families are themselves communities. A great deal can be done within the home to invest in children. Families can start investing in children early by spending quality time with them and remaining consistent. Families can engage with their children through shared reading, asking questions, and joining in on children's activities. Shared reading is an appropriate activity for home communities because it connects children with their caregivers, allowing them to form strong relationships through literacy. Developmentally, this is beneficial to children because it exposes them to literacy and forms relationships with caregivers. By asking children questions, we form conversational bonds between children and families as we help children to develop language skills. Families can ask children questions about how their day went, things they did in a day, and questions about shared reading. It is also helpful to engage with children at home by joining in on activities such as play. Family participation helps self-esteem by expressing an interest in children and the things they like to do. This indicates to children their worth, value, and that they are cared for. In addition, allowing children to help with meals, cooking, and setting the tables is a way to engage children in family activities.

School systems can make early investments by ensuring early childhood institutions provide high-quality education and care to young children. Early childhood facilities should consist of staff who are experienced, trained, and possess the necessary skills to appropriately nurture, educate, guide, and care for young children. Programs should also be age and developmentally appropriate to the students they serve and should support children in developing essential tools needed throughout development (Marion 2011). Program needs include, but are not limited to consistent daily schedules; nutritious meals; adequate time for indoor and outdoor play; opportunities to develop peer relationships; and access to a variety of gross and fine motor activities such as blocks, puzzles, and art supplies. Classrooms should also be designed with multiple stations such as art centers, science centers, and literacy centers. An appropriate early childhood classroom should meet the needs of young children while allowing them to learn actively through experiences.

Mesosystem: Relationships among Communities

Children have direct contact and interaction with so many communities that it is reasonable to expect that these communities will at some point intersect. Moreover, it is critical that these communities share a strong rapport for the sake of the child.

Aside from laying a strong foundation for the education and care of children, school and home should also ensure an equally strong foundation in their relationship with one another. Educators, childcare providers, families, and other professionals serving children should also serve families by forming a collaborative partnership to meet children's needs. This requires effort from both communities, as they share equal responsibility for ensuring children's welfare. Factors that contribute to strong collaborative partnerships are communication, family involvement, and school involvement. Together, these practices help communities to build and maintain healthy partnerships and healthy community environments for children.

Communication

School and home communities should have consistent communication with one another regarding children. In fact, it is typical for these communities to have daily contact. It is helpful for professionals to keep families informed of issues pertaining to the child, such as school events, lessons, school performance, and any strengths and weaknesses observed in the classroom. It is also important to communicate any changes in behavior, as these can hold several possible meanings, such as illness or a change in another environment.

In turn, families should communicate their concerns with school communities, sharing occurrences outside of school that could influence changes in the school environment. Any changes in family patterns and routines should be shared, since one of the most effective ways children learn is through recognizing patterns (Zadina 2014). Consistent behavior and schedules are forms of patterns where any change can be influential on a child, making it important for schools and families to be observant and communicate.

Family and School Involvement

Aside from communicating, school and family should work with one another by becoming involved in each other's events as they care for children.

Families should avail themselves of the opportunities schools offer for their involvement, such as volunteering, fundraising, accompanying children on field trips, and serving on parent-teacher councils. In the early years, schools can make many services available to families, such as home visits and other types of interventions.

Home visits were proven effective in a study conducted by Campbell, Brooks, Hosokawa, Robinson, Lin, and Krieger (2015), which examined Healthy Homes, a program that conducts home visits to teach families self-management care for asthma. The study looked at children aged 3–17, their caregivers, and home visits made by a community health worker. The study found these home visits produced positive outcomes for children's health.

There are other ways for schools to become involved with families, as these options may not be accessible. If the child remains in the same school, current and incoming educators can work with families in creating transition plans. Schools and families can also schedule conferences to discuss transitions; communicate and plan with third parties, such as therapists; and plan events allowing joint participation between schools and families. Members of the school community should also have knowledge of available resources to be able to refer to families in the event further assistance is needed that cannot be provided within the school community.

Exosystem: Keeping a Balance

Children can be as impacted by environments they are indirectly connected to as they are with those they are directly connected to. That is the basis of the exosystem. When a child has contact with someone who is impacted by a community they are a part of, the child may be impacted also. A common example of this is a caregiver impacted by his or her work environment (Paquette and Ryan 2001). Although the child may not work, a family member does, and the impact is felt by not just that family member but by the entire family. Work schedules can keep family members away from home, or a sudden change in a work schedule may require the entire family to make adjustments. Similarly, in the school community, maternity leave, illness, or other events that occur outside of school may require a teacher to be absent for an extended period. This can cause change and adjustment for students.

Although children are not directly involved with the changes described above, they are impacted in ways that can cause changes in behavior. It is important to maintain a healthy balance for children, despite these changes, and the best way to provide balance is to maintain consistency in implementing activities and to continue to invest in them. For example, a parent's or caregiver's new work schedule may prevent them from participating in family activities at certain times. Efforts should be made to adjust the times those family activities are implemented so both the child and family continue to spend quality time together. When a teacher is absent from school, activities should be conducted in the same manner so children continue to utilize and develop their skills while the teacher is absent.

It is also critical to provide children, particularly young children, with explanations regarding any change in circumstances because they learn through them (Marion 2011). Children function best when occurrences make sense to them, and that only happens when they are given an explanation. Once children have an explanation, they can understand their environment and what is taking place within it. Adults can effectively provide explanations to children about changes occurring within their communities by using language that is age and developmentally appropriate to communicate: the event taking place, why the event is taking place, and how the event will be dealt with.

Macrosystem: Culture in Investing

Because the macrosystem consists of cultural components that influence the child, it should also influence the way communities invest in children. The macrosystem should impact the reasoning and purpose behind activities that a community plans for its children. The investments communities make in children's activities should have a purpose because these activities form a culture among children. Communities should take several factors into consideration when investing and planning community activities for children and should have a set of ideals that serve as the basis for their activities. Examples of these ideals can include culture, traditions, beliefs, and expectations for children and families.

Families can form practices based on their beliefs and cultural norms, which can create a home environment that supports their relationships with children. Many have common practices that include designating certain times for togetherness, such as meals, praying, family game night, and family vacations. Schools and other educational facilities demonstrate their values by creating student and parent handbooks and philosophy statements that indicate the school culture and the reasons for their practice. Educators may also have personal teaching philosophies and may maintain written documents that express their educational beliefs. Religious institutions may have mission statements describing factors that influence their purpose. Communities should also include the norms and values of other communities when planning. For example, school communities should consider cultural differences at home that may be represented in their school, as these may influence the way children function in the classroom.

Chronosystem: Considering the Positive and Negative

Children can be influenced by events that occur in environments they have no direct contact with, such as a parent's job. However, events occurring in a child's direct environment can be just as influential. These events can either be positive or negative and can either benefit children or pose a threat to their well-being. It is important for communities to consider all events and to develop strategies to aid children in coping with adverse events while reinforcing the benefits of positive events.

Positive Events

There are events that can be beneficial to children's growth and development, and communities should ensure children have access to these through careful planning and providing children with the opportunity to participate. Extracurricular activities are a common example. Field trips, walking trips, cooking activities, and presentations for families (such as art galleries featuring children's work) are all events teachers can plan to expose children to a variety of experiences that benefit their self-esteem, learning, and development.

Negative and Other Events

Just as impactful as positive events, negative and other events can threaten children's well-being. Examples of negative events include divorce, traumatic events, and natural disaster. Other events may not be negative but are just as influential, such as moving to a new city or school. These events can require children to adjust and may impact them socially and emotionally. However, children may not know how to adjust and recover from these situations, so they rely on their communities to help them. Communities should exercise great care in handling these events, since the care approach can also affect children's resiliency Compassion is an important factor in helping children to adjust and transition during change. It helps children to know they have a place, are acknowledged, and worthy of respect (Marion 2011). Compassion is shown by acknowledging children's emotions, allowing them to express those emotions, communicating appropriately, and being consistent with effective guidance and coping strategies.

DISCUSSION AND RECOMMENDATIONS

Communities are comprised of individuals and events that impact children's lives in several areas, including growth, development, education, morals, and self-esteem. A community's adult individuals are also impacted by the events that take place within their communities. The difference, however, is that adults are further along developmentally than children, and they have the skills they need to cope and to maintain healthy relationships. Adults are also in positions to make decisions regarding the welfare of children. The following recommendations are suggested for consideration when discussing and creating strong, healthy communities for children.

Viewing Oneself as a Community Member

As demonstrated by Bronfenbrenner's ecological systems theory, human beings make up a community. This theory holds that there are five systems that influence children. These systems are comprised of environments that contain people who are connected to children; therefore, these ecological systems or environments are synonymous with *community*.

The first step in creating healthy communities for children is for individuals to acknowledge themselves as a part of a community. In doing so, they should remember that several communities hold equal importance with one another, and that a community is not just one specific place, but several. School, home, church, and other environments that involve children's time and physical presence are all communities—any individual connected to these environments in any way is a part of that community.

Children are Members of the Community

Each person is entitled to be involved in his or her communities (Moran, Gibbs, and Mernin 2017). Children have a place in society and the communities in which they live. Children have a place in the home, school, religious institutions, and other communities they are part of. Children are not able to lead communities, but they are members of these communities and need to be led. Children also can make contributions to their communities. Adults should be mindful to keep children involved in their communities by arranging activities and guiding them in these activities. Children's activities should allow them to build upon their independence, self-help, decision-making, and problem-solving skills. This should start with small activities planned by adults, eventually leading to children planning their own activities with adult guidance. This method was successful in Canada's Community Action Projects (2016) competition, which built relationships between community organizations and children through youth-led community projects that utilized physical education activities.

Reflect, Examine, and Fulfill the Role of Community Leader

Any adult member of a community with children is a leader. Adults have the responsibility of effectively guiding children in ways that nurture their development and support their well-being. These individuals should conduct themselves appropriately in and out of the presence of children and should model the behavior they aspire to instill in the children they serve. Individuals should also be cognizant that their actions, decisions, and dialogue carry a substantial amount of weight with children, who can be impressionable. When creating stable communities, adults should be mindful of the ways in which they carry themselves, and their practices should reflect the philosophies and ideals they desire for children to have. These philosophies should not just entail goals for children, but should also strive for children to develop compassion for their communities (Jasinski and Lewis 2016).

Work Together and Start Early

Although there are several communities that function separately, they should intersect at some point concerning the child. It is helpful for communities to work together in serving children. Sometimes communities are unable to meet the needs of children individually, but collaborative efforts can meet children's needs in ways that a single community cannot. Communities should strive for strong partnerships by strengthening communication and involvement with one another. They should also begin making investments early, because the earlier communities begin investing in children, the better equipped children will be in the future. Early investment helps children to be more prepared for school and to become well-rounded individuals with morals that guide them throughout development, even as adults.

It is also helpful to teach children about their communities early so they can serve them in the best possible way. For example, local libraries in Nigeria used community engagement to promote child literacy by donating books to rural schools that had small libraries and few resources to invest in children's literacy and education (Osuchukwu and Edewor 2016). This engagement resulted in increased book donations, and in motivation to enlist other communities to support school literacy. Based on these results, Osuchukwu and Edewor (2016) recommended that public libraries integrate with schools and enlist the help of other communities.

CONCLUSION

Together, children and adults form many communities, at home, in school, at church, on sports teams, and in community centers like the Boys and

Girls Club. Children can contribute to communities but are not in a position to guide them: It takes the support of adults to guide children in becoming productive members of their communities. Through effective adult guidance, children learn about their communities while learning to respect and to serve them. Children gain the skills they need to serve their communities through high-quality care and education, and cannot begin learning about and contributing to their communities until these communities invest in them. Communities should begin investing in children in the early years to ensure their needs are met, and to teach morals while building self-esteem, self-awareness, and awareness of others. These investments help children to be resilient while navigating through frustrations and difficult times. Well-rounded children may have moments of difficulty but can self-regulate through them. With these skills, children can work individually and collectively with their peers in their communities and can continue to do so as adults.

REFERENCES

Bronfenbrenner, Urie. 2009. *The Ecology of Human Development*. Harvard University Press.

Campbell, Jonathan D., Marissa Brooks, Patrick Hosokawa, June Robinson, Lin Song, and James Krieger. 2015. "Community Health Worker Home Visits for Medicaid-enrolled Children with Asthma: Effects on Asthma Outcomes and Costs." *American Journal of Public Health 105*, no. 11: 2366–2372.

Hou, Weimin, Anita Komlodi, Wayne Lutters, Karoly Hercegfi, Jennifer J. Preece, and Allison J. Druin. 2015. "Supporting Children's Online Identity in International Communities." *Behaviour & Information Technology 34*, no. 4: 375–391. https://doi.org/10.1080/0144929X.2014.948490.

Jasinski, Igor, and Tyson E. Lewis. 2016. "The Educational Community as Intentional Community." *Studies in Philosophy and Education 35*, no. 4 (2016): 371–383.

Kostadinov, Iordan, Mark Daniel, Michelle Jones, and Margaret Cargo. 2016. "Assessing Change in Perceived Community Leadership Readiness in the Obesity Prevention and Lifestyle Program." *Health Promotion Journal of Australia 27*, no. 3 (2017): 208–214. https://doi.org/10.1071/HE16050.

Marion, Marian. 2011. *Guidance of Young Children*. Upper Saddle River, NJ: Prentice Hall.

Moran, Thomas E., Danette C. Gibbs, and Lauren Mernin. 2017. "The Empowerment Model: Turning Barriers into Possibilities." *Palaestra 31*, no. 2 (2017).

Osuchukwu, Ngozi P., and Nelson Edewor. 2016. "Make the Children Read: Participatory Rural Approach in School Libraries in Umueri, Nigeria." *Library Philosophy & Practice (e-Journal)*. 1–19. http://digitalcommons.unl.edu/libphilprac/1384.

Paquette, DeDe and Ryan, John. 2001. "Bronfenbrenner's Ecological Systems Theory." Accessed January 9, 2012. http://www.cms-kids.com/providers/early_steps/training/documents/bronfenbrenners_ecological.pdf.

Rolnick, Art, and Rob Grunewald. 2003. "Early Childhood Development: Economic Development with a High Public Return." *The Region 17*, no. 4 (2003): 6–12.

Xu, Yaoying. 2011. "The Effects of Teaching Primary Caregivers to Conduct Formative Assessment on Caregiver-Child Social Interaction and Children's Developmental Outcomes." *Early Child Development and Care 181*, no. 4 (2011): 549–571. https://doi.org/10.1080/03004431003620066.

Zadina, Janet. 2014. *Multiple Pathways to the Student Brain: Energizing and Enhancing Instruction*. John Wiley & Sons.

Chapter 15

A Human Sciences Career in Transition

Continuity and Reinvention in Health Equity

Penny A. Ralston

INTRODUCTION

This chapter focuses on the continuity and reinvention of my career in the human sciences. I have served the profession for 46 years, starting as a public school home economics teacher and now as a public health researcher. How did this career evolve? What were the constants and how did reinvention occur along the way? What advice do I have for others as they transition into new careers? These are questions that will be addressed in this chapter.

The focus on continuity and reinvention draws from theories related to life course development and successful aging. The human sciences body of knowledge posits that life course development is an important integrative element. Life course development refers to "changes in individuals and families (and other social units) over historical time" (Nickols et al. 2009, 270) and includes the interrelated concepts of human development across the life span and social institutions that create transition points for individuals as they develop. Further, each individual has a life trajectory comprised of the sequence of events and transitions from birth to death (Nickols et al. 2009). These life trajectories reflect interplay with social institutions and can be influenced by history during an individual's development.

Within life course development, the continuity theory of aging states that as people age, they usually maintain the same interests, activities, and behaviors as in earlier life (Atchley 1989). More recently, successful aging theorists have built on this theoretical framework to propose that successful aging involves not only continuity but also innovation, in that aging itself can be a time of growth and creativity (Rowe and Kahn 1997). It is this sense

of growth and creativity, or reinvention, that undergirds my career path as
outlined below.

THE FOUNDATION AND EVOLUTION

Key themes that guided my life were established during my early years
where I was raised on a farm in Indiana. Farm life was epitomized by daily
hard work that included taking care of farm animals and three gardens, and
preserving food (e.g., canning vegetables, slaughtering animals, and freezing
meat). The 215-acre farm required my parents' managerial oversight and constant labor; thus, I developed a strong work ethic. During those years, I also
developed a desire to do well academically. Education was highly valued by
my family because both of my parents had not had the opportunity to finish
high school. My parents were impressed with friends who had educated their
daughters and were determined that they would do the same. As a result, I
was encouraged to do well in school and received several academic honors
(I earned membership to the National Honor Society and graduated high
school as class salutatorian) and I received mentoring from teachers and
community members. I also developed leadership skills by being elected to
several offices, including president of my 4-H Club, president of our school's
National Honor Society, and countywide treasurer of 4-H Junior Leaders.
As an African American youth in a predominantly White high school, this
was quite an achievement. Thus, I developed the confidence that I could
compete with anyone. Being involved in these organizations also helped me
to understand the importance of community. This was particularly important
since my home life was not perfect. I had loving parents but economic problems put much pressure on the family. Further, my father had complications
of diabetes that led to several hospital stays, amputation of both legs, and
blindness. He passed away when I was 16 years old. Thus, the community
became a place where I developed supportive relationships and could grow.
As I entered college at Ball State University, the key themes of work ethic,
academic excellence, leadership, and community were my foundation to
move forward.
    The following years were, in many ways, a repeat of my early years in
terms of key themes. I was a student leader (president of my sorority, Delta
Sigma Theta, and an officer in our chapter of Mortar Board national honor
society) and an academic achiever (recipient of the Emens Award, the highest
honor given to an undergraduate at Ball State University). I double-majored
in home economics and social studies, and I taught both for three years in
Marion, Indiana, following graduation from Ball State. I went on to graduate
school at the University of Illinois, where I completed my master's degree

and was encouraged to stay on for the doctorate. I had the wonderful opportunity to work with Judy Brun, Mildred Griggs, and Hazel Spitze—all nationally recognized teacher educators. I remember clearly a meeting with Judy
Brun, who was a class instructor at the time, and the one sentence she shared
that changed my life: "Penny, you think quite well. You should consider staying at Illinois and getting the doctorate." Mildred Griggs, who was one of the
first African American faculty I had ever had, was my role model. Griggs was
a young rising star in the field, and I watched her every move. I took inspiration that I could be like her someday. I completed the doctorate under her
guidance as my major professor. Along the way, she introduced me to several national leaders. I was then hired as an assistant professor at Iowa State
University, where for nine years I enjoyed a very supportive professional
environment and was promoted to associate and then full professor. I also was
given numerous opportunities to develop leadership skills, and I found myself
chairing committees and truly caring more about group achievements. I had
the opportunity to collaborate and do outreach with cooperative extension
colleagues. One major effort was the gerontology workshop series, where I
worked with my gerontology mentor, Edward Powers, and others. Several
educational seminars were held around the state to inform extension agents
and other professionals about different topics on aging. Again, I had several
impactful mentors, including Ruth Deacon, then dean of the College of Home
Economics at Iowa State University. She was not a day-to-day mentor, but
someone who could influence a junior faculty member in brief encounters. I
marveled at how she was always in the right place and saying the right thing
to provide support and guidance in my career.

LEADERSHIP IN THE HUMAN SCIENCES

After being promoted to full professor and feeling the need to develop
my personal life, I began seeking other possible career opportunities. I
received a letter that I had been nominated for a department chair position
at the University of Massachusetts at Amherst. I got out a map to see where
Amherst was located. At the same time, Carlie and Gary Tartakov, new
arrivals from UMass-Amherst to Iowa State, had become good friends, and
of course encouraged me to follow up on this opportunity. This resulted in
securing the position, meeting (and one year later marrying) my loving husband Chester Davis, and learning how to lead an academic department for
five years in a very political environment.

During the UMass-Amherst years, I was also developing as a leader in
the human sciences. Under the guidance of several mentors such as Leola
Adams, Virginia Caples, and Julia Miller, I was encouraged to get involved

in the American Home Economics Association (AHEA). I was elected to the Council on Certification, where I learned firsthand the politics of AHEA. In 1988, the council faced major opposition to a proposed change in structure (we proposed a resolution to have more autonomy from AHEA; the proposal passed the following year without opposition). This exposure led to other opportunities to serve the profession, including, among others, serving as chair of the higher education agency member unit, as vice president for standards, and in 1995–1996 as president of the association, which by then had been renamed the American Association of Family and Consumer Sciences (AAFCS). Serving as the first president after the name change, I developed a platform to move the profession into this new phase by fostering greater continuity and visibility (focus on the early childhood initiative); promoting research (cosponsorship of the national conference on social change, public policy, and community collaborations); and encouraging unity and a renaissance among our members, especially since the name change left some feeling disappointed and somewhat wounded.

In addition to AAFCS involvement, I served for several years on the Board on Human Sciences (BoHS) of the then National Association of State Universities and Land-Grant Colleges, now called Association of Public Land-grant Universities. Perhaps my most impactful role was as chair of the federal relations committee for the BoHS, where we hired our first lobbyist and secured earmark funding for an early childhood initiative at the National Science Foundation. We also developed a pilot research funding program for junior faculty and held trainings to help faculty obtain federal funding.

At the same time that I was evolving as a leader in the human sciences, I was also moving up the administrative ladder in higher education. In serving as chair for the division of home economics at UMass-Amherst, I assumed a unit that had only pieces of a traditional home economics program (we had faculty in family studies, consumer economics, and merchandising) and a history of discord. The student body of over 400 students was primarily merchandising majors. We were housed in a college of agriculture and probably survived because of the large enrollment, which the college needed at the time. I was asked to come in and "fix" the department. As a department, we had to develop a common mission, vision, and conceptually sound organizational structure, and to identify a new name. We also had to hire new faculty, enhance student experiences, and gain more visibility on campus for research. These were all tall orders, especially since soon after I was hired in 1987, we suffered five budget rescissions. Nevertheless, we were successful in righting the ship, and when I left in 1992 we had achieved most of our goals. We developed a new focus and strategic plan for the department, revamped our name (Department of Consumer Studies), and hired nationally recognized faculty such as Sheila Mammen and Patricia Warner. I was also particularly proud of the faculty lecture series we established, where we recruited John Kenneth Galbraith to lecture on campus.

Due to successful leadership at UMass-Amherst and my growing visibility in AAFCS, I was recruited to apply for the deanship of the College of Human Sciences at Florida State University. This was again a challenging environment as I followed a strong leader, Margaret Sitton, who had served as dean for 20 years. During my 14-year tenure as dean, enrollment more than tripled, from 900 in 1992 to 3,250 in 2006. Faculty members received over 35 awards for teaching and research and generated close to $2 million annually in new contract and grant awards. Over $18 million was raised in two capital campaigns, with the college's endowment increasing fourfold (from $2 million to $8 million), including two eminent scholar chairs and four endowed professorships. Other noteworthy achievements included a $5.3 million renovation of the Sandels Building and $1 million received for the Office Depot Technology Complex. Under my watch, the FSU Family Institute was established, the college implemented a living learning center (a dormitory-based learning community), and new programs such as athletic training were established.

While serving as dean, I worked collaboratively with faculty at other universities to develop and administer several projects to recruit and graduate students of color. These included Mentoring Multicultural Students for the Health Professions, where over 150 students have completed the program with a 95% graduation rate and with substantial placements in graduate and professional schools; and SciencPrep, a collaborative project with historically Black universities to provide undergraduate students in the human sciences exposure to research and graduate education. Both projects were funded by the United States Department of Agriculture with grants totaling $500,000.

In addition to student development, I also began focusing on the community. This work was propelled when I cochaired a planning committee for a community-wide health and wellness program for Black families, sponsored by the Tallahassee chapter of The Links, Inc. The program, which focused on improving health awareness and health behaviors, received support from the medical community, local churches, hospitals/care facilities, and universities. In total, close to 700 people attended between 1999 and 2004. The program received a recognition award from The Links, Inc. national organization and served as the springboard to other health-related activities in the community. In 2007, the Day of Dialogue on Minority Health (DoDMH) grew out of this seminar. It is now an eight-county, church-based coalition that holds annual health seminars to improve health of local populations with events rotating among the counties.

These, along with many other experiences, helped me to further develop my leadership skills, especially multidisciplinary collaborations and political savvy, and to establish a passion for community-based work.

TRANSITION TO HEALTH AND
OPPORTUNITIES FOR INNOVATION

Thus far, my life trajectory has been epitomized by work ethic, academic excellence, leadership, and community. One could say that, based on the consistency of those themes, my life has reflected the continuity theory of aging. Yet the next phase, as I enter my later years, begins to demonstrate innovation. Further, these activities are ones I would not have considered in my early years. As posited by the successful aging theorists, older age can bring about growth and creativity that reflects an accumulation of knowledge, skills, and wisdom (Rowe and Kahn 1997).

FORMING THE BHL CENTER

As I entered my 14th year of being a dean at Florida State University, I began to think about the next phase of my life. Too young to fully retire, I reflected on what I really enjoyed doing because, at the end of the day, it comes down to the processes of life. In other words, enjoyment is about how we like to pass the time and with increasing years we realize that time is short. On an out-of-town trip, I sat in a restaurant alone and pondered my next steps. I outlined on a napkin what an entity might look like that served the community but also could help the university. Florida State University, like many other comprehensive research universities in the mid-2000s, was on a path to become one of the top 25 public research universities in the country. Federal research dollars were a part of the metrics that would help reach this goal. I also thought about how much I enjoyed my work in planning the health seminars for The Links, Inc. Putting these two themes together—community and health research—led to the idea of a center that would focus on improving the health of medically underserved populations. I played around with different names for the center but finally settled on the Center on Better Health and Life for Underserved Populations. Although a mouthful, I found later that the students enjoyed shortening the title to BHL Center.

What were the health problems in the community that would demonstrate a need for the BHL Center? At the time, the North Florida counties were a textbook example of health disparities. Health disparities can be defined as differences in the health status and/or disease risk of different groups of people (Adler 2006). Using cardiovascular disease as an example, while death rates from heart disease declined 46.1% in Caucasian men between 1979 and 1998, the decline for African American men during this period was only 33.3%. During this same period, African American women also experienced a lower decrease in mortality rates from coronary heart disease compared to Caucasian women: 26.6% compared to 40.1% (CDC 2017). These same disparities were noted in North Florida counties, which became a targeted area for the BHL Center (Florida Department of Health 2007). What can universities do to address health disparities? As I considered the focus of the BHL Center, I concluded that to have ultimate impact, the activities would need to be both "hands on" in the community and sophisticated enough to garner competitive funding. In contemplating how to bring these two possible goals together, it made sense to make intervention research the focus. Thus, the mission of the BHL Center is to improve health of underserved populations through research and program development. The specific goals are to (a) conduct research on health disparities and underserved populations that informs the program development process; (b) develop, implement, and evaluate community-based programs to address health disparities in underserved populations; and (c) train students to work with underserved populations.

When the BHL Center became official at the university in June 2006, I was able to secure $25,000 in start-up funds from the provost and a one-year sabbatical. I used this year to make contacts with community stakeholders and health professionals, locally as well as nationally, and to begin to seek funding for support. The first year was difficult. I had overhead expenses for the Center (space rental, a full-time assistant director) but only the start-up funds and a small grant. I was given a graduate student assistant by my department chair, and while this was a major benefit, struggling to pay rent and make payroll was stressful. Yet somehow, we made it through; sometimes using my own funds.

IMPACTFUL EVENTS

Two impactful events occurred in the first year that helped to launch the BHL Center. First, I attended several national health conferences that year and learned about the community-based participatory research (CBPR) process. CBPR is a partnership approach to research that involves the community on an equal basis in all aspects of the research process. Drawing on the work of Kurt Lewin, Orlando Fals Borda, and Paulo Freire, the CBPR process focuses on community needs and values to determine the direction of the research and the processes that are used (Israel et al. 2005). CBPR was consistent with my own values about the importance of community and thus this approach was embraced by the BHL Center.

The second impactful event was receiving a grant funding announcement from Ann Mullis, a fellow faculty member in my department. The funding opportunity was from the National Institutes of Health and outlined a request for a five-year grant to conduct research to improve the health of an underserved population using CBPR. In my last year as dean, I had submitted a couple of grants to the United States Department of Agriculture that focused on improving dietary outcomes of African Americans using church-based approaches. Neither was funded, but I used the substance of the previous proposals to develop a new one for NIH.

The contacts I had made through the DoDMH enhanced this effort. I met with Arrie Battle, a community health stakeholder from Gadsden County, who had attended the inaugural DoDMH in 2007. We worked together to determine strategies for involving county churches in the project. Gadsden County, adjacent to Leon County (where Florida State University is located), is majority minority with major health disparities. Thus, including this county in the grant proposal would serve populations that needed health interventions the most.

GARNERING FEDERAL FUNDING

The grant was submitted in October 2007. As we approached 2008, much was happening nationally and internationally as the Great Recession was underway. For a couple of reasons, I felt that only a miracle would make it possible for the grant to be funded. First, this was my first NIH proposal and I knew the difficulty of getting funding from this federal agency from my work as dean. Second, there was the possibility of funds being limited at the federal level due to the Great Recession. I received a score of 3.0 and learned that it was a good score but not necessarily a fundable score. Then I began to get emails and telephone calls from the program officer requesting additional information. In June 2008, we received confirmation that the grant was funded in the amount of $1.75 million. Needless to say, there was joy in North Florida! With the indirect funds from the grant, I could now pay the rent on our space for five years, and I also had at least half of the funding needed to pay for an assistant director and a half-time graduate assistant.

With the BHL Center's overhead expenses in place, we could now get to work. At the same time we received the NIH grant, we also received a one-year grant in the amount of $215,000 from a local health maintenance organization to develop a church-based health project focused on blood pressure control. In this project, we worked with families in three churches to implement "Check Your HYPErtension," a six-week program that included weekly interactive sessions (Ralston et al. 2015). This project gave us important information on intervention development as we started the preliminary work on the NIH project.

For the NIH grant, we worked with Ms. Battle to recruit four churches in Gadsden County and identified two in Leon County. Ms. Battle also helped us to organize an advisory group in Gadsden County since we had fewer contacts and relationships there. This group identified churches to target in this county and chose a name for the project: Health for Hearts United. The community shortened the name to "Healthy Hearts."

Using a quasi-experimental longitudinal design, the Healthy Hearts study targeted 300 midlife and older African Americans in the six churches (three treatment, three comparison), including a subsample of 100 participants selected for clinical assessments (Ralston et al. 2014). Using an interactive, iterative process with health ministries formed in the treatment churches, an 18-month, theory-driven intervention was developed. As outlined in Ralston et al. (2017), the intervention included three components (awareness building, clinical learning, and efficacy development), four key messages (eat better, move around more, reduce stress, and take charge of your health), and three implementation strategies (church initiated, staff-initiated, and joint church-staff programming).

Data were collected in four phases (baseline, 6, 18, and 24 months) from 257 participants ($\geq$45 years, including 104 clinical subsample) who were randomly sampled from six churches in the two counties. The resulting retention rates of 89.5% (overall sample) and 72.9% (subsample) showed positive outcomes for health behaviors, clinical measures, and selected biomarkers. Although both treatment and comparison groups improved, there were significant improvements for those in the treatment groups on several variables.

With these positive outcomes, we were able to secure a follow-on grant from NIH that provided $1.4 million in funding to disseminate the best practices from the previous project. This dissemination project used a three-phase model: training, planning, and delivery. Participants included pastors and health leaders (n=168) from 30 churches in the two-county area (20 Gadsden and 10 in Leon) who delivered CVD awareness events to 586 outreach participants. Preliminary outcomes from this project are very positive.

STATEWIDE AND NATIONAL VISIBILITY

With these and other grants and activities, the BHL Center developed both state and nationwide visibility. One such opportunity arose in 2007, when I heard Dr. Louis Sullivan, MD (former U.S. secretary of health and human services) speak about the newly formed Sullivan Alliance. The alliance was formed to address concerns of minority underrepresentation in the health professions, as outlined in the Sullivan Commission report (2004). Upon learning about state initiatives being formed to affiliate with the Sullivan Alliance, I met with him briefly after his talk and asked if he would be interested in having Florida involved in this effort. He of course said yes, and I returned to Florida A&M University to engage colleagues Cynthia M. Harris and Cynthia Hughes Harris (administrators of public health and allied health, respectively), as well as Dr. Rebecca Pauly, MD, at the University of Florida. This team then planned an inaugural statewide meeting to determine whether or not we should go forward with a Florida affiliate of the Sullivan Alliance. With agreement from over 100 people in attendance, the Florida Alliance for Health Professions Diversity (FAHPD) was launched. Since its establishment in 2007, FAHPD has engaged close to 900 high school through master's-level students in symposia that have rotated around the state. It also provided 90 of those students with intensive summer experiences. In tracking those students over time, we see that they are, in fact, entering the health professions, including medicine, public health, and related disciplines.

In addition to this work, I was asked by Chuck Wells, a long-term colleague now working for the Florida Department of Health, to serve on the Biomedical Research Advisory Council (BRAC), which at the time administered over $40 million in competitive state research grants in Florida. Through serving on BRAC, I was able to spearhead the development of the *Health Disparities Research Agenda for Florida* in 2011. A statewide summit launched this effort by bringing together leading health disparity researchers. Following the summit, a 30-member Health Disparities Research Advisory Committee was formed to develop the research agenda (FL CURED 2011).

The document that resulted from the advisory committee's work highlighted substantive areas of health promotion, health services, and cancer as the priority research foci for Florida. It was shared with Florida legislators, and through the efforts of Representative Joe Gibbons (District 100), we secured a total of $800,000 in start-up funding in fiscal years 2013 and 2014. The funding launched the Florida Health Equity Research Institute (FL HERI), a statewide virtual entity that includes 13 higher education partners that work collaboratively to implement the research agenda.

FL HERI has four cores, including (1) administrative, (2) community engagement, (3) education and training, and (4) research. The cores are, respectively, led by Lee Green (Moffitt Cancer Center), Angela Adams (Central Florida Pharmacy Council), Cynthia M. Harris (FAMU), and Folakemi Odedina (University of Florida). We partnered with the FAHPD to carry out the work of the education and training core. As this chapter is being written, government relations work is underway to secure $1 million in state funding for FL HERI in the upcoming year.

LESSONS LEARNED

So, what have I learned as I have entered this new, innovative phase of my life? I would like to close this chapter with some wisdom I learned along the way as I established a new venture in health equity. In addition, these are life lessons because they also represent what I have learned from a life course perspective:

- *Have a passion for the new venture.* As we get older, time is not on our side. There is no time to waste on "filler" activities or distractions. If you have not done so already, figure out what you love and focus your new venture around it.
- *Think big and aspirational.* How we spend our time in later years will vary by individual interests, but for me having a social purpose is of utmost importance. I want to know that others—not only those I am serving locally—will benefit. So, I developed a Center that serves locally but has implications for the state and the nation.
- *Plan carefully and practically.* Although a broad vision is important, starting a new venture requires attention to details. Similar to starting a business, I had to develop the concept and the action plan, including a proposed budget. I also knew that I would have to start small.
- *Mentor yourself.* You may find that there is no one left to mentor you, so mentor yourself! Find out what you need, strategize to get the resources, and go for it.
- *Take calculated risks.* In starting a new venture, sometimes taking risks is important to the overall viability of your project. As an example, I knew that the Center's location would be important to the clients we would serve. Further, I wanted autonomy in choosing the work environment, so instead of asking the university to find space for the Center, I decided to rent space. That decision had financial consequences, but it provided independence and lessened the disruption of potential moves due to funding issues or campus politics.
- *Handle uncertainty.* Starting a new venture means that there will be uncertainties. Will grants be funded? Will students be interested? Would the community welcome our effort? Learning how to manage these uncertainties began with having faith in the project and knowing that it was related to my life's purpose.
- *Enjoy the process every day.* The *process* of life becomes increasingly important with age because long-term goal setting is not as relevant. If the passion is focused and you have planned appropriately, then the process of building your new venture makes every day special. You are doing what you love . . . your life's work.

REFERENCES

Adler, Nancy E. 2006. "Overview of Health Disparities." In *Examining the Health Disparities Research Plan of the National Institutes of Health: Unfinished Business*. Washington, DC: Institute of Medicine. https://www.nap.edu/catalog /11602/examining-the-health-disparities-research-plan-of-the-national-institutes -of-health.

Atchley, Robert C. 1989. "A Continuity Theory of Normal Aging." *The Gerontologist 29*, no. 2: 183–190. https://doi.org/10.1093/geront/29.2.183.

Center for Disease Control and Prevention. 2017. "Fact Sheet. Division for Heart Disease and Stroke Prevention, Data & Statistics." Accessed December, 2020. https://www.cdc.gov/dhdsp/data_statistics/index.htm.

Florida Center for Universal Research to Eradicate Disease (FL CURED). 2011. "Health Disparities Research Agenda for Florida." Accessed December, 2020. cancer.ufl.edu/files/2012/08/FL_CURED.pdf.

Florida Department of Health. 2007. "Behavioral Risk Factor Surveillance System." Retrieved from: floridahealth.gov/.

Israel, Barbara A., Eugenia Eng, Amy J. Schulz, and Edith A. Parker. 2005. *Methods in Community-Based Participatory Research for Health*. New York: Jossey-Bass.

Nickols, Sharon Y., Penny A. Ralston, Carol Anderson, Lorna Browne, Genevieve Schroeder, Sabrina Thomas, and Peggy Wild. 2009. "The Family and Consumer Sciences Body of Knowledge and the Cultural Kaleidoscope: Research Opportunities and Challenges." *Family and Consumer Sciences Research Journal 37*, no. 3: 266–283.

Ralston, Penny A., Tammye Farmer, Iris Young-Clark, and Catherine C. Coccia. 2015. "Blood Pressure Control for African American Parents and Children: Feasibility and Initial Outcomes of a Faith-Based Intervention Pilot Study." *Journal of Health Disparities Research and Practice 9*, no. 2: 47–65.

Ralston, Penny A., Jennifer L. Lemacks, Kandauda KAS Wickrama, Iris Young-Clark, Catherine Coccia, Jasminka Z. Ilich, Cynthia M. Harris, Celeste B. Hart, Arrie M. Battle, and Catherine Walker O'Neal. 2014. "Reducing Cardiovascular Disease Risk in Mid-Life and Older African Americans: A Church-Based Longitudinal Intervention Project at Baseline." *Contemporary Clinical Trials 38*, no. 1: 69–81.

Ralston, Penny A., Iris Young-Clark, and Catherine Coccia. 2017. "The Development of Health for Hearts United: A Longitudinal Church-Based Intervention to Reduce Cardiovascular Risk in Mid-Life And Older African Americans." *Ethnicity & Disease 27*, no. 1: 21–30.

Rowe, John W., and Robert L. Kahn. 1997. "Successful Aging." *The Gerontologist 37*, no. 4: 433–440. https://doi.org/10.1093/geront/37.4.433.

The Sullivan Commission. 2004. "Missing Persons: Minorities in the Health Professions." A report of the Sullivan Commission on Diversity in the Healthcare Workforce. Accessed December, 2020. https://www.semanticscholar.org/paper/Mi ssing-Persons%3A-Minorities-in-the-Health-A-Report-Sullivan/9931aefb7d51582 145ade6d938979a3a96b193d1.

Chapter 16

Family and Consumer Sciences in the Middle

Opportunities for Guiding Career Development

Jacqueline M. Holland

INTRODUCTION

"What do you want to be when you grow up?" It is natural for adults to ask, explore, and engage in conversation with young people on this question. Some children have a precise picture or idea of a future career, while for others the desired profession remains to be formed or defined. Exploring issues of this sort begins in preschool and continues into adolescence. The family is often a contributing factor in determining a career selection (Emmanuelle 2009; Kumar and Hruda 2001; Maor and Cojocaru 2018). As the child gets older, teachers may also influence career pathways (Kumar and Hruda, 2001; Seward and Gaesser 2018). Taylor, Wang, Van Brackle and Kaneda (2003) concluded that sex-role stereotyping and maturation also influence career decision-making. Blackhurst (2008), when studying future aspirations of elementary and middle school students, found that females rather than males tended to aspire to careers in which college preparation was necessary. Taylor et al. (2003) found that culture affected the career choice of children in the United States and Japan. U.S. children tended to select careers that were focused on self, while those in Japan favored occupations that reflected self and others, thus mirroring the self-oriented U.S. culture and the group-oriented Japanese culture, respectively. Regardless of how careers are selected, there are still choices that must be made to move forward on a career path. The purpose of this research was to conduct an exploratory study of middle school children's development toward career choices. The questions addressed in this study included: (1) Does family and consumer sciences

(FCS) affect the self-efficacy and career development of eighth grade middle school students, and if so, how? (2) What FCS supports and resources contribute to the self-efficacy of students' needs to pursue career interests? and (3) What human social factors influence students enrolled in FCS?

LITERATURE REVIEW

A career is described as a lifetime of work and roles related to a particular occupation in which one participates (Super 1980; Jordan and Whaley 2004; McKay 2019). Students today face a world in which they may experience several professions. Some professionals advocate high school as the correct time to introduce career development, while others support this introduction in the elementary and middle school years (Virtue 2010). Almost everyone will have a career; therefore, the sooner one discovers an interest that is supported by a career path, the more excellent will be the quality of life and attitude toward work (Holland 2011; Taylor et al. 2003). The statement by legendary author Henry David Thoreau (1854), "Go confidently in the direction of your dreams. Live the life you have imagined," can be the driving force of every person considering a career pathway (Harris-Bowlsbey, Suddarth, and Reile 2008). The FCS is a content area that supports career development. This chapter investigates the potential contributions of FCS in students' career choices.

Presently, many young people in the United States lack a level of self-efficacy necessary to initiate the steps to pursue a career. Self-efficacy maintains that people have a "self-system" that enables them to exercise control over their thoughts, feelings, and actions (Bandura 1989, 1). Students who do not have a clear or decisive idea of a career will experience an adverse effect in their work experience, self-efficacy, life satisfaction, and self-esteem (Creed, Prideaux, and Patton 2005). By contrast, in situations where career development support occurs, students became equipped to select an occupation conducive to their success (Hirschi and Läge 2008). A lack of self-efficacy and purpose can be a roadblock for young people who are moving toward a career goal.

During the middle school years, students ages 12–14 are enrolled in a variety of subjects. Core academic subjects include mathematics, language arts, science, and social studies. Additional courses may consist of art, FCS, physical education, health, foreign language, music, and other specialty subjects. In many schools, however, adolescents do not acquire assistance in gaining knowledge that better equips them to select career pathways that support their interests and abilities (Brogan 2010; Brown 2002). From the viewpoint of an educational leader, this is a concern; it is crucial that systems are established in the learning environment to assist students in identifying desires and developing the mindset toward a future career. The period of early adolescent development sets the stage for high school, so it is imperative for education leaders to focus on equipping students for their future.

Several frameworks associated with career development address the steps that are foundational to pursuing a career. Human development explores the concepts of self-efficacy and purpose, which are foundational in life. Career development represents the whole constellation of psychological, sociological, educational, physical, economic, and chance factors that combine to influence the nature and significance of work across the entire life span of any given individual. According to Rivera and Schaefer (2009), many view career developments as an integral part of students' academic preparation, as well as their social and personal growth. These developmental stages are based on historical perspectives that include the works of Pope (2000), Parsons (1909), Holland (1959), and Super (1980).

The theory of vocational choice is one of the foundational works on an individual's personality and the work environment (Holland 1959; Nauta 2010). According to Holland, each individual has a distinct personality that determines the given career to which he or she is attracted. The personal styles (RIASEC) are Realistic (R), Investigative (I), Artistic (A), Social (S), Enterprising (E), and Conventional (C).

According to Holland (1992), there are four basic assumptions that support the theory of vocational choice. First, most people in society can be categorized using one of six types above. Second, there are six categories of environments using the same terms: realistic, investigative, artistic, social, enterprising, and conventional. Third, people pursue environments that permit them to demonstrate their talents and abilities, express their attitudes and values, and take on agreeable challenges and roles. Fourth, the interface between one's personality and the characteristics of the environment regulates one's behavior (4).

Other researchers emphasize the role of self-concept as a person develops a career choice (Super 1957; Mack 2020). Everyone develops a self-concept that characterizes how they see themselves, how they would like to be seen, and how they think others view them (Harris-Bowlsbey 2008). Many factors go into the development of the self-concept, including environment, culture, experiences, family, and events. Super (1980) and Bhatt and Pujar (2020) emphasize that the kind of reinforcement one receives determines the perception of how well one does in a specific task or area. Having a purpose can influence how well one completes a task.

Every person has a purpose for living. Damon (2008) defined purpose as "a stable and generalized intention to accomplish something that is at the same time meaningful to the self and consequential for the world beyond the self" (33). Damon (2008) research revealed several principles/features about purpose. The concept of purpose begins in early adolescence. When purpose is absent, a belief system becomes challenging for youth. Also, identified purpose in childhood can lead to moral commitment and positive social behavior (Damon, Menon, and Bronk 2003).

The Social Learning Theory as described by Bandura (1977, 1989) maintains that human learning is derived through modeling. This framework, also known as social cognitive theory, is a method to understand human thinking, emotions, action, and motivation with the assumption that people shape their environments, rather than just reacting to them (Bandura, 1977, 1989, 1995; Maddux and Gosselin 2003). Bandura's work and research with Social Learning Theory steered him to include cognitive components of motivation and self-regulation. This new development led to a concept that he named Social Cognitive Theory, which included self-efficacy as a core aspect (1989). Self-efficacy maintains people have a self-system that enables them to exercise control over their thoughts, feelings, and actions (Bandura 1989). Bandura (1977) defined the term as a belief or beliefs about the ability to "organize and execute the courses of action required to produce given attainments" (3).

Career planning has been shown to benefit students in many ways. It supports young people in discovering their strengths and talents (Holland 2011). Often, students leave high school without certainty regarding their career path. Some may have a specific desire that has not been vetted by considering their strengths. Students can experience careers while in high school through career and technical education programs of study. Darche and Stam (2012) discovered that students who participated in such programs obtained firsthand experiences in a desired career and gained technical skills and college credit that propelled them into the postsecondary experience. A 10-year longitudinal study was conducted by Hewlig (2004) with students beginning in second grade. The results showed that these students were able to identify a career choice upon graduating from high school.

Adolescents develop in four areas. These include (a) physical; (b) intellectual; (c) social, emotional, and moral; and (d) psychological (Damon, Eisenberg, and Lerner 2006; National Middle School Association 2010; Pruitt 1999). Knowing that middle school students develop in the areas above, it is essential that schools maintain programs, initiatives, experiences, and a culture that supports the successful development of this age group. In its publication, *This We Believe: Keys to Educating Young Adults*, the National Middle School Association (2010) provided several goals that all middle schools should implement to develop a self-actualized young adolescent. They include (a) thinking rationally and critically and expressing thoughts clearly; (b) reading deeply to independently gather, assess, and interpret information from a variety of sources; (c) exploring music, art, and careers and recognizing their importance to personal growth and learning; (d) developing strengths, particular skills, talents, or interests and developing an emerging understanding of one's potential contributions to society and to personal fulfillment; and (e) forming the interpersonal and social skills needed to learn, work, and play with others harmoniously and confidently (11–12).

The National Association of State Administrators for Family and Consumer Sciences (n.d.), an organization for FCS administrators and professionals, developed the U.S. national standards for FCS in 1995 and continues to update. These measures, which reflect diverse philosophies and approaches to educational delivery systems, concluded that the mission of FCS education is to prepare students for opportunities to develop knowledge, skills, attitudes, and behaviors to experience successful lives. The standards that relate to career development include:

- Strengthening the well-being of individuals and families across the life span
- Becoming responsible citizens and leaders in family, community, and work settings
- Managing resources to meet the material needs of individuals and families
- Balancing personal, home, family, and work lives
- Using critical and creative thinking skills to address problems in diverse family, community, and work environments
- Successful life management, employment, and careers development
- Functioning effectively as providers and consumers of goods and services
- Appreciating human worth and accepting responsibility for one's actions and success in family and work life

The vision and mission statements have been widely publicized and used since that time and have significantly affected the direction taken by the FCS curriculum and program development for secondary education at national, state, and local levels.

METHODOLOGY

The study involved 41 eighth grade students and two FCS teachers using the Primary Academic Motivational Beliefs Survey (PAMBS) and focus groups. PAMBS was adapted from the Motivated Learning Strategies Questionnaire to measure students' self-efficacy and career development (Pintrich and De Groot 1990). Sample questions included:

- It is important for me to learn what is being taught in this class.
- My motivation is sparked through lessons and activities in this class.
- Understanding the topics taught in this class is important to me.

- Doing well in this class will help me have a satisfying career when I grow up.
- I feel good about myself as a student in FACS.

Some of the questions were adapted to include FCS terminology, and a few additional queries related to FCS. The FCS teachers were also interviewed prior to meeting the students to ascertain their curricula, instructional strategies, and motivation techniques used. Student feelings about FCS and the FCS teacher were also explored. The qualitative data focused on the responses acquired through the focus group interviews. Interviews with two different sets of students and their teachers occurred at each school. Video and audiotapes were analyzed using coding and thematic techniques. Audiotapes were transcribed to capture all verbal responses, then transcribed sessions were investigated further and coded to identify themes and key phrases in support of the study. Videotapes were viewed to add clarification to the audiotapes and to capture body language and other innuendos that participants exhibited. Students and teachers remained anonymous, as fictitious names were reported with the data.

Quantitative data from the PAMBS were analyzed using the Statistical Package for the Social Sciences, a data analysis computer program. According to Schreiber and Asner-Self (2010), an analysis of variance (ANOVA) examines the variability in scores when there are more than two groups (256). Howell (2010) reported it as the most used statistical measurement in research, partly because the number of means measured among variables can be limitless. This was a one-way ANOVA with repeated measures across the four themes. The themes reflected in the survey included self-efficacy, academic achievement, career development, and student perception of the FCS teacher.

QUANTITATIVE FINDINGS: ANALYSIS OF VARIANCE

Students participated in the PAMBS, which reflected self-efficacy, career development, FCS class, and instruction by the FCS teacher. In examining the effects of self-efficacy, academics, career development, and student perception of the teacher, students rated each of the questions supporting the four themes. Six questions represented self-efficacy and six were related to career interest, each having a total of 30 points. The 11 questions about academics made up a total of 55 points, and 9 questions about the FCS teacher represented 45 points. As a result, each student's academic and teacher scores were transformed linearly to equivalent scores based on a total of 30 points. The purpose of the transformations was to permit direct comparisons among the four themes.

The overall ANOVA with repeated measures indicated that the mean of at least one theme is significantly different from the mean of at least one other theme, $F(3, 120) = 43.13, p < .001$. The application of the Greenhouse-Geisser correction still resulted in $p < .001$.

The Greenhouse-Geisser procedure was used for the degrees of freedom to evaluate this test. The results were 1.959 and 78.370. This procedure was employed if the assumption of sphericity was violated (Howell 2010, 446).

To determine precisely which means were significantly different from other means, the researcher performed six post hoc tests via paired t-tests with the Bonferroni correction. The Bonferroni correction protects the integrity of the .05 alpha level; for a mean difference to be statistically significant at the .05 level, the obtained p must not exceed .008 (.05/6). The tests were conducted to compare the following themes: self-efficacy against academics, self-efficacy against teacher, self-efficacy against career, academics against teacher, academics against career, and teacher against career.

The mean difference of 4.38 (SD = 5.26) indicates that self-efficacy is significantly greater than academics, $t(40) = 5.33, p < .001$; the mean difference of 8.06 (SD = 4.07) indicates that self-efficacy is significantly greater than teacher, $t(40) = 12.69, p < .001$; the mean difference of 5.29 (SD = 6.32) indicates that self-efficacy is significantly greater than career, $t(40) = 5.36, p < .001$; the mean difference of 3.69 (SD = 2.81) indicates that academics is significantly greater than teacher, $t(40) = 8.42, p < .001$; and the mean difference of -2.77 (SD = 4.55) indicates that career is significantly greater than teacher, $t(40) = -3.90, p < .001$. Last, the mean difference of .92 (SD = 3.87) indicates there is no significant difference between academics and career $t(40) = 1.52, p = .137$.

QUALITATIVE FINDINGS: FOCUS GROUPS

Several recurring elements became evident in examining self-efficacy, career development, FCS course, and student perception of the FCS teacher. Results from the survey supported the first theme of self-efficacy in students, which shows self-efficacy with the highest mean score at 24.29. That compares to career, with a mean of 19.00 (a difference of 5.29); teacher, with a mean of 16.23 (a difference of 8.06); and academics, with a mean of 19.92 (a difference of 4.37). Focus group and survey results indicated that students had a very strong sense of self-efficacy. During the focus groups, the term confidence was used in the place of self-efficacy to provide students with a more precise understanding. Of the 25 students who participated in the focus groups, all responded positively when asked if they were confident. Students defined confidence as "You don't care what people judge you by," "believing in yourself," and "Something you are really sure of and have basic confidence in yourself."

According to Bandura (1995), people differ in the areas of life in which they cultivate their sense of efficacy. Students were quite confident in their ability to reach goals. These goals related to future careers, as well as academic success. Student responses included:

- "People praising me for . . . what I do, like saying I did a good job."
- "Just the way that my parents have faith in me, and some of my teachers, and my brother, he has faith in me as well."
- "Being surrounded by positive people. My family . . . they always have me in situations, so I just be confident. Like, OK, I got this."

These comments supported Bandura's (1995) social learning theory that verbal persuasion given by another can deepen self-efficacy.

In relationship to the theme of career development, about 80% of the students who participated in the focus group were able to name a profession they wanted to pursue: medical field (4), athlete (1), veterinarian (1), business (2), education (1), restaurant and chef (3), government and military (2), lawyer, artist, military, dancer, engineering, pilot, graphic arts designer, housewife, CIA agent, manager, and "I'm not sure."

In support of Holland (1959), Keller and Whiston (2008) reported that parent behaviors are related to the career interests of their children through a series of events within the child's environment. The researchers determined that children's exposure to varied activities in the home and community, whether broad or limited, influences their career choices. One student expressed her interest in dance:

I just like to continue to dance, because if I stop dancing for a long time, then I will kind of get out of shape and stuff. I dance all the time. I know a lot of family that dance, so they help me to try to get into school to dance.

Most students knew what it took to achieve their goals, and in some cases, were already taking steps to reach them. When asked what they were doing to reach their career goals, a sampling of responses included:

- "I'm doing research; my stepmother is helping me" [to become a pediatrician].
- "Well, to go to college and get a major in business management. And to go into the military."

Although a few comments from the survey identified FCS as affecting a future career ("good way to improve your future and find a successful career" and "good jobs with cooking"), on a broader scope, it appeared that FCS had little to do with students' career development. Students never identified their FCS teacher as being instrumental in assisting them to pursue a career. During a focus group session, when students were asked about their experiences in FCS, several students responded that they liked the class, as represented by the below comment:

> You get a better understanding of how to work together because we get put into groups; so I think it will be a good lesson to learn for when we grow up.

Though not directly related to a specific career, FCS does provide a skill necessary for workplace success: working well with others. With regard to the theme of FCS course, student responses varied. Approximately 76% indicated they felt good about themselves as students in FCS. FCS educators have played a valuable role in guiding youth in life skills. Student responses from the survey and focus group interactions regarding FCS included:

- "Good way to improve your future and find a successful career."
- "I'm learning life skills."
- "Awesome, very exciting place to learn cool stuff when tired with math and reading."
- "The basics you need if you were living on your own."

The fourth theme, students' feelings about their FCS teacher, also varied. Balfanz (2009) reported FCS offers high student engagement and provides opportunities to experience short-term success. In public schools, FCS educators play a valuable role guiding youth in life skills. When students were asked their feelings about FCS, the responses applied to the teacher. Favorable and unfavorable comments from students in both schools included:

- "The teacher helps you."
- "Others wished they had gotten the chance to take the class."
- "Hard assignments.'
- "Love it."
- "Mean/strict teacher."
- "Look forward to going to class."

CONCLUSION AND DISCUSSION

Maddux and Gosselin (2003) discovered self-efficacy beliefs are not just concerned with abilities separate from circumstances; rather, the beliefs are what the person can do within the circumstances of the situation. This implies that students have a high view of themselves and their ability to accomplish forthcoming tasks. This finding agreed with data results from the focus group interviews with students, who were very forthright as they communicated how they acquired confidence, and the steps they were taking to reach their goals. Survey results and post hoc tests used to compare themes revealed that students rated academics and career higher than the teacher. In addition, their responses on self-efficacy were greater than academics, teacher, and career. Three questions were explored. The first question was does FCS affect the self-efficacy and career development of eighth grade middle school students, and if so, how? The investigation suggests that with this group, FCS has some effect on career development; nonetheless, parents and peers tended to have a greater impact on how students felt about their ability to move forward on a desired goal than teachers. This could be because students spend more time with family and peers than teachers, which strongly affects their efficaciousness. However, students stated that FCS was a good way to improve one's future and find a successful career. The second question was what FCS supports and resources contribute to students' self-efficacy in pursuing career interests? Study results indicate that FCS was associated with many of the skills students identified as being able to help them. The curriculum and related activities could have contributed to these identifying markers for FCS. This again illustrates the positive effect FCS has on student self-efficacy. The final question was "What human social factors influence students enrolled in FCS?" One contributing factor that influenced student enrollment was school administrators who selected students for the classes. This decision was often based upon academic requirements. Secondly, teachers influenced the students. Regardless of the student's view of the teacher, they saw value for themselves in the FCS class. A final contributing factor was self-efficacy. Self-efficacy, along with purpose, played a dominant role in what students could achieve in the class, based on how they felt about their ability to do so (Bandura 1977; Damon 2008; Magnavita 2002; Michael 2019).

The study also found that students could identify specific behaviors that helped them to achieve goals. These included working hard, getting good grades, having a positive attitude and behavior, support from family and friends, and focus on education. Effective strategies implemented through FCS contributed to students' self-efficacy and increased their knowledge of related career pathways. Nevertheless, with this group, FCS had little or no effect on career development. Although teacher behavior had some effect on student self-efficacy, it did not go as far to develop their efficaciousness when related to career development. On the contrary, parents and peers showed a more dramatic effect on the students' sense of self and their ability to pursue a desire. Indirectly, strategies used by the FCS teacher in instructional planning provided students with a skill-set transferable to the workplace, and similar experiences that require working with others.

Given that only two schools participated in this study (one teacher having the students from the beginning of the school year and the other beginning midyear), the sample could have affected the results. Additional students and teachers in the sample may have resulted in a different outcome. Further research should include restructuring survey questions to delve deeper into how FCS affects student self-efficacy. Another study might also further explore students' understanding of self-efficacy as compared to confidence. Extending the study to compare other middle school grades enrolled in FCS (sixth and seventh) could also alter the results. This would provide another lens to ascertain the effectiveness of FCS with younger adolescents.

REFERENCES

Bandura, Albert. 1977. *Social Learning Theory*. Englewood Cliffs, NJ: Prentice Hall.

Bandura, Albert. 1989. "Human Agency in Social Cognitive Theory." *American Psychologist 44*, no. 9 (1989): 1175. https://doi.org/10.1037/0003-066X.44.9.1175.

Bandura, Albert. 1995. *Self-Efficacy in Changing Societies*. New York, NY: Cambridge University Press.

Blackhurst, Anne and Richard W. Auger. 2008. "Precursors to The Gender Gap in College Enrollment: Children's Aspirations and Expectations for Their Futures." *Professional School Counseling 11*, no. 3: 149–158. https://doi.org/10.1177/2 156759X08011003C1.

Brogan, Deirdre Tara. 2010. "Stuck in the Middle: Career Progress, Motivation, and Engagement Among Urban Middle School Students." PhD diss., Boston College.

Brown, Duane and Associates. 2002. *Career Choice and Development* (4th ed.). San Francisco, CA: Jossey-Bass

Bhatt, Maneesha, and Lata Pujar. 2020. "Influence of Self-Concept and Parenting on Adolescents Identity Development." *International Journal of Social Sciences Review 8*, no. 4–6: 158–160.

Creed, Peter A., Lee-Ann Prideaux, and Wendy Patton. 2005. "Antecedents and Consequences of Career Decisional States in Adolescence." *Journal of Vocational Behavior 67*, no. 3: 397–412. https://doi.org/10.1016/j.jvb.2004.08.008.

Damon, William. 2008. *The Path to Purpose: Helping our Children Find Their Calling in Life*. New York, NY: Free Press.

Damon, William, Nancy Eisenberg, and Richard Lerner. 2006. *Handbook of Child Psychology: Vol. 3. Social, Emotional, and Personality Development* (6th ed.). Hoboken, NJ: John Wiley & Sons.

Damon, William, Jenni Menon, and Kendall Cotton Bronk. 2003. "The Development of Purpose During Adolescence." *Applied Developmental Science 7*, no. 3: 119–128. https://doi.org/10.1207/S1532480XADS0703_2.

Darche, Svetlana, and Brad Stam. 2012. "College and Career Readiness: What Do We Mean? Maria's Story." *Techniques: Connecting Education and Careers 87*, no. 3: 20–25.

Emmanuelle, Vignoli. 2009. "Inter-Relationships among Attachment to Mother and Father, Self-Esteem, and Career Indecision." *Journal of Vocational Behavior 75*, no. 2: 91–99.

National Association of State Administrators of Family and Consumer Sciences (n.d.). "Family and Consumer Sciences National Standards 3.0." http://www.lead fcsed.org/national-standards.html.

Harris-Bowlsbey, JoAnn, Barbara H. Suddarth, and David M. Reile. 2008. *Facilitating Career Development*. Broken Arrow, OK: National Career Development Association.

Hewlig, Andrew A. 2004. "A Ten-Year Longitudinal Study of the Career Development of Students: Summary Findings." *Journal of Counseling and Development 82*, no. 1: 49–57.

Hirschi, Andreas and Läge, Damian. 2008. "Using Accuracy of Self-Estimated Interest Type as a Sign of Career Choice Readiness in Career Assessment of Secondary Students." *Journal of Career Assessment 16*, no. 3: 310–325. https://doi.org/10.1177/1069072708317372.

Holland, John L.1959. "A Theory of Vocational Choice." *Journal of Counseling Psychology 6*, no. 1: 35. https://doi.org/10.1037/h0040767.

Holland, John. L. 1992. *Making Vocational Choices* (2nd ed.). Odessa, FL: Psychological Assessment Resources.

Holland, Jacqueline. M. 2011. "Career Development Planning: Getting Students on the Right Path." *Techniques 86*, no. 2: 8–9.

Howell, David C. 2010. *Statistical Methods for Psychology* (7th ed.). Belmont, CA: Cengage Wadsworth.

Jordan, Ann K. and Whaley, Lynn T. 2004. *Investigating Your Career*. Mason, OH: Thompson South-Western.

Kumar, Revathy, and Ludmila Z. Hruda. 2001. "What do I Want to Be When I Grow Up? Role of Parent and Teacher Support in Enhancing Students' Academic Confidence and Educational Expectations." In *Annual Meeting of the American Educational Research Association*.

Mack, Stan. 2020. "How Does Your Self-Concept Affect Your Career?" Accessed May 1, 2017. https://work.chron.com/selfconcept-affect-career-23438.html.

Maddux, James E. and Jennifer T. Gosselin. 2003. "Self-efficacy." In *Handbook of Self and Identity*, edited by Mark R. Leary, and June Price Tangney, 218–238. New York, NY: Guilford Press.

Magnavita, Jeffrey J. 2002. *Theories of Personality*. New York, NY: John Wiley.

Maor, Shifra, and Stefan Cojocaru. 2018. "Family as a Powerful Factor That Influences Career Choice in Nursing." *Social Research Reports 10*, no. 1: 7–22.

McKay, Dawn R. 2019. "The Two Meanings of Career." Last modified June 15, 2019. https://www.thebalancecareers.com/what-is-a-career-525497.

Michael, Rinat. 2019. "Self-efficacy and Future Career Expectations of At-risk Adolescents: The Contribution of a Tutoring Program." *Journal of Community Psychology 47*, no. 4: 913–923. doi:10.1002/jcop.22163. https://doi.org/10.1002/jcop.22163.

National Middle School Association. 2010. *This We Believe: Keys to Educating Young Adults*. Westerville, OH: Author.

Nauta, Margeret M. 2010. "The Development, Evolution, and Status of Holland's Theory of Vocational Personalities: Reflections and Future Directions for Counseling Psychology." *Journal of Counseling Psychology 57*, no. 1: 11–22. https://doi.org/10.1037/a0018213.

Parsons, Frank. 1909. *Choosing a Vocation*. Boston, MA: Houghton Mifflin.

Pintrich, Paul R., and Elisabeth V. De Groot. 1990. "Motivational and Self-Regulated Learning Components of Classroom Academic Performance." *Journal of Educational Psychology 82*, no. 1: 33.

Pope, Mark. 2000. "A Brief History of Career Counseling in the United States." *Career Development Quarterly 48*, no. 3: 194–211. https://doi.org/10.1002/j.2161-0045.2000.tb00286.x.

Pruitt, David. 1999. *Your Adolescent: Emotional, Behavioral, and Cognitive Development from Early Adolescent Through the Teen Years*. New York, NY: Harper Resource.

Rivera, Lourdes M. and Schaefer, Mary Beth. 2009. "The Career Institute: A Collaborative Career Development Program for Traditionally Underserved Secondary (6–12) School Students." *Journal of Career Development 35*, no. 4: 406–426.

Schreiber, James B. and Asner-Self, Kimberly. 2010. *Educational Research*. Hoboken, NJ: John Wiley.

Seward, Kristen, and Amy H. Gaesser. 2018. "Career Decision-Making with Gifted Rural Students: Considerations for School Counselors and Teachers." *Gifted Child Today 41*, no. 4: 217–225. https://doi.org/10.1177/1076217518786986.

Super, Donald E. 1957. *The Psychology of Careers*. New York, NY: Harper and Row.

Super, Donald E. 1980. "A Life-Span, Life Space Approach to Career Development." *Journal of Vocational Behavior 16*, no. 3: 282–298.

Taylor, Satomi Izumi, L. Weiping Wang, Anita VanBrackle, and Toshiko Kaneda. 2003. "What I Want to Be When I Grow Up: A Qualitative Study of American and Japanese Children's Occupational Aspirations." *Child Study Journal 33*, no. 3: 175–186.

Thoreau, Henry David. 1854. *Walden; or, Life in The Woods*. Boston, MA: Ticknor and Fields.

Virtue, David C. 2010. "A View from the Middle." *Middle School 42*, no. 1: 2.

Chapter 17

Only One in the Room

Reflections on the Career of Shirley Hymon-Parker, PhD

Shirley Hymon-Parker and Kenneth Gruber

INTRODUCTION

Shirley was the youngest of eight children, with five sisters and two brothers. She grew up on a farm in Warrenton, North Carolina. Her parents were sharecroppers. They grew food crops to sustain the family while harvesting tobacco and cotton for the landowner. When her father died, Shirley was just 12 and her mother had to take on the role of primary breadwinner for the family. This left a lasting impression on Shirley that she would carry with her on her journey through life. At age six, Shirley was already working—wanting to help out the family and not wanting her mother or other members of her family to pay for things she wanted or needed. This early mindset of self-sufficiency molded her philosophy that "when opportunity knocks—don't just accept it, but learn everything about it."

As a young girl and as a teenager, when not doing farm work, Shirley adopted her mother's multifaceted work ethic and earned money through various jobs: babysitting, driving a school bus, waitressing at restaurants after school and on weekends, and working at a local pantyhose factory. The overarching lesson she gained from her farm experience was that *she did not want to stay on the farm.* Having picked cotton all day for as little as $2, Shirley concluded that farm work was just too hard!

EDUCATION

Shirley was first in her family to attend a four-year college. At North Carolina Central University (NCCU), she earned a Bachelor of Science degree in home economics, with an emphasis in clothing and textiles. She then turned her attention to graduate school. Cornell University was interested in increasing its minority enrollment and recruited Shirley. She was interested in a career in high fashion design and wanted to pursue that major at Cornell. Shortly after being accepted, she discovered that a degree in high fashion was not offered; instead she could pursue a degree in functional apparel design. Although it wasn't exactly what she wanted, functional apparel design had a broader impact than high fashion, preparing its majors beyond couture design to such mass audience functions as uniforms for firefighters and athletic teams. For a resourceful girl who, out of necessity, grew up designing and sewing most of her own clothes, Shirley concluded that functional apparel would still provide design opportunities to use in preparing for her career. With the prestige of attending Cornell and not wanting to disappoint her family, Shirley decided that functional apparel design and a Cornell degree would be an "acceptable" educational choice.

Shirley found graduate school more challenging than she expected. For one, she was the only African American student in her classes. In fact, among some 30 graduate students in the College of Design and Environmental Analysis, there were only two other students who identified as minorities— both male, one Asian and one Jewish. During that first semester, those guys became Shirley's school family. The trio would hang out together and share the miseries and triumphs of their semester in graduate school.

Being in the minority wasn't the only challenge that first semester. Shirley was not doing well on class tests. She had always done very well in under-graduate studies and had graduated cum laude from NCCU. As an undergraduate, she prepared for exams by methodically taking notes on her readings and course lectures, making audio tapes of her notes to use as study guides, and committing great amounts of material to memory. At Cornell, though, her study preparation approach was not working and she performed poorly on her first few tests in design classes. This failure concerned her to the point that she considered withdrawing from Cornell. She even wrote home asking if it would be all right if she left school. Fortunately, before she made the decision to leave, a female faculty member invited her to lunch and talked with Shirley about her test performance. The professor quizzed Shirley on the test material and found that Shirley knew the information but that her ability to think about how to answer the questions needed development. At the faculty member's suggestion, Shirley joined a study group to learn more effective study methods, including orally reviewing lessons before the group. With the study-group experience and mentoring from the professor, Shirley altered her study habits, began doing well in her classes, and changed her mind about leaving Cornell.

Shirley went on to complete an MS from Cornell University, with a major in apparel design and a minor in human relations and public policy. From there, she enrolled at the University of Maryland, College Park (UMCP) and earned a PhD, with an emphasis on education policy, planning, and administration. She later returned to UMCP to complete and receive a doctoral certificate in gerontology.

Out of college, Shirley began her professional career as a fashion-buyer intern/assistant buyer and department store manager for Hecht's (now Macy's). Shirley worked closely with all levels of the retail operation, including department managers, store managers, buyers, divisional merchandise managers, and general merchandise managers. Her work with Hecht's ranged from domestics to women's apparel and provided a foundation for her knowledge about fashion buying, merchandising, and advertising that she later incorporated into the fashion merchandising program she established at the University of Maryland Eastern Shore (UMES).

EDUCATIONAL CAREER

Shirley has served in a variety of educational positions. At the time of this writing, she serves as interim dean, College of Agriculture and Environmental Sciences (CAES) at North Carolina A&T (NCAT) University, having previously served CAES as associate dean for research. At the UMES (Princess Anne campus), Shirley was professor and chair, Department of Human Ecology; associate research director—1890 programs, School of Agricultural and Natural Sciences; associate professor, Department of Human Ecology; assistant professor, Department of Human Ecology; and fashion merchandising program coordinator/lecturer, Department of Human Ecology. At Hood College, she served as instructor for the home economics department.

In her first academic position, Shirley joined UMES as a lecturer in the fashion merchandising program. She was soon charged with developing the fashion merchandising program and was named the program's coordinator. In 1987, Shirley left UMES to start a family and began teaching in the home economics department at Hood College in Frederick, Maryland. There she served as an instructor, teaching retail buying, advertising, and promotion courses. A year later she returned to UMES to resume her career and advanced through the ranks.

TEACHING

The courses Shirley has taught cover a range of topics that include fashion merchandising and design; fashion illustration; research methods; social psychology of food, clothing, and shelter; supervisory management; human development; and family and consumer sciences (FCS) teacher education.

She also has had a keen interest in developing technology in the classroom as a teaching aid, and in connecting to the classroom through distance learning. Shirley has been a strong advocate for technology as a medium for instruction, learning, and connection.

While at UMES, Shirley established a project to teach merchandising through funding from a USDA 1890 Capacity Building Grant. The project, a student-operated campus-based retail boutique called "The University Shoppe," specialized in selling such college-themed merchandise as clothing, jewelry, paintings, and ceramics. It included products designed and crafted by students and artisans from the local community. Fashion merchandising students were responsible for completing the operational aspects of the store, including selecting and managing inventory, advertising, pricing, and sales. Interior design students were tasked with designing the boutique space and completing minor renovations with assistance from campus facilities staff. The store continues to operate 19 years later as a student-run enterprise.

A few years later, Shirley had her fashion buying and merchandising class renovate the thrift store at MAC Inc. Area Agency on Aging in Princess Anne, Maryland. The students transformed a damp, dreary basement strewn with stacks of clothing into an elegant, brightly painted, and organized boutique filled with stylish clothing, shoes, and accessories. Supported with donated materials from local merchants, the boutique continues to thrive.

RESEARCH

Her research interests have included reducing the incidence of obesity among children in childcare centers, enhancing economic development of rural communities through the establishment of small businesses, improving fashion retail to better prepare students for employment, the role of minorities in fashion merchandising and textiles, the effectiveness of existing fashion merchandising curriculums in preparing students for entry-level management positions in retail, and the quality of well-being of the rural southern elderly. Shirley's approach to research has always been to focus on unaddressed needs in her department/school, the profession, and the community. For example, she pursued fashion merchandising and child development program grants to advance new curriculum, support the training of professionals in these disciplines, and expand experiential learning experiences for students. Her undergraduate research grants were written to prepare students for graduate studies and to provide training in conducting research. Rural entrepreneurship grants were written to provide business training for women and minorities on the Eastern Shore of Maryland. In sum, her research interests and efforts have followed a path of building capacity for others.

ADMINISTRATIVE EXPERIENCE

Early in her tenure at UMES, Shirley developed a strong interest in administration and realized that she possessed many of the skills and traits necessary to be an effective administrator. This revelation of managerial aptitude inspired her to shift her career focus to higher education administration, through which she has enjoyed great success and accomplishment.

As a young interim department chair at UMES, Shirley had the opportunity to attend a weeklong training seminar for new agricultural college administrators and department chairs. When Shirley got to the seminar, once again she found that she was the only African American among about 20 other trainees. By the end of the first day, she got the distinct impression that one of the trainers did not think she belonged to the workshop. During a number of interactive sessions, the trainer never called on Shirley to participate or share her responses to activities. Despite her efforts to be called on or to provide input, the session leader chose to ignore her or cut her off. This bothered her. She knew she was qualified to be at the session, as did her fellow trainees. They encouraged Shirley to share her ideas from group sessions despite the trainer's avoidance of her contributions. This experience taught Shirley to respect her own abilities and to find and use her voice even when others didn't want to hear it.

As an administrator at UMES, Shirley was instrumental in developing two distance education programs. One was the 2+2 child development program offered at Chesapeake Community College (75 miles away). The program targeted nontraditional students who work full time and complete their degrees via distance education. The program received the 2006 ADEC Webb-Godfrey-Hill Excellence in Distance Education Award. The second program involved hosting professional classes at the Baltimore Museum of Industry for FCS teachers that needed FCS courses for teacher certification.

ACADEMIC PROGRAM DEVELOPMENT

During Shirley's 26 years at UMES, she developed several academic programs that increased the university's visibility and enrollment. These academic offerings included the study abroad program in collaboration with the London College of Fashion, and the Fashion Institute of Technology's (FIT) Visiting Student Program (VSP). FIT-VSP was among the more popular programs for fashion merchandising students, as it was a dual degree program in advertising and marketing communications established in collaboration with the FIT in New York City. This program afforded eligible students an opportunity to spend one year in New York at FIT to obtain a second degree (AAS) in advertising and marketing communications.

The study abroad program enabled fashion students to engage in two-week study tours to Paris and London, and/or an eight-week summer study abroad program in London in conjunction with the London College of Fashion. In both programs, Shirley worked closely with the university's registrar, financial aid, and business offices to reduce the financial burden and ensure a smooth transition on- and off-campus for students participating in these programs. She also developed detailed guidebooks and websites to aid university administrators, students, parents, and faculty in understanding and navigating enrollment in these programs.

These programs' origins owe much to Shirley's creativity and tenacity as that "one person in the room." Princess Anne, where UMES is located, is a small seaside town on Maryland's Eastern Shore. To provide fashion merchandising experience, Shirley needed to find stores for students to learn retail, marketing, and consumer behavior. At the time Shirley was trying to develop the fashion program, there were no major stores or a mall in Princess Anne. The closest town with some fashion merchandising internship opportunities was in Salisbury, 14 miles away. Shirley looked in Salisbury for businesses to offer intern experiences for her students, but she also looked across the bay to Washington, D.C., and Alexandria, Virginia; and northbound to Philadelphia, Pennsylvania and New York. She soon identified and arranged for many retail and merchandising experiences for her students.

As Shirley sought to develop an exciting and competitive fashion program at UMES, she was referred to a professor at FIT—Alfred Sloan. Shirley told him of her vision and plans for the UMES fashion program and sought his experience to help get the program on the right track. He was willing to help develop the potential of the program and came for a visit. He apparently liked what he saw. In a few short years, UMES had a program relationship with FIT, with a small group of UMES students enrolling annually for a year of study at FIT and graduating UMES with two degrees—an associate of arts degree in advertising and marketing communications from FIT, and a bachelor of science degree in fashion merchandising from UMES.

Shirley was also responsible for leading the reorganization of the child development program at UMES, which became the second largest enrolled program in the department. Initially, UMES and Salisbury State University were interested in a joint child development program, enabling students attending either institution to earn a degree on either a teacher education or nonteacher education track. The curriculum development and course negotiations took more than two years. After a plan had been worked out, final approval was not granted by the Maryland Higher Education Commission. Salisbury State, which had a special education degree program, decided to implement the early childhood education track. Meanwhile, UMES faculty turned their attention to the child development, nonteacher certification track. This renewed program focus led to the successful development of a model childcare laboratory. Courses connected to Title III and Department of Health and Human Services grant-funded programs were also transformed to support two permanent child development faculty.

Shirley also provided leadership in developing a doctoral program in food science and technology at UMES—the only one of its kind in the state and the only one at an 1890 land-grant institution. The program was considered so vital to the region and campus that a new $16 million building was built to house it. Other academic-related program activities included coordinating and conducting numerous fashion study tours (including Europe) and field trips, identifying and supervising student internship sites, and establishing and operating two student-centered businesses on campus that provided opportunities for students to get hands-on experience.

Shirley has been a strong advocate of service learning, and for the development of research and scholarship skills among undergraduates. When she was a young graduate student at Cornell University, she recalled being very unprepared for conducting graduate-level research. She hadn't received instruction on the basics of research nor on how to conduct and write a research study. Believing that promising undergraduate students should not enter graduate school without foundational experience, Shirley, as an UMES administrator, partnered with administrators and faculty from Kansas State, Michigan, and Kappa Omicron Nu honor society to apply for a USDA Challenge Grant to support an undergraduate research program. The application was not funded, but Shirley was undeterred, later writing a USDA 1890 Capacity Building Grant that was accepted to establish an undergraduate research program in the Department of Human Ecology at UMES.

Shirley carried this vision to NCAT, and within a year after joining the university as the associate dean for research in the School of Agriculture and Environmental Sciences (SAES), Shirley and a committee of four faculty members established the Undergraduate Research Scholars Program (URSP) in 2010. This structured, formalized program was the first of its kind at the university. It was created to provide select groups of rising juniors and seniors with the opportunity to learn the research process through a multilayered intensive research course. Scholars develop and implement a research project, present findings, develop potential manuscripts for publication, and participate in a series of monthly seminars focused on research processes. Since Shirley joined NCAT, she has championed funding and proposals to expand opportunities for undergraduate research and to establish the SAES URSP.

RECOGNITION OF SCHOLARSHIP AND
SERVICE TO THE PROFESSION

Shirley's achievements have been widely recognized. In 1984 and again in 1986, she was recognized as an Outstanding Young Woman of America. The award honors the remarkable accomplishments of women and their achievements—past and present—in their homes, communities, and professions that positively contribute to a better America.

In 1994, she received the University of Maryland Eastern Shore Chancellor's Teacher Scholar Award, followed in 1996 by the Outstanding Teacher Award presented by the UMES Alumni Association. In 1997, she received NCCU's Department of Human Sciences Outstanding Alumni Award, recognizing outstanding alumni achievement and leadership. That same year she was presented the Home Economist of the Year Award by the Maryland Association of Family and Consumer Sciences. Recipients of this award are recognized for exemplary service and creative endeavors as a FCS educator.

In 2006, she received the ADEC-Webb-Godfrey-Hill Distance Education Award of Excellence, recognizing excellence, innovation, and impact in distance education programs. Then, in 2010, the American Association of Family and Consumer Sciences presented Shirley with Distinguished Service Award. The award recognizes a member's superior achievements in FCS and outstanding contributions to the FCS profession.

PROFESSIONAL ACHIEVEMENTS

Shirley has authored or coauthored 31 peer-reviewed journal articles and book chapters and has been a contributing author to several educational textbooks, handbooks, monographs, newsletters, proceedings, and technical reports.

Her work as a FCS administrator led to the reestablishment of a child and family development lab school to support the UMES child and family development program. She also engaged her first-year experience class (HUEC 100) students in implementation of an after-school program for students in grades 1–5 at the Seton Center in Princess Anne, Maryland (1999). Shirley has been actively involved in planning and advisory boards:

- Agricultural Development Farmland Prevention Trust Fund advisory committee
- NC Agromedicine Institute board of directors
- NC Biotechnology Center advisory council

- Association of Public and Land-Grant Universities: board on agriculture assembly, policy board of directors (member and secretary), experiment station section, and experiment station committee on policy
- 1890 Association of Research Directors: chair, director-at-large, and 13th Biennial Research Symposium cochair
- American Association of Family and Consumer Sciences: board of directors (director-at-large), higher education unit (chair and nominating committee chair), annual conference committee, and annual conference committee task force
- Board on Human Sciences board of directors
- National Coalition for Black Development in Family and Consumer Sciences: vice president, membership committee chair, fellowship and grants committee chair
- 1890 Council of Administrators of Family and Consumer Sciences secretary and treasurer

Consistent with her philosophy of taking advantage of opportunities, she has been willing, more than once, to be the only woman, the only African American, or the only African American woman to serve on a board or a committee. She takes great pride in doing this and encouraging other minority women to follow her lead.

SHIRLEY'S HUSBAND AND FAMILY

Shirley is married to Eugene (Gene) Parker of Berlin, Maryland. They have two adult children: daughter Jocelyn and son Alex. Gene and the children have been Shirley's greatest advocates and supporters. Gene, who had a long career in law enforcement and was a police captain, also took on the household chores while Shirley worked on her doctorate and traveled for work. They were always there to cheer her on and let her know how proud they were of her work.

Gene and Shirley grew up in large families where hard work was the norm, but never at the cost of getting the best possible education. Shirley set lofty goals for herself and as she reached one milestone, new opportunities continued to emerge and she was encouraged by her family to pursue them. She did.

Although she often felt throughout her career that she was the "only one in the room" in the physical sense, she never was. Shirley always knew that she had spiritual and emotional support from God, her family, supervisors, and colleagues. They listened to her, encouraged her, cried with her, cheered her on, and reminded her that she could not only achieve, but excel. She feels that she is who she is because of her life experiences and the people who loved her—especially her mother, Theresa Hyman, her greatest mentor. Theresa Hyman never worked fewer than three jobs at any one point in her life, including work as a farmer, café manager, cook, caterer, domestic, eldercare provider, and factory worker. Shirley learned her work ethic, people skills, kindness, and passion for the work she wanted to do in life from her greatest inspiration, her mother.

REFERENCE

Hymon-Parker, Shirley. 1999. "Establishment of an Interdisciplinary Collaborative Degree Program in Early Childhood Studies." In *Serving Children and Families Through Community-University Partnerships: Success Stories*, edited by Chibucos, Thomas R., and Richard M. Lerner, 139–142. Springer, Boston, MA.

Part V

TECHNOLOGY

WAVE OF THE PRESENT AND FUTURE

Technology has provided some amazing experiences in and out of the classroom. As family and consumer sciences professionals, we seek to prepare students to fill multiple current and future roles as individuals, family members, and community members within a diverse global society. Through the use of technology, we prepare students to balance work and family life and to manage the challenges of living and working in a technological society. This section offers examples of research, along with inspiration to enhance student learning through technology

Chapter 18 introduces a conceptual model for thinking about family engagement with media and the role media plays in shaping children's lives.

Chapter 19 shares what has worked for one school system, and for family and consumer science teachers as they increase the use of technology in secondary classrooms.

Chapter 18

Media, Technology, and the Family

Exploring the "CASIE" Model of Media Use in Youth Development

Lacey J. Hilliard, Danielle C. Stacey, AnneMarie McClain, Milena Batanova, and Richard M. Lerner

INTRODUCTION

This chapter introduces a conceptual model for thinking about ways that families can engage with media, and the role media plays as a context for shaping children's lives.[1] In doing so, the authors describe myriad opportunities for families to optimize media use and promote positive development, as they underscore the need for adults and youth to be critical media consumers. Through this discussion, the authors describe the practical applications of a theoretical grounding in relational developmental science and discuss implications for future work in developmental science and media development.

Computers are useless. They can only give you answers. (Pablo Picasso)

As developmental scientists, we approach the role of media and technology in the home through a relational developmental lens, meaning that the most important aspects of a new gadget are the *how* and the *why*; for example, how is it used, and why? How and why do users relate to digital devices, and do these relations between individuals and media/technology impact their development? Are other relations affected by a person's interactions with media/technology? For instance, does a child's engagement with media affect her relationship with her parents? If so, does this impact change the course of the parent-child relationship and/or the development of either the parent or the child? Are relationships between parent and child occurring while using a device related to other instances of their exchanges with each other?

There is currently little research to answer these questions about media/
technology engagement, parent-child relations, and child development (Bers
and Kazakoff 2013; Calvert 2015). This absence of systematic research
highlights the salience of Picasso's seemingly enigmatic epigram quoted
above. That is, one can think about media/technology and their content as
inadequate for elucidating human development, unless the study of such
devices is coupled with research that seeks to understand coactions between
the person and the device, along with users' relationships and the reasons
for them. Therefore, the real potential of experiencing media/technology
lies in the *how* and *why*, in understanding how and why media/technology
impacts human development. It also lies in advancing knowledge about the
relationship between a person and her media/technology context, and among
the people within this context, as—together—these links shape the course of
human development (Overton 2015).

This chapter introduces an organizing framework for thinking about the
ways in which families can engage with media, and the role that media plays
as a context for shaping children's lives. This discussion will describe opportunities for families to optimize media/technology use and promote positive
development and will underscore the need for media-literate adults and youth
(i.e., those who are able to recognize and evaluate the complex messages we
receive via media; Livingstone 2004). First will be a description of the theoretical approach used, followed by a discussion of the ways this theoretical
approach applies to the context of media/technology (especially within the
family and parent-child relations). The chapter then moves to a model for
media and technology engagement in the home and concludes with recommendations for future research and application.

A THEORETICAL APPROACH TO UNDERSTANDING
MEDIA/TECHNOLOGY AND HUMAN DEVELOPMENT

Contemporary developmental science involves the description, explanation, and optimization of within person change, and of between-person
differences in within-person change across the life span (Baltes, Reese,
and Nesselroade 1977; Lerner 2012). Today, the cutting edge of theory in
developmental science involves the use of the relational developmental systems (RDS) metatheory to devise and test models that link youth, families,
communities, and the broader ecology of human development, including
media/technology. RDS metatheory emphasizes that human development
occurs within a system involving an integration of levels of organization,
from biology/physiology through culture, the physical ecology, and history
(Overton 2015). The key ideas in RDS metatheory involve the view that

development across life involves mutually influential individual context relations; these relations constitute the basic unit of analysis within human development.

Of course, individual relationships are one (key) instance of individual context relations. In other words, other people are key parts of the context of human development. Moreover, because all relations within the developmental system are embedded in history (i.e., the arrow of time, temporality, runs through all levels and relations within the system), the potential for change (either stochastic or systematic) is ubiquitous. The potential for change is a critical part of the developmental system. As such, the possibility of at least some systematic change in individual context relations, of what may be termed *plasticity*, means that one can be optimistic that the application of developmental science (through programs and policies) can promote positive human development and further social justice.

Plasticity in the RDS has an impact of both traditional features of human development (such as parent-child relations or family socializing practices), as well as recently emerged features of the ecology of human development (such as the enormous growth of electronic media in the lives of children and families). As such, policies or programs aimed at promoting positive development for diverse individuals and families may be appropriate targets for innovation. Accordingly, the RDS metamodel may be a useful frame for describing, explaining, and optimizing the impact of media and technology on the lives of children and families. This chapter presents a model drawn from RDS metatheory to provide a means to make these contributions to developmental science and its application.

INTRODUCING THE CASIE MODEL

The authors contend that these contributions are timely due to the ubiquity of media in the lives of children and families. The contemporary life of youth and families is marked by an unprecedented growth in the presence of electronic media (Bers 2012; Bers and Kazakoff 2013). Children have become media consumers and technology users at very early ages (Center on Media and Child Health 2005; Gutnick et al. 2011; Rideout and Hamel 2006) and spend more time with digital media today than with any other waking activity (Roberts and Foehr 2008). However, there is little research about how the new digital landscape might impact the positive development of youth, and why some youth may use certain media in more beneficial or adaptive ways than others. There is thus an absence of a strong evidence base to use in advising parents about how to promote positive outcomes from their children's media/technology use.

To help move toward the creation of information pertinent to the potential impact of media/technology on the development of child-parent relationships, and on human development more generally, the authors introduce the CASIE model of media use. This model capitalizes on both the individual context and the individual facets of the developmental system, as depicted within the RDS metamodel. That is, from an RDS-based perspective, youth and families may engage with media/technology by using it to establish or maintain social relationships, or to communicate or connect with others (C); activate (urge, impel) others to behave (A); serve the interests of self or others, including social movements or institutions (S); inform others of a knowledge- or evidence-base, or persuade them through opinion or argumentation (I); or (of course) to entertain media viewers (E). Each component of the model may provide instances of individual use and exploration as well as engagement with family members.

Examples of these CASIE model components draw both from the literature of child, adolescent, and family development in general, and from past and ongoing research. This review facilitates conclusions about how parents may be involved with the media engagement domains described by the CASIE model. For instance, parents must be critical consumers of media and must enhance their own media literacy, defined as the ability to access, analyze, and engage in critical thinking about media messages to make informed decisions about issues relevant to their lives (Hobbs 2010). Such media literacy helps them to model and mentor comparable knowledge and skills in their children.

THE ROLE OF THE FAMILY IN MEDIA USE

The following sections discuss the relevance and importance of media and technology across all families, highlight challenges involved with ubiquitous media and technology use, and provide ideas for addressing such challenges. Each component of the CASIE model is described, accompanied throughout by details and examples that are drawn from previous research and the authors' ongoing studies.

MEDIA USE BY CHILDREN AND FAMILIES

New media/technology platforms are developed and dispersed quickly, such that it is difficult for experts and researchers to offer relevant research-grounded recommendations or guidelines (Takeuchi 2011). Rideout et al. (2013) notes a jump in young children's reading on mobile devices (30%, up from 4% in 2011). However, children spend less time reading or being read to on these devices than they do with other activities. For example, television is still the dominant medium for children aged eight years and under. According to a nationally representative survey by Common Sense Media in 2013, 58% of children watch TV at least once a day, 17% use mobile devices, 14% use computers, and 6% play video games, all at least once a day (Rideout et al. 2013). Of course, these trends are changing rapidly and, as such, it is imperative that researchers and educators provide guiding principles that can transcend the changing landscape of mobile applications (apps), online games, interactive media, and creative media content.

Researchers have previously discovered that parents and caregivers who coview television programming with their children can help guide children's attention to the salient features of any given show (e.g., Reiser, Tessmer, and Phelps 1984; Reiser, Williamson, and Suzuki 1988). As the current landscape of television viewing is constantly shifting, more platforms deliver media into homes than ever before and children are often engaged with media by themselves, at earlier ages, and for longer periods of time (Takeuchi 2011). Thus, the crux of the way in which coviewing experiences apply must be adapted to these new digital settings. The Learning in Informal and Formal Environments Center coined the term "joint media engagement" to extend the notion of coviewing beyond watching television to more broadly describe what happens when people learn together with media across a variety of settings (see life-slc.org/).

Due in large part to lower costs of devices, household ownership of technological devices is now comparable between lower-income and minority families and middle- to upper-class and White families (Rideout et al. 2013; Livingston 2011). The vast majority of 8- to 18-year-olds have a computer at home, regardless of race or parent education. Eighty-seven percent of parents with no more than a high school education, and 97% of parents with a college degree, own a computer (Rideout, Foehr, and Roberts 2010). Regardless of whether they come from one or two-parent households and independent of their parents' education levels, however, there are differences in the media use of 8- to 18-year-old Black, Hispanic, and White children. White children engage in approximately 8.5 hours of daily media use, whereas Black and Hispanic children have been found to spend 13 hours with media (Rideout, Foehr, and Roberts 2010).

The increase in affordable digital technologies offers new opportunities to coengage children and parents—especially those from underserved populations—with high-quality educational content. However, equity concerns persist for reasons that transcend mere access to these tools. This "participation gap" reflects the differential use of education media (Jenkins et al. 2009; Neuman and Celano 2012; Watkins 2011). For instance, one report showed that 35% of lower-income parents of children ages 0–8 have downloaded educational mobile apps, as compared to 75% of higher-income parents (Rideout et al. 2013). Furthermore, the degree or extent to which such apps and other education media are used by parents and their children together (i.e., joint media engagement) is largely unknown. Therefore, it is important for experts studying, developing, and promoting digital tools to consider strategies to close the participation gap, and further, to ensure that the educational media content provides relevant, enriching, and developmentally appropriate material for families, some or much of which may also be used through joint engagement.

THE CASIE MODEL OF MEDIA USE

As previously noted, there are five key facets of media use included in the CASIE model. These facets reflect five principal ways in which media is used to communicate or connect, activate others to act, serve other communities, inform others or provide information, and entertain. Each of these categories can be experienced through joint media engagement, and in turn, how shared media experiences influence—and are influenced by—individual (e.g., children's social and emotional well-being, character development, and media literacy) and contextual (e.g., family relationships, home environment) factors. Embedded in the *how* is also exploring the *why*, or why the processes of influence operate in the ways that they do.

The impact of parent facilitation and/or parent-child shared media use in regard to the five facets of the CASIE model may impact both the attributes of the individual (the child and/or the parent) and the family or broader contextual variables. As these influences evolve across time, they may be part of a feedback loop to influence subsequent media use. Thus, individuals and their contexts are part of an ongoing bidirectional system that reflects recursive relations within the RDS.

Communicate or connect. The first domain of media use involves communicating or connecting with others. Examples of this domain include using platforms to video-chat with family and friends (e.g., Skype or FaceTime) and sharing experiences through social media platforms (e.g., Facebook, Instagram, or Twitter). Media use in this domain can increase participation with others through new online communities, offer enhanced maintenance of preexisting communities, and promote opportunities for joint media engagement and adult mentoring to a wider, more geographically diverse network of communities, thereby exposing youth to diverse points of view (Kahne et al. 2012). Most youth use online networks to extend the friendships that they navigate in the familiar contexts of school, religious organizations, sports, and other local activities (Boyd 2014). They can be "always on," in constant contact with their friends via texting and social networking sites, supported by widely available high-speed broadband internet connections. The majority of youth use new media to "hang out" and extend existing friendships (Ito et al. 2009).

Social media use has permeated childhood and adolescence, and these online connections are integral to the social lives of youth. The number of social media site users more than doubled from 33% of the online population in 2008 to 69% of the online population in 2012 (Smith 2013). Through online interaction with others, social media use can help contribute to competence by providing a platform that promotes discussion and the production of media content relevant to important positive relationships. For instance, multiplayer online role-playing games, Facebook events, blogging platforms, and video sharing sites all offer new platforms for users to actively participate, collaborate with, and help other individuals in a variety of ways (Thackery and Hunter 2010).

Due to the nature of this type of media engagement, it may be difficult for parents to engage with youth—particularly older youth—about their online activities. By establishing open communication about access, time spent, and the nature of online communications, parents can guide children to connect to others through social media in positive ways. Furthermore, parents can evaluate their own behaviors and the literal and metaphorical messages they send to their children in the ways they connect with others online. Models of appropriate media use have generally referred to demonstrating a healthy media diet by balancing online digital communication and media consumption with face-to-face activities with peers (Hiniker et al 2015; Livingstone and Helsper 2009; Thoman and Jolls 2005). Parents can also model appropriate media use by encouraging responsibility, safety, and positive connection online, while engaging in and encouraging their own offline conversations.

Activate. The second CASIE domain involves urging or impelling others to behave. Examples of this domain include using digital platforms to promote involvement in politics and activism, and to increase attention to and awareness of issues all over the world. Media literacy helps contribute to knowledge-building and promotes competence in one's ability to understand, analyze, and produce media content. News media use is an example of how media activates consumers and is especially effective in promoting political awareness (Pasek et al. 2006). Youth who watch news on television, or read newspapers in school or at home, demonstrate higher civic knowledge. Joint engagement with the news and subsequent discussions with parents could be a possible explanation for this increased knowledge (Amadeo, Torney-Purta, and Barber 2004).

Adults and youth are engaging in online activism (or cyber activism), which is the process of using internet-based communication and socializing techniques to create, manage, or promote citizen-based movements to generate awareness, protest, or promote a certain goal or cause (McCaughey and Ayers 2013). In his text on critical literacy, Morrell (2015) describes two instances in which communities of youth engaged in such activism toward a larger social movement; specifically, youth organizing and mobilizing in revolt of the Zapatista Liberation Army in Mexico, and the successful movements to disrupt World Trade Organization meetings in Seattle in the late 1990s. In both examples, Morrell describes the creativity, leadership, and fervor with which youth used social networks and online technologies to affect change. More contemporary examples include campaigns to challenge the ways in which toy companies use gender stereotypes to package and sell products (Turbett 2012) and a group of young people known as the DREAMers, who have formed an online (and offline) community to advocate for undocumented immigrant youth rights (Nicholls 2013). The Arab Spring is also an ideal example of how and why digital technologies and social media can be used to activate social change. Known as a revolutionary wave of protests and demonstrations that began in Tunisia in 2010 and quickly spread around the Arab world, the Arab Spring became a movement largely founded on youth using social media like Facebook and Twitter to share their voices and concerns with their oppressive institutions (Gerbaudo 2012).

Participating in online activism involves many steps: learning about the issue, identifying the stakeholders and barriers, feeling compelled toward action, understanding possible action steps to enact change, navigating digital platforms to promote an idea or cause, and persisting in getting the word out. All these steps necessitate scaffolding, encouragement, and instrumental assistance (e.g., getting access to information or the devices to organize). Parents can be a critical asset to helping youth navigate these issues or can work alongside their children to learn the skills together.

Serve. The third domain of the CASIE model involves serving the interests of self or others, including social movements or institutions. Examples of serving through media use involve the discovery of and participation in volunteerism and community events. Although many parents, educators, and researchers have argued that social media use is leading to a narcissistic and self-centered society, some activities prompted by social media use have been found to increase empathy in users (Kahne, Lee, and Feezell 2010). Activity fostered by media use may also translate to real-world action. For instance, in a recent study of social media use and political action, higher online sharing and trust were associated with greater offline intent to participate in political activities (Kweon and Lee 2013). By taking on roles of media content production and media consumption, therefore, youth can use their contextual resources to provide service to others. Parents can model ways in which they serve their communities and help others via media/technology, and can help their children to find ways to engage in positive participation online.

Inform. The fourth use of media in the CASIE model is to inform others of a knowledge- or evidence-base, or to persuade others through opinion or argumentation. Examples of this domain include using media to seek information about life skills, health and safety, child development milestones, and educational topics. Research has shown that children who use educational media learn more in the short term (Penuel et al. 2009) and do better in school later on compared to children who do not use educational media (Anderson et al. 2001).

The authors' work at the Institute for Applied Research in Youth Development (Tufts University) serve as examples of educational media that provides tools to promote growth in knowledge and engage discussion about challenging topics. It should be noted that, while the two projects described below may also serve as examples of media being used to communicate or connect (and even to activate), the authors posit that they best exemplify the *Inform* aspect of the CASIE model.

The first example is the Arthur Interactive Media Buddy Project, a media-based program designed to promote character development and social and emotional well-being in elementary school students (see Batanova et al. 2016 and Bowers et al. 2015 for discussion and findings based on the initial pilot work). The program uses cross-grade buddies and interactive technology (such as online games and comics) based on the television series *Arthur* to help students explore multiple perspectives and situations, discuss difficult topics, and consider the impact or consequences of different decisions on individuals' feelings and behaviors.

The second example is the *Quandary* Game study (Hilliard et. al 2018). *Quandary* is an online game that engages middle-school-aged students in ethical decision-making and supports the development of skills that will help students to recognize ethical issues and deal with challenging situations in their own lives. The project involved having adolescents play *Quandary* episodes and discuss topics that arose from the game play. Researchers then assessed the potential impact of watching the episodes on moral thinking and the ability to take the perspective of others.

The digital tools exemplified by the Arthur interactive features and the *Quandary* video game were designed and tested within a school-based setting; however, the content and purpose of the products are to spur conversations about difficult topics, such as having empathy for others, forgiving someone when they have upset you, and making decisions that involve varying consequences for other individuals (e.g., making a decision when you cannot make everyone happy). The games are designed with moral-, social-, and character-building facets in mind but, in returning to the opening points of this chapter, the tools alone are not enough to foster these attributes. Instead, relational factors are the keys to success with digital tools. For instance, how do children interact with these games and comics? How can others (older youth, parents, other adults) help children navigate difficult topics?

There are, notably, many similar technology-based tools available for youth and families. One needs only to search for "educational games" on the internet or in an online app store to see the myriad of available content. In addition, there are many online tutorials created to provide information on a topic. It is important for educators and media experts to consider developmental science when creating such digital products. For example, how might children's developmental capacities affect the engagement and effectiveness of an educational game? What role should parents play in scaffolding difficult topics? How can this be fostered within the media/technology itself?

Entertain. The final CASIE domain of media use is perhaps the most ubiquitous. Entertainment through media use includes watching television shows or movies, browsing websites, engaging with apps, reading for enjoyment on an electronic reader, and playing video games.

Research shows that the nature of parent-child entertainment media is ever-changing alongside the landscape of new media. Children engage with media/technology in new ways, and through platforms their parents had no access to growing up. As such, Takeuchi (2011) noted that there is less intergenerational play within families of young children and adolescents. In the recent Common Sense report mentioned earlier (Rideout et al. 2013), parents with children aged 3–10 years reported that among all activities they enjoy doing with their children, watching television was the most often cited (89% of parents in the study's sample), then reading books (79%), followed by playing board games (73%). The high ratings for these activities, when compared with children's daily use of media/technology (such as using apps and playing video games), indicate that parents may not be capitalizing on opportunities to engage with their children using the digital activities their children most seek out.

This research in contemporary media uses has implications for both producers and consumers of entertainment media. How can one capitalize on children's interests to foster shared media use? By seeking out opportunities to engage with their children by playing or learning alongside them, parents can show support, care, and interest in their children's media/technology interests. In fact, research also demonstrated that using educational media with adult guidance leads to greater learning than if used alone (Koolstra and Lucassen 2004; Reiser, Tessmer, and Phelps 1984).

Are there ways to create entertainment media that encourage adaptive relational processes between parents and children? As researchers, how can we examine the role of shared attentional focus on media as a catalyst for positive development? The following section provides some evidence for the pathways of the CASIE model and highlights areas that necessitate further study.

RECOMMENDATIONS FOR FUTURE RESEARCH

The goal of this chapter was to propose a model of media use within the family that is based on tenets of relational developmental science metatheory (Overton 2015). This model conceptualizes the ways in which family media engagement can optimize individual development and family relationships. The authors assert that media can be used to connect and communicate, activate, serve, inform, and entertain, and that all of these uses can help to promote positive development and family relationships through joint engagement between parents and children.

The authors stress that the goal in developing this model of media use is to spur related research. Each aspect of the model should be evaluated empirically with children and parents from a broad range of ages, social groups, and backgrounds. Future research should also examine whether and how the components of the model interact with one another (e.g., how do parents differentially approach joint media engagement by means of using media for entertainment but also connection? Are different contexts more conducive to engaging conversations?). Undoubtedly, there are additional individual differences and situational factors that affect how parents approach media use with their children in particular settings.

Based on the authors' research and the myriad examples of important work cited in this chapter, it is evident that parents must be critical consumers of media and enhance their digital literacy if they are to model and mentor comparable knowledge and skills in their children. In the context of enhanced digital literacy, and as effective models and mentors, parents should appraise their children's media use and seek ways to positively engage all instances of these media (as in the CASIE model) in the lives of their children. Parents should identify positive content in media to enhance communication with their children about difficult topics or developmental challenges, for example, coping with or responding to students who bully, rejecting negative portrayals of diverse individuals or groups, and gaining the skills needed to live positively in a world marked by diverse people and cultures.

Resources for families also need to be created and disseminated in manners that recognize and fit the diversity of parents and their media use. Educators, researchers, and digital designers should aim to adapt a model that embraces such diversity in the ecology of families and in their media use. Core issues that remain to be addressed involve media developers (e.g., what are ways to develop and adopt media that promote the relational processes between parents and children?) and researchers (e.g., how can we further examine the role of joint media engagement on the parent, child, and family?). Specifically, how and why do specific types of media use provide catalysts for positive youth development and family relationships among specific groups of people, and under what circumstances and channels are they most effective and most beneficial to diverse families?

CONCLUSIONS

We live in a society wherein media and technology are becoming not only ubiquitous, but highly salient contexts for human development. Indeed, in the world's youngest generations, the media/technology context may be the one in which they spend most of their waking hours, both in and out of school. Our challenge as developmental scientists (and as parents, mentors, and citizens) is to maximize the opportunities for positive exchanges with media and technology, and to thereby assume that this salient and seemingly ever-growing setting for youth and families will provide burgeoning opportunities for thriving and healthy development in diverse people of our nation and world.

Research and applications aimed at this vision of a positive role for media and technology may be usefully framed by the model presented in this chapter. However, other models of youth and parent relationships with media/technology should be created and tested. In this way, future cohorts of developmental scientists may use their ingenuity and generativity to identify multiple pathways to enhance the positive development of youth and families through media/technology engagement and literacy.

NOTE

1. Preparation of this chapter was supported in part by grants from the John Templeton Foundation and the Templeton Religion Trust.

REFERENCES

Amadeo, Jo-Ann, Judith Torney-Purta, and Carolyn Henry Barber. 2004. "Attention to Media and Trust in Media Sources: Analysis of Data from the IEA Civic Education Study." Medford, MA: The Center for Information and Research on Civic Learning and Engagement. https://circle.tufts.edu/sites/default/files/2019-12/FS_AttentionTrustinMediaSources_2004.pdf.

Anderson, Daniel R., Aletha C. Huston, Kelly L. Schmitt, Deborah L. Linebarger, and John C. Wright. 2001. "Early Childhood Television Viewing and Adolescent Behavior: The Recontact Study." *Monographs of the Society for Research in Child Development 66*, no. 1: vii–147. https://www.jstor.org/stable/3181552.

Bakes, Paul B., Hayre W. Reese, and John R. Nesselroade. 1977. *Life-span Developmental Psychology: Introduction to Research Methods*. Monterey, CA: Brooks-Cole.

Batanova, Milena, Edmond P. Bowers, Lacey J. Hilliard, Jonathan M. Tirrell, Danielle C. Stacey, AnneMarie McClain, and Richard M. Lerner. 2016. "Examining Cross-Age Peer Conversations Relevant to Character: Can a Digital Story About Bullying Promote Students' Understanding of Humility?" *Research in Human Development 13*, no. 2: 111–125.

Bers, Marina Umaschi. 2012. *Designing Digital Experiences for Positive Youth Development: From Playpen to Playground*. Cary, NC: Oxford University Press.

Bers, Marina Umaschi, and Elizabeth R. Kazakoff. 2013. "Developmental Technologies: Technology and Human Development." In *Handbook of Psychology, Vol. 6: Developmental Psychology* (2nd ed.), edited by Richard M. Lerner, M. Ann Easterbrooks, Jayanthi Mistry, and Irving B. Weiner, 639–657. Hoboken, NJ: John Wiley & Sons Inc.

Bowers, Edmond P., Lacey J. Hilliard, Milena Batanova, Danielle C. Stacey, Jonathan M. Tirrell, Katherine Wartella, and Richard M. Lerner. 2015. "The Arthur Interactive Media Study: Initial Findings From a Cross-age Peer Mentoring and Digital Media-based Character Development Program." *Journal of Youth Development 10*, no. 3: 46–63.

Boyd, Danah. 2014. *It's Complicated: The Social Lives of Networked Teens*. Chicago, IL: Yale University Press.

Calvert, Sandra L. 2015. "Children and Digital Media." In *Handbook of Child Psychology and Developmental Science*, edited by Marc H. Bornstein, Tama Leventahl, and Richard M. Lerner, 375–415. Hoboken, NJ: Wiley.

Center on Media and Child Health. 2005. "The Effects of Electronic Media on Children Ages Zero to Six: A History of Research." The Henry J. Kaiser Family Foundation. Accessed December, 2020. https://www.kff.org/other/issue-brief/the-effects-of-electronic-media-on-children/.

Gerbaudo, Paolo. 2012. *Tweets and the Streets: Social Media and Contemporary Activism*. London: Pluto Press.

Glenn, Heidi. 2012. "*Girls, Boys and Toys: Rethinking Stereotypes in What Kids Play With*. National Public Radio." Last modified December 17, 2012. https://www.npr.org/sections/thetwo-way/2012/12/17/167452439/girls-boys-and-toys-rethinking-stereotypes-in-what-kids-play-with.

Gutnick, Aviva Lucas, Michael Robb, Lori Takeuchi, Jennifer Kotler, Lewis Bernstein and Michael H. Levine. 2011. *Always Connected: The New Digital Media Habits of Young Children*. New York: The Joan Ganz Cooney Center at Sesame Workshop.

Hilliard, Lacey J., Mary H. Buckingham, G. John Geldhof, Patricia Gansert, Caroline Stack, Erin S. Gelgoot, Marina U. Bers, and Richard M. Lerner. 2018. "Perspective

Taking and Decision-making in Educational Game Play: A Mixed-methods Study." *Applied Developmental Science* 22, no. 1: 1–13.

Hiniker, Alexis, Kiley Sobel, Hyewon Suh, Yi-Chen Sung, Charlotte P. Lee, and Julie A. Kientz. 2015. "Texting while Parenting: How Adults Use Mobile Phones while Caring for Children at the Playground." In *Proceedings of the 33rd Annual ACM Conference on Human Factors in Computing Systems,* 727–736. New York: ACM. https://doi.org/10.1145/2702123.2702199.

Hobbs, Renee. 2010. *Digital and Media Literacy: A Plan of Action.* Washington, DC: The Aspen Institute.

Ito, Mizuko, et al. 2009. *Hanging Out, Messing Around, and Geeking Out: Kids Living and Learning with Media.* Cambridge, MA: MIT Press.

Jenkins, H., Ravi Purushotma, Margaret Weigel, Katie Clinton, and Alice J. Robison. 2009. *Confronting the Challenges of Participatory Culture: Media Education for the 21st Century.* Cambridge, MA: MIT Press.

Kahne, Joseph, Nam-Jin Lee, and Jessica Timpany Feezell. 2012. "Digital Media Literacy Education and Online Civic and Political Participation." *International Journal of Communication* 6: 1–24.

Koolstra, Cees M., and Nicole Lucassen. 2004. "Viewing Behavior of Children and TV Guidance by Parents: A Comparison of Parent and Child Reports." *Communications* 29, no. 2: 179–198.

Kweon, Sang Hee, and Seo-young Lee. 2013. "A Study on Empathy, Credibility, and Political Attitude in Social Media: Focused on the Relationship between Empathetic Intention and the Motivation of Belonging on Intended Pro-Social and Political Behavior." *Advances in Journalism and Communication* 1, no. 3: 26–40.

Lerner, Richard M. 2012. "Developmental Science: Past, Present, and Future." *International Journal of Developmental Science* 6, no. 1–2: 29–36.

Livingstone, Sonia. 2004. "Media Literacy and the Challenge of New Information and Communication Technologies." *The Communication Review* 7, no. 1: 3–14.

Livingstone, Sonia, and Ellen Helsper. 2009. "Balancing Opportunities and Risks in Teenagers' Use of the Internet: The Role of Online Skills and Internet Self-efficacy." *New Media & Society* 12, no. 2: 309–329.

McCaughey, Martha, and Michael D. Ayers, eds. 2013. *Cyberactivism: Online Activism in Theory and Practice.* New York: Routledge.

Morrell, Ernest. 2015. *Critical Literacy and Urban Youth: Pedagogies of Access, Dissent, and Liberation.* New York: Routledge.

Neuman, Susan B., and Donna C. Celano. 2012. *Giving our Children a Fighting Chance.* New York: Teachers College Press.

Nicholls, Walter J. 2013. *The DREAMers: How the Undocumented Youth Movement Transformed the Immigrant Rights Debate.* Stanford: Stanford University Press.

Overton, Willis F. 2015. "Process and Relational Developmental Systems." In *Handbook of Child Psychology and Developmental Science, Volume 1: Theory and Method,* edited by Overton, Willis F., and Peter CM Molenaar, 9–62. Hoboken, NJ: Wiley.

Pasek, Josh, Kate Kenski, Daniel Romer, and Kathleen Hall Jamieson. 2006. "America's Youth and Community Engagement: How Use of Mass Media is Related to Civic Activity and Political Awareness in 14- to 22-year-olds." *Communication Research 33*, no. 3: 115–135.

Penuel, William R., Shelley Pasnik, Lauren Bates, Eve Townsend, Lawrence P. Gallagher, Carlin Llorente, and Naomi Hupert. 2009. *Preschool Teachers Can Use a Media-rich Curriculum to Prepare Low-income Children for School Success: Results of a Randomized Controlled Trial*. New York and Menlo Park, CA: Education Development Center, Inc., and SRI International.

Reiser, Robert A., Martin A. Tessmer, and Pamela C. Phelps. 1984. "Adult-child Interaction in Children's Learning from Sesame Street." *Educational Communication and Technology Journal 32*, no. 4 (Winter): 217–223. https://www.jstor.org/stable /30218146.

Reiser, Robert A., Naja Williamson, and Katsuaki Suzuki. 1988. "Using Sesame Street to Facilitate Children's Recognition of Letters and Numbers." *Educational Communication and Technology Journal 36*, no. 1 (1988): 15–21.

Rideout, Victoria J., Ulla G. Foehr, and Donald F. Roberts. 2010. *Generation M2: Media in the Lives of 8 to 18 Year Olds*. Menlo Park, CA: Henry J. Kaiser Family Foundation.

Rideout, Victoria, and Hamel, Elizabeth. 2006. *The Media Family: Electronic Media in the Lives of Infants, Toddlers, Preschoolers and Their Parents*. Menlo Park, CA: Henry J. Kaiser Family Foundation. Accessed December, 2020. https://www.kff .org/other/the-media-family-electronic-media-in-the/.

Rideout, Victoria, Melissa Saphir, Seeta Pai, Allison Rudd, and Jenny Pritchett. 2013. "Zero to Eight Children's Media Use in America 2013." Washington, DC: Common Sense Media. Accessed December, 2020. https://www.commonsenseme dia.org/research/zero-to-eight-childrens-media-use-in-america-2013.

Roberts, Donald F., and Ulla G. Foehr. 2008. "Trends in Media Use." *The Future of Children 18*, no. 1 (Spring): 11–37. https://www.jstor.org/stable/20053118.

Smith, Aaron. 2013. *Civic Engagement in the Digital Age*. Washington, DC: Pew Research Center.

Takeuchi, Lori M. 2011. *Families matter: Designing Media for a Digital Age*. New York: The Joan Ganz Cooney Center at Sesame Workshop.

Thackeray, Rosemary, and MaryAnne Hunter. 2010. "Empowering Youth: Use of Technology in Advocacy to Affect Social Change." *Journal of Computer-Mediated Communication 15*, no. 4: 575–591.

Thoman, Elizabeth, and Tessa Jolls. 2005. *Literacy for the 21st Century: A Framework for Learning and Teaching in a Media Age*. Malibu, CA: Center for Media Literacy.

Watkins, S. Craig. 2011 "Digital Divide: Navigating the Digital Edge." *International Journal of Learning and Media 3*, no. 2 (2011): 1–12.

Chapter 19

Technology Enhances Secondary Family and Consumer: Sciences Instruction

Maggie A. Caples and Nadine Smith

INTRODUCTION

In the authors' school system, the integration of technology to improve instruction has been an ongoing process, progressing from the provision of computers for each teacher to roll out of the provision of an individual computer device for each student. This chapter examines: (1) how to use technology for instruction; (2) pros and cons of using technology in family and consumer sciences (FCS) classrooms to improve instruction; and (3) ethical issues related to the use of technology in the classroom, including the use of technology provided by the school system.

In addition to the technology provided by the school system, students can bring their own devices. It has been a challenge to use both school and personal devices to enhance instruction, rather than allowing the devices to distract students during class. Past and current school system administrations have supported the use of technology to prepare students to become globally competitive and prepared with twenty-first-century skills for career and college readiness.

The goal of this chapter is to share what has worked for the school system, and for FCS teachers as they increased the use of technology in their secondary FCS classrooms. The journey through this "technology explosion" as individuals, educators, and parents has been enlightening and exhausting but rewarding. Technology has provided some amazing experiences in and out of the classroom, and the authors are grateful to be part of the reform taking place in education and FCS instruction.

IS TECHNOLOGY A RESOURCE OR A RESTRAINT FOR TEACHERS?

Technology can be both a resource and a restraint. For example, as a resource technology can help teachers learn computer skills, conduct online research, and locate premade lessons and worksheets to help integrate technology across the curriculum. Educators should consider getting help using various devices and learning the intricate operating details of the internet. A few examples include: (1) learning the latest updates of computer hardware and software; (2) understanding the difference between, for example, a podcast and a blog; (3) researching interesting projects online; and (4) using the computer to extend activities. Teachers should encourage students to use technology in and out of school. The possibilities are endless when it comes to how the internet, computers, and other forms of modern technology can benefit classroom instruction.

Technology is essential and pervasive in educational settings. Instructors are trying to learn how to incorporate technology to improve instruction and student outcomes. A major question often asked is, "Can we change and improve the way we deliver instruction through the use of technology?" The answer is "yes," but training is needed for instructors, staff, and students. When a school system introduces technology into classrooms, assumptions should not be made about the skill level of the school-based staff. The career of education involves people of different genders, ages, and backgrounds; skill level and comfort with the use of technology among these groups may differ significantly. School systems should be mindful that everyone comes with different technological experiences and resources. Currently, the use of technology has increased drastically in the workforce; therefore, students need these skills to prepare for college and careers.

Computer literacy encompasses some of the twenty-first-century skills students need to learn to be globally competitive. There are many important issues surrounding technology and education. When discussing education and technology, these issues are easy to group under two categories, pros and cons. The pros relate to giving students 24-hour access to current global information, communication, and networking capabilities through YouTube, social media, the internet, and various search engines. Today's students can retrieve information instantly. The internet and software applications may also help organize students by keeping books, notes, and a multitude of other important resources together within reach of their fingertips. Technology is also used by teachers to comply with students' Individual Education Plans, because it can help personalize and modify instruction to accommodate students' differing needs. For example, Newsela (newsela.com) is a free internet resource that provides the same articles on various reading levels. It also provides quizzes that are graded automatically, providing instant feed-back to the student and teacher. Digital technology is a tool that may fulfill each student's educational needs by helping to individualize, differentiate, and improve the way he or she is taught today. Technology has also given students the option to complete classes online if interruptions occur to their daily lives. Today, thanks to educational technology, more students are able to complete graduation requirements and proceed with postsecondary plans. Technology has opened up the world to our students like never before, and the experiences can benefit many students in a positive manner.

Technology has increased communication between home and school. In our school system, parents now have access to their students' grades and cur-riculum online. This information is housed in a single user-friendly platform designed for easy access to student data, assessments, curriculum, instruc-tion, reporting, and analysis. Teachers can communicate with parents more frequently and can offer more descriptive feedback regarding student prog-ress through the school system's online portal. The site also offers academic advice, suggestions for resources (human and nonhuman), opportunities for educational growth, and a wealth of information about the district's leader-ship goals and mission. Technology has made the school system's leadership initiatives transparent and accessible to all who have a stake in the welfare of the students.

Although the emergence of technology in the educational realm has been beneficial for many, there are caveats to technology initiatives that could reap some negative outcomes. Since student access to technology has increased, some have observed a decrease in activities that build verbal communication and social skills. When an educator is mindful of this dilemma, collaboration and communication can be purposefully incorporated into instruction.

Other cons for technology use in the classroom include ethical issues, such as cheating, plagiarism, and bullying. In some cases, cheating has increased because technology has made this behavior easier to accomplish. For exam-ple, cell phones can be used to take pictures of test questions, to text questions and answers to friends, and to search the internet for answers and shortcuts to assignments. Technology also allows students to access large audiences for inappropriate behaviors including bullying or public attacks on an individu-al's reputation. Once a comment or picture is posted, it is virtually impossible to delete. Unfortunately, naive students risk the chance of mortgaging their future over an inappropriate post from the past.

According to David Volpi, MD, PC, FCS, technology can impact students physically in a negative manner (Meece 2012). Doctoral student Sara Thomée and her colleagues at the University of Gothenburg's Sahlgrenska Academy in Sweden conducted four studies to investigate the effects of heavy computer and cell phone use on the sleep quality, stress levels, and general mental health of young adults. Thomée and her team asked 4,100 young adults ages 20–24 to fill out questionnaires. They also interviewed 32 of those who were considered heavy information and communication technology (ICT) users. The results revealed that intensive use of cell phones and computers can be linked to an increase in stress, sleep disorders, and depressive symptoms in young adults (Thomée 2011). Volpi noted that a combination of both heavy computer use and heavy mobile technology use makes the associations even stronger (Meece 2012).

Additional health concerns arising today for frequent users are carpal tunnel syndrome, neck and back stress, eye strain known as "blue screen syndrome," and exposure to electromagnetic emissions. Regulation for screen use is recommended because of the possibility of developing computer vision syndrome, once seen in office workers and now also seen in students (Meece 2012). Some teachers have observed anxiety-produced stress when students had to put cell phones away out of sight during instruction. As cited above, researchers have observed obsessive, addictive, and unhealthy behaviors concerning technology that are not beneficial to the developing child.

Educators have other concerns with technology that are legitimate and should be taken seriously. These concerns include hacking, viruses, stress and anxiety caused by learning about technology, wear and tear on equipment, disposal of old equipment (impact on the environment), and what happens when the technology does not work. Research has been conducted on student achievement when using paper and pencil versus technology for testing and other academic tasks. Noyes and Garland (2008) reported finding that some students performed better with paper and pencil than with technology when testing. Shapley et al. (2006) found in a study of Texas sixth graders that the use of technology when testing produced higher student achievement. There are two schools of thought on the impact of using paper and pencil versus technology for testing, and the verdict is still out on this issue.

Ethical concerns arise around copyright issues, accessing inappropriate materials, security of learner information and maintaining privacy, software piracy, and digital citizenship. Other issues will arise as we continue to advance and develop new technology for the classroom. Educators should consider teaching ethical issues related to technology in addition to the content curriculum. If a school system wants to prepare globally competitive students who communicate using technology in a safe and respectful manner, the students should be taught digital citizenship. Westheimer and Kahne (2004) suggested three types of digital citizens: responsible, participatory, and justice oriented.

NATIONAL AND SCHOOL SYSTEM PERSPECTIVES
ON THE USE OF TECHNOLOGY IN THE CLASSROOM

The introduction of personal computers and the development and advancement of other technological tools, such as cell phones and the internet, have transformed the way individuals learn, live, and work. From the invention of microwave ovens to remote access to lock our doors and check our houses, technology has revolutionized our lives. Nowhere is this change more evident than in how we deliver education. Buzzell and Pintauro (2003) stated:

"Many experts acknowledge that the U.S. educational system is in the process of being fundamentally reshaped by technology. Although the internet has existed since the early 1970s and personal computers have long been in many classrooms, they initially had relatively little impact on educational reform" (201). They continued that the internet "allowed personal computers to evolve from machines used to perform word processing, data analysis, or graphics manipulation to global information and communication networking tools." (201)

The continued growth of equal access to the web was fueled by passage of the federal Telecommunications Act of 1996, which helped bring internet access to communities, agencies, and schools across the country. This act was the first significant overhaul of United States telecommunications law in more than 60 years. This act represented a major change in American telecommunication law, because it was the first time the internet was included in the broadcasting and spectrum allotment (Federal Communications Commission. n.d.). Telecommunications companies nationally and internationally continuously work to increase the speed, scope, and range of the internet to provide access for all.

Technology is a part of every aspect of our personal lives. Every day, new uses are developed for technology to improve teaching and learning. Technology can bring the world to the classroom in real time.

AT THE NATIONAL LEVEL

The International Society for Technology in Education (ISTE) has developed national technology standards and performance indicators for teachers and students. According to the introductory statement to the ISTE Standards for Teachers, "Effective teachers model and apply the ISTE Standards for Students . . . as they design, implement, and assess learning experiences to engage students and improve learning; enrich professional practice;

and provide positive models for students, colleagues, and the community" (International Society for Technology in Education, n.d.). According to ISTE, all teachers should meet the technology standards and performance indicators included in the list. The current ISTE Standards for Teachers are as follows:

1. Facilitate and inspire student learning and creativity.
2. Design and develop digital age learning experiences and assessments.
3. Model digital age work and learning. (International Society for Technology in Education, n.d.)

The current ISTE Standards for Students (International Society for Technology in Education, n.d.) include the following standards, along with what students should know and be able to do:

1. *Creativity and innovation.* Students demonstrate creative thinking, construct knowledge, and develop innovative products and processes using technology.
2. *Communication and collaboration.* Students use digital media and environments to communicate and work collaboratively, including at a distance, to support individual learning and contribute to the learning of others.
3. *Research and information fluency.* Students apply digital tools to gather, evaluate, and use information.
4. *Critical thinking, problem-solving, and decision-making.* Students use critical thinking skills to plan and conduct research, manage projects, solve problems, and make informed decisions using appropriate digital tools and resources.

The skills identified by the Partnership for 21st Century Skills (P21) include learning and innovation skills; information, media, and technology skills; and life and career skills. Information, media, and technology skills include information literacy, media literacy, and ICT literacy. ICT literacy skills include:

1. Using digital technology, communication tools, and/or networks appropriately to access, manage, integrate, evaluate, and create information in order to function in a knowledge economy.
2. Using technology as a tool to research, organize, evaluate, and communicate information, and the possession of a fundamental understanding of the ethical/legal issues surrounding access to and use of information.

These skills are considered to be important for the U.S. workforce to be successful in the global economy. Students must be twenty-first-century learners to be globally competitive graduates.

The National Education Association (NEA) is a founding member of the P21. The partnership, chaired by the NEA executive director, includes a range of business partners, various education-related organizations, and media groups. The six elements of twenty-first-century learning identified by the 'P21' partnership are as follows:

1. Emphasize core subjects.
2. Emphasize learning skills.
3. Use 21st century tools to develop learning skills.
4. Teach and learn in a 21st century context.
5. Teach and learn new 21st century content.
6. Use 21st century assessments that measure core subjects and 21st century skills. (National Education Association. n. d.)

The Council of Chief State School Officers (2006) identified the essential knowledge and skills that students must have to be successful in life and employment in this young century. Students need to be twenty-first-century learners to develop these skills.

White House ConnectED Initiative. In June 2013, President Obama announced the ConnectED initiative, designed to enrich K-12 education for every student in America. The White House ConnectED Initiative states, "Preparing America's students with the skills they need to get good jobs and compete with other countries relies increasingly on interactive, personalized learning experiences driven by new technology." According to the website for the ConnectED Initiative, ConnectED empowers teachers with the best technology and the training to make the most of it, and empowers students through individualized learning and rich, digital content (White House ConnectED Initiative 2013).

AT THE SCHOOL SYSTEM LEVEL

When Dr. S. Dallas Dance was appointed superintendent of the Baltimore County Public Schools (BCPS) in Maryland, the system developed *Blueprint 2.0: Our Way Forward 2013–2014 through 2017–2018*, the five-year strategic plan for the school system. *Blueprint 2.0* incorporates components of the twenty-first-century learning skills and other national standards related to academic achievement and technology integration. The BCPS Theory of Action states: "To equip every student with critical 21st century skills needed to be globally competitive, BCPS must ensure that every school has an equitable, effective digital learning environment, and every student has equitable access to learning and developing proficiency in a second language" (Baltimore County Public Schools. n.d., 2). Kevin Kamenetz,

Baltimore County executive, stated, "If we are to prepare our students to compete in the 21st century workforce, we must change the way we educate them to reflect our everchanging world" (Baltimore County Public Schools. n.d., 9). One of the BCPS priorities identified in *Blueprint 2.0* is to transform school facilities into twenty-first-century learning environments. The system had already supplied computers to administrators and teachers and equipped classrooms with a variety of technology equipment. Now it has embarked on several initiatives, with plans to equip every administrator, teacher, and student with their own personal computer device. Schools are in the process of developing more innovative ways to deliver instruction in the digital environment.

Christina DeSimone is a FCS teacher in the BCPS. In addition to teaching FCS, she has served on the board for the Maryland Association of Family and Consumer Sciences (MAFCS) for several years, most recently as MAFCS president in 2013–2015. She has made presentations on using technology in FCS classrooms at AAFCS, state, and local meetings. As a new teacher, her principal was so impressed with her use of technology for FCS instruction that he had her conduct a professional development session on how to use technology for teaching for the entire school staff. She wrote (C. DeSimone, personal communication, April 19, 2016):

> The importance of technology in family and consumer sciences programs can-not be overstated. Technology integration is a vital part to the survival of FCS programs. If we are going to stay relevant in today's changing school environ-ment it is critical we change with the times by implementing technology in useful and authentic ways. The challenge for FCS programs is to figure out how to implement technology in a way that will add benefit to the overall learning experience while not degrading the integrity of skills we have been teaching for the last 100 years. How do we use technology to add to the traditional FCS experience with all its many programs?

PAST AND CURRENT PERSPECTIVES ON USING TECHNOLOGY FOR INSTRUCTION

Think back through education history. As each technology advance has been introduced for instruction, many of the same questions have been raised:

1. Will this replace the classroom teacher?
2. Will this increase academic achievement or dummydown the curriculum?
3. How will I find time to learn how to use this and still teach?

The current technology explosion is no different. Ditto machines gave way to copiers and printers. The chalkboard gave way to interactive white boards. Overhead projectors gave way to LCD projectors and optic view projectors. Instructional television, the wave of the future for instruction in the 1960s, has been replaced by the internet in classrooms and relegated to use for the morning announcements. Typewriters were exchanged for laptop or desktop computers. With each of these changes in instructional technology, teachers had a steep learning curve and had to be supported with professional development to learn how to use the new innovation.

According to Pitler, Hubbell, Kuhn, and Malenoski (2007), teachers are enthusiastic about embracing new technologies as they have seen positive student results. However, teachers feel unsure about how to effectively incorporate technology into the curriculum. Zuniga (2009) reported that the three most common factors hindering teachers from the integration of computer technology into their classrooms were the lack of high-quality training, lack of time, and fear of computer technology. In that same study, other teachers reported that when under pressure about student state test scores, computer integration into the classroom became a secondary priority. According to Buzzell and Pintauro (2003), using technology can help a teacher move from being a good teacher to being a great teacher. They stated that digital classrooms create a shift from a teaching paradigm to a learning paradigm.

With the introduction of each equipment innovation for instruction, cost has been a factor. Computer technology integration is no different. Here is a series of questions, not totally inclusive, that must be considered. What are the initial purchase costs? Can teachers work with what they have or is it necessary to purchase new equipment? What facility changes are necessary to support and use this equipment (i.e., wiring, data drops, WiFi)? How many will be needed for effective instruction and student use? What consumable supplies will be needed? How much must be budgeted for repair and replacement costs? Will one per classroom or department be enough, or will more be needed?

Our school system went from the implementation of computer labs and/or a few computers in each classroom to the current 1:1 initiative to supply each teacher and student with their own personal computer device. A few other U.S. school systems are experimenting with the 1:1 initiative to make instruction more engaging, flexible, innovative, creative, and conducive to student learning. The goal is to create more interesting, individualized instruction that will lead to improved student achievement and students ready with the technology skills needed for the twenty-first century.

Equity, likewise, has raised issues to address with the introduction of each new instructional technology. Which schools and students will have the latest innovative equipment in their classrooms? How will the system get all teachers to adopt the new technology? Which students will get to use the new equipment? Will it be saved for the gifted and talented classes, or will the special education classes have experience with it also? Will the schools in wealthier areas of the school system have more technology for instruction than schools located in lower socioeconomic areas? Which programs in the school will get to use the equipment?

In the beginning, schools installed computer labs to provide computers for student use. However, FCS teachers often had difficulty scheduling classes in the computer lab because the core academic areas got first preference for use. The authors' system has sought to provide FCS teachers with their own classroom technology equipment. Using computers for testing is also a priority. When testing occurs, the school can use any of the computers in the school, regardless of funding for the equipment. During this time the teachers don't have access and must make alternative plans for their lessons.

Technology for teaching and learning was one of the equity issues raised through stakeholder forums held to develop *Blueprint 2.0: Our Way Forward 2014–2018*. It is important to ensure equal and fair access to all schools and students, and it is important for all students to learn how to use various aspects of technology to be college and career ready.

Whereas the main focus of this chapter has been on integration of computers and other technology devices, it is important to remember that technology in FCS is more than computers. For each FCS content strand there are technology advances. It is useful to point out to students the technology in use in their daily lives, for example, things individuals take for granted, such as the microwave oven (which revolutionized food preparation). Various modern food processing techniques, such as freeze drying, have made specific perishable foods available anywhere at any time, even on the battlefield. The fabric for our clothes, furnishings, and even highway construction are examples of technology in daily life. The finishes and other technology-based innovations allow fabrics to be customized according to the intended use; that is, clothing can be customized for different sports and space travel. The processes of daily living for individuals and families have been changed by the introduction of computers and technology. For example, using a cell phone to lock and set house alarms from a remote location (housing), watching babies via cameras and phones (parenting), holding meetings through the internet (communications), depositing checks via a smart phone (financial literacy), and smart appliances (interior design, housing, and equipment). For teachers, there are electronic grade books and electronic curriculum guides. Every aspect of how we teach and learn in FCS has been touched and improved by technological advances.

CREATIVE IDEAS FOR USING
TECHNOLOGY IN FCS CLASSROOMS

The introduction of technology into the FCS classroom is not new. This discipline has always been on the forefront of introducing technology to improve homes, communities, and families. Whether the technology is evolving from a needle and thread to a computerized sewing machine, hand-mixers to electric mixers, or an infant simulator to a web-based software parenting program, FCS has tried to expose students to authentic, hands-on experiences using technology. For example, infant simulators have been upgraded to a web-based software program that utilizes realistic scenarios to allow students to virtually rear a child from birth to 18. An exploratory study of 66 high school students compared the impact of web-based simulation on student achievement. The study group of the 66 students in the web-based simulation was compared to students who learned parenting skills by traditional means. The results of the study found that the students in the web-based simulation group had an improvement of one letter grade on posttest assessments and they raised their scores from 66% to 77%. This study suggested that web-based technology could be a valuable tool for FCS educators (Anderson, Webster, and Czapek 2015).

Teachers need to be willing and purposeful as they integrate technology into the curriculum instead of viewing it as an add-on, a second thought, or an occurrence. Technology should be viewed as a catalyst for learning to raise awareness, start conversations, change minds, or drive change. A shift in mindset needs to occur from using technology as a replacement for books to using technology as a tool or strategy to engage learners (Richardson 2013). An educator's goal should be to cultivate lifelong learners, not discourage learning. Teachers should incorporate creative instructional strategies to use technology and the internet instead of utilizing them as a speedy retrieval machine regurgitating facts. For example, a creative strategy would be to use one of the many free programs available online such as polls, blogs, games, videos, web quests, and interactive sites developed to help stimulate creativity and intellectual growth.

Best practices for educational strategies are also enhanced by the technologies our students *bring* into the family consumer sciences classrooms. For example, personal cell phones have added a whole new dimension to teaching, and if managed well, the teacher can capitalize on this technology. There are many uses for the cell phone in the classroom. These uses include, but are not limited to: Skype (or FaceTime), taking pictures (extremely helpful tool to students who have challenges writing or taking notes), using a calendar, note taking, accessing the internet, getting directions, emailing, texting, polling, recording, filming, calculating, accessing music and television, using electronic books, and other applications. The Teacher Academy of Maryland (TAM) program used Skype to allow TAM high school students to tutor elementary school students several miles away in math, and the math grades improved. The program won a national award.

Cell phones partnered with various other devices give school systems freedom to initiate strategies such as "flipping the classroom." Flipping a classroom involves technology and gives students who are challenged with school assignments another way to learn. In a flipped classroom, a teacher videotapes his or her lesson and expects students to view the lesson at home as homework. The students attend school the next day and apply what they learned at home to an assignment that produces an authentic performance-based product. Creating the video and allowing students to view it at home may produce a beneficial outcome for the students. First, the students may view the video more than once until understanding occurs. Second, someone at home also may view the video and learn with the students so that he or she can offer guidance if needed. Lastly, students have time to think and prepare good questions without the pressure of a bell signaling the next class.

PROFESSIONAL DEVELOPMENT FOR INSTRUCTIONAL TECHNOLOGY USE

In order to maximize the use of technology in FCS programs, proper training should be offered to teachers and staff. The authors' school system offers professional development often and provides various opportunities to teachers and staff. The training sessions and times vary to accommodate teacher schedules. Training is given on a continual basis on such topics as technology equipment, software programs, instructional strategies and techniques, educational policies, best practices, grading and assessments, curriculum, health and personal well-being, and related topics. Teachers are given opportunities to attend conventions and seminars to learn about new instructional practices and technological advances.

POLICY ISSUES

S. Dallas Dance, PhD, superintendent of BCPS, stated, "The overarching purpose of our school system—the sole reason we exist—is to prepare globally competitive graduates. This is a large goal, but we can get there by being strategic in our focus and by being deliberate in our action" (Baltimore County Public Schools. n.d., 12). One of those strategic actions has been to provide technology-rich learning environments so that students have access regardless of race, special education status, gender, ethnicity, sexual orientation, English Language Learner, or socioeconomic status. On March 11, 2014, the Board of Education gave contract authority to lease teacher and student devices to support the vision of providing equitable technology to all. This policy was a shift from purchasing the equipment, and in some instances led to higher cost per computer because updates, repairs, and other factors were built into the lease contracts.

Funds from some grants required a purchase of equipment, not a lease, so decisions were made to continue those purchases for the immediate future. The school system is working out policies on how technology can be acquired based on the source of funding. A central system was implemented to standardize what computer devices can be purchased. This innovation was a change from the time when an office could order different computers based on their choice of equipment for a classroom or laboratory and the funding source. One policy issue is determining what programs will be allowed to purchase equipment rather than leasing it. Another is to identify who decides what model of computer can be purchased. For career and technology programs, there is some differentiation of what model can be purchased if the content office can justify that a different computer is needed based on program software needs. However, movement is from individualized office purchases of technology equipment to all purchases supporting the school system's five-year plan for the 1:1 rollout to give every teacher and student a device by 2017–2018.

Another policy action the school system took is to improve the infrastructure in buildings system-wide to provide equitable wireless access to the internet by making WiFi available in every building and every classroom. More bandwidth was acquired to support simultaneous access for every student and teacher in the school, regardless of their location in the building. This change also supports the system's vision to move from hardcopies of books to eBooks with the 1:1 rollout.

TECHNOLOGY IMPACTS CHANGES IN SOCIETY

At the time of this writing, the authors' school system is the 25th largest in the United States. Many other school systems have visited to evaluate the 1:1 conversion model. The system aspires to demonstrate how the learning environment can be individualized for different learning preferences, and how it can have positive effects upon closing the student achievement gap. This focus has the potential to reshape the U.S. public education system. As noted earlier, Buzzell and Pintauro (2003) stated that the U.S. educational system is in the process of being fundamentally reshaped by technology. Students will be able to learn differently. Teachers will be able to use different processes for their instructional and administrative duties, such as recording and reporting grades and keeping parents informed about their students' progress. This change may lead to increased communication capabilities. Just as the introduction of new technologies changed how we work and play in our personal lives, the new technologies have the potential to change the way teaching and learning occur in the classroom.

CURRENT SCHOOL SYSTEM TECHNOLOGY INITIATIVES

One major technology initiative in the authors' school system is Students and Teachers Accessing Tomorrow (STAT), and the one to one (1:1) conversion for computer devices is a part of that. This innovation institutes a multiyear transformation of classrooms into a complete twenty-first-century technology learning environment. Work has begun to redesign curricula in the core content areas to redefine what instruction will look like in a blended learning environment, while placing a stronger emphasis on critical thinking and analytical skills. The focus is on reimagining teaching and learning to maximize the potential of every student in every school. The technology associated with STAT through the 1:1 conversion *supports* this shift in teaching and learning, but it is not the focus. The school system is reexamining the dynamics between educators and students, how space is used, and where and when learning occurs. The computer device is one of many tools that enhances the customization and personalization of teaching and learning for all students. From classroom instruction to designing digital curriculum, learner-centered environments, along with personalized learning through technology, better meet the needs of individual students to raise achievement and close gaps. The rollout of 1:1 devices for students began in selected elementary schools in 2014–2015, in selected middle schools in 2015–2016, and in selected high schools in 2016–2017. This rollout will continue for all schools K-12 through the 2017–2018 school year. At that time all administrators, teachers, and students will have a personal computer device.

The schools selected for initial rollout at each level are called Lighthouse Schools. Elementary schools were the first in the school system to receive individual digital learning devices for students, to implement 1:1 personalized and blended learning, and to create an innovative, comprehensive digital learning culture (Baltimore County Public Schools. n.d.). The Lighthouse Schools serve as models for the additional schools in the rollout. This change has required additional teacher resources for staffing, professional development, planning, and furniture. Support has been provided by STAT teachers housed in the Lighthouse Schools to help school staff develop and implement the new instructional methods needed to successfully create the new learning environment possible with the 1:1 conversion.

THE FUTURE

The internet and technology devices have infiltrated almost all aspects of daily life, changing how we communicate, work, play, shop, make travel plans, and learn (Buzzell and Pintauro 2003, 213). It is no longer a choice as to whether to bring technology into our learning environments. Gaining experience with technology is a crucial component of education programs. National documents speak to the need for technology skills for teachers and students to prepare graduates for the twenty-first century. It is a natural fit for FCS programs.

Will technology help produce equity in our schools and classrooms? It will if we ensure that all students have equal access to technology regardless of their zip code or what courses they take. The 1:1 initiative will provide technology resources equitably, but all teachers must be willing to learn how to create a different learning environment using technology in innovative ways for the instruction to be equitable across the system. School systems will have to continue to provide professional development and support to help teachers explore how to integrate technology to change teaching and learning. Colleges and universities will have to train future educators differently so they are ready to take their place in technology-rich teaching environments. The expanded use of technology in classrooms has the potential to transform America's classrooms. It is up to each school system to put structures in place to make that happen.

In the conclusion of his article reporting on the government's National Technology Plan, Donlevy (2005) sums up what is needed as schools and school systems implement technology-rich environments:

Dramatic advances in information technology continue to affect all levels of society. To compete in a global economy, students need to have academic skills but also the technological sophistication to navigate in an increasingly digitized world. Schools must embrace the new technologies to transform teaching and learning and draw upon the new multimedia formats. Schools, too, must involve technologically sophisticated students in their planning efforts, since students often arrive at school with expertise beyond the level of their teachers and program administrators. (107–109)

As Donlevy's report notes (45), "public schools that do not adapt to the technology needs of students risk becoming increasingly irrelevant." We cannot do less in FCS programs. We must embrace new technologies and ensure that FCS classrooms lead the way for implementation, or mirror the technology-rich environments found in the rest of the school building. The field of FCS was founded on the application of science to improve the lives of individuals, families, and communities. Ellen H. Richards, considered to be the founder of the field of home economics (now FCS), used her knowledge of science to improve lives and living conditions. The FCS profession should continue to be on the forefront of using the most current technologies to improve lives and living conditions, including for teaching and learning in today's FCS classrooms.

To conclude, education has developed a vision to prepare students to take their place in the global economy. The authors' local school system made a commitment to become the best system in the nation, and the leadership has committed to using all resources necessary to accomplish this goal. Closing the achievement gap is a priority, and introducing cutting-edge technology is seen as one way to expand opportunity for all.

REFERENCES

Anderson, Julius W., Carrie M. Webster, and Christine Czapek. 2015. "Using My Virtual Child in FCS Secondary Education." *Journal of Family and Consumer Sciences 107*, no. 4: 35–40.

Baltimore County Public Schools. n.d. "Blueprint 2.0: Our Way Forward 2014-2018." Accessed December, 2020. https://www.bcps.org/.

Buzzell, P., and S. J. Pintauro. 2003. "Learning with Technology." In *Creative Instructional Methods for Family & Consumer Sciences, Nutrition & Wellness*, edited by Valerie M. Chamberlain, and Merrilyn N. Cummings, 214–201. New York: Glencoe McGraw-Hill.

Council of Chief State School Officers. 2006. Accessed December, 2020. https://ccsso.org/.

Donlevy, Jim. 2005. "Teachers, Technology and Training: Envisioning the Future: The U.S. Department of Education's National Technology Plan." *International Journal of Instructional Media 32*, no. 1: 107–109.

Federal Communications Commission. n.d. "Telecommunications Act of 1996." Accessed May 1, 2020. https://fcc.gov/telecom.

Meece, Mickey. 2012. "Lenses to Ease the Strain from Staring at Screens." *The New York Times*, Mar 14, 2012. https://www.nytimes.com/2012/03/15/technology/personaltech/easing-eye-strain-with-the-right-lenses.html.

National Education Association. n.d. "21st Century Skills". Accessed May 1, 2020. https://www.nea.org/.

Noyes, Jan M., and Kate J. Garland. 2008. "Computer- Vs. Paper-Based Tasks: Are They Equivalent?" *Ergonomics 51*, no. 9: 1352–1375. https://doi.org/10.1080/0 0140130802170387.

O'Neill, Barbara. 2016. "Thirty Terrific Technology Tools for Teaching Personal Finance." *Journal of Family and Consumer Sciences 108*, no. 1: 39–43. http://dx .doi.org/10.14307/JFCS108.1.39.

Pitler, Howard, Elizabeth Ross Hubbell, Matt Kuhn and Malenoski, Kim. 2007. *Using Technology with Classroom Instruction that Works*. Alexandria, VA: Association for Supervision and Curriculum Development.

Richardson, Will. 2013. "Technology–Rich Learning: Students First, Not Stuff." *Educational Leadership 70*, no. 6: 10–14. https://www.cbsd.org/cms/lib010/PA0 1916442/Centricity/Domain/2713/Students%20First%20Not%20Stuff.pdf.

Shapley, Kelly S., Daniel Sheehan, Keith Sturges, Fanny Caranikas-Walker, Briana Huntsberger, and Catherine Maloney. 2006. "Effects of Technology Immersion on Teaching and Learning: Evidence from Observations of Sixth-Grade Classrooms." Texas Center for Educational Research. https://www.semanticscholar.org/paper /Effects-of-Technology-Immersion-on-Teaching-and-of-Shapley-Sheehan/d05a6 d5338b9928ffc726365a097edcbeaa3a396.

Simpson, Brain. 2015. "Gambling on Technology in the Classroom." *The Baltimore Sun*, December 1, 2015. https://www.baltimoresun.com/opinion/op-ed/bs-ed-d ance-technology-20151201-story.html.

Thomée, Sara, Annika Härenstam, and Mats Hagberg. 2011. "Mobile Phone Use and Stress, Sleep Disturbances, and Symptoms of Depression among Young Adults- A Prospective Cohort Study." *BMC Public Health 11*, no. 1: 66. http://dx.doi.org/10 .1186/1471-2458-11-66.

Westheimer, Joel, and Joseph Kahne. 2004. "Educating the Good Citizen: Political Choices and Pedagogical Goals." *PS: Political Science and Politics 37*, no. 2: 241–247. https://www.jstor.org/stable/4488813.

White House Connected Initiative. 2013. Accessed May 1, 2020. https://obamawh itehouse.archives.gov/issues/education/k-12/connected.

Zuniga, Ramiro. 2009. "Teacher Perspectives on the Current State of Computer Technology Integration into the Public School Classroom." PhD diss., The University of Texas-Pan American.

Index

About the Contributors

Milena Batanova is the research and evaluation manager at Making Caring Common, a project of the Harvard Graduate School of Education. She oversees the development and evaluation of empathy-based strategies for K-12 schools, and her work uses an applied developmental approach to examine what individual contextual factors contribute to the different components of empathy as well as reduced bullying and victimization. Milena was a research assistant professor at the Institute for Applied Research in Youth Development at Tufts University and obtained her PhD in health behavior and health education from the University of Texas at Austin.

Nina Lyon Bennett holds a PhD in child and family development from the University of Georgia, and her undergraduate and master's degree in sociology from Clark Atlanta University, where she began her career in higher education. She is currently assistant dean for Academics in the School of Agriculture, Fisheries and Human Sciences at University of Arkansas at Pine Bluff. She has presented at several national conferences, is a published author, a certified life coach, and has earned graduate certificates in social gerontology, women's studies, and family financial planning. Dr. Lyon Bennett has also received several professional certifications and awards, including the American Association of Family and Consumer Sciences (AAFCS) certification in Human Development & Family Studies and is a 2016 graduate of the Food Systems Leadership Institute.

Maggie A. Caples earned a Bachelor of Science degree in home economics education at Hampton Institute (now Hampton University), a master's degree in home economics education at Virginia State University, and a doctorate degree in curriculum and instruction at the University of Maryland, College

Park. Currently, she is the retired supervisor of family and consumer sciences (FACS) for the Baltimore County Public Schools, where she supervised programs and courses for FACS, criminal justice, culinary arts, homeland security, and the Teacher Academy of Maryland. She has taught FACS courses at several HBCUs (Hampton University, Virginia State University, Howard University, Morgan State University, and University of Maryland Eastern Shore). She was married for 50 years and has two daughters, a grandson, and two great-grandchildren.

LaTonya J. Dixon is an assistant professor in the area of Nutrition and Hospitality Management (NHM) within the Department of Family and Consumer Sciences (FCS) at Alabama A&M University. She received her Bachelor of Science degree in dietetics from Oakwood College (now Oakwood University) in 2003 and master's and doctoral degrees in food science from Alabama A&M University in 2005 and 2010, respectively. Through this appointment she is involved in teaching, disease prevention research, and the academic advisement of NHM students. She is actively involved in the AAFCS, the Academy of Nutrition and Dietetics, and the National Organization of Blacks in Dietetics & Nutrition. In the past, she has held several positions in the food industry, including food safety director and quality assurance supervisor.

Kenneth Gruber is a social/research psychologist with over 37 years of research and program evaluation experience. He is senior research scientist at the UNCG Center for Youth Family and Community Partnerships. His areas of specialty include data collection design and methodology, statistical analysis, program evaluation, technical writing assistance, and grant application review. His professional work is mostly in the area of program evaluation and the use of this information for program development and applied research. He has been deeply involved in community health topics publishing research on chronic illnesses, nutrition, adolescent pregnancy prevention, impact of diet on health and weight management, health access for uninsured adults, and environmental factors in the home and asthma.

Lacey J. Hilliard is an assistant professor and director of the Social Development and Social Issues Lab in the Applied Developmental Psychology program at Suffolk University. Lacey earned her PhD in developmental psychology from the Pennsylvania State University. Her program of research is focused on understanding how families and educators approach challenging social issues with children, including the social cognitive development of intergroup attitudes and how children process and respond to information about social groups. She has led the creation, implementation, and evaluation of educational media and technology-based interventions designed to help children and adolescents navigate social challenges and ethical dilemmas in schools.

Jacqueline M. Holland, CFCS, is associate professor and interim department director for Family and Consumer Sciences at Morgan State University, Baltimore, Maryland. Throughout her career in education, she has been a family and consumer sciences teacher (FACS), school administrator, and district supervisor for FACS programs in the Prince Georges County School District, Maryland. Dr. Holland was the 2016-2019 president of the National Coalition for Black Development in Family and Consumer Sciences. the She was the 2017-2018 president of the American Association of Family and Consumer Sciences, one of six women of color elected to this role in the 112-year history of the organization. A recent recipient of the AAFCS Distinguished Service Award, she also manages the Community of Diversity, Equity, and Inclusion for the organization.

Shirley Hymon-Parker is the associate dean for research in the College of Agriculture and Environmental Sciences (CAES) at North Carolina Agricultural and Technical State University. She served as interim dean for CAES from 2015 to 2018 and helped lead major outreach to North Carolina communities, farmers, youth, and other individuals through programs administered through Cooperative Extension at N.C. A&T. Hymon-Parker received her bachelor's degree in clothing and textiles from North Carolina Central University, her master's in design and environmental analysis from Cornell University, and a doctorate in administration and supervision from the University of Maryland, College Park.

Vanessa P. Jackson is chair and professor in the Department of Retailing and Tourism Management in the College of Agriculture, Food, and Environment at the University of Kentucky. She also serves as the director of faculty diversity and inclusion in the college. Her current research focuses on soft skill development for student competitiveness in entry-level positions in the human sciences. Dr. Jackson has also conducted and published research on African American women in academic leadership and the barriers they experience.

Ethel G. Jones is currently serving as the director for the School of Human Ecology at Louisiana Tech University in Ruston, Louisiana. Dr. Jones has a significant record of core accomplishments and distinctions from having served as a leader in many professional organizations, where she has made significant contributions in the area of professional accreditation. She has written and published numerous professional scholarly publications. Dr. Jones received a plethora of honors as a teacher and professor throughout her work history at the secondary and collegiate levels. Her encouragement and dedication to helping students and young professionals be successful continue to be noteworthy.

Alice F. Joyner serves as chairperson of the Department of Family and Consumer Sciences at Virginia State University. Dr. Joyner also has a long history as an extension agent with the Virginia Polytechnic Institute State University cooperative extension system working to transform lives and communities. She holds a BS degree in family and consumer sciences with a concentration in foods and nutrition, an MS degree in career and technical education with a concentration in family and consumer sciences, and a Doctor of Education (EdD) in higher education leadership.

Richard M. Lerner is the Bergstrom Chair in applied developmental science, the director of the Institute for Applied Research in Youth Development, and professor in the Eliot-Pearson Department of Child Study and Human Development at Tufts University. He received his PhD in developmental psychology from the City University of New York. Dr. Lerner's work integrates the study of public policies and community-based programs with the promotion of positive youth development and youth contributions to civil society.

Brenda A. Martin is chairperson of the Department of Human Sciences at the University of Arkansas at Pine Bluff. Dr. Martin received her BS degree in fashion merchandising from the University of Arkansas at Pine Bluff, her MA degree in career and technical education from Western Michigan University, and her PhD in workforce education from The Pennsylvania State University. In 2014, Dr. Martin was awarded the Chancellor's Distinguished Teaching Award and was selected to participate in the USDA-NIFA visiting scholars' program in 2017. Dr. Martin was recently award the 2020 Family and Consumer Sciences Outstanding Educator Award from the American Association of Family and Consumer Sciences-Arkansas Affiliate.

Debra L. Mayfield received the Bachelor of Arts degree in communications and fine arts from Howard University, Washington, D.C., and the Juris Doctorate from the University of Southern California, Los Angeles. After receiving the Juris Doctorate, she became employed in the Hollywood film industry for almost a decade at Creative Artists Agency, Three Sisters Entertainment, and Paramount Studios with CBS's number-one shows *JAG* and *NCIS*. After leaving the film industry, she became employed in environmental law and policy at the environmental law organization, Earthjustice, in

Washington, D.C. Currently, she is a PhD student at Georgetown University, pursuing a degree in the area of U.S. history, focusing on slavery, reconstruction, and women's studies.

Juanita Mendenhall currently serves as the international director of the Disaster Assistance Partnerships for Home Economics/FCS Programs in Developing Countries, a council committee of the International Federation for Home Economics (IFHE) that began service in 2010. Both her bachelor's and master's degrees in home economics are from Indiana University. Mrs. Mendenhall served on the IFHE executive committee in various capacities for over 12 years, including one four-year term as executive committee representative for the Americas and another as vice president for the region of the Americas. Mendenhall also taught many special courses for Indiana and Purdue Universities, St. Francis College, and Sir Arthur Teacher Training College in St. Lucia, West Indies, where she taught teachers of home economics for the Caribbean.

AnneMarie McClain is a doctoral candidate in the Communication Arts Department at the University of Wisconsin-Madison. AnneMarie's program of research explores how to best leverage and design media to promote positive outcomes among children—particularly children of color, of LGBTQ+ identities, and of lower-income backgrounds. She has conducted studies about Black families' strategies for using media for ethnic-racial socialization and Black parents' preferences for representation in their children's media. AnneMarie is a former elementary school teacher and has worked with hundreds of children and families and their schools as a researcher and liaison for various projects in child development labs at Tufts University, Harvard University, and UW-Madison.

Julia R. Miller Arline is professor and dean emeritus of Michigan State University in East Lansing, Michigan, where her work in the human sciences and other disciplines focused on administration and management, instruction (face-to-face and online), as well as research and outreach locally, nationally, and internationally. Her expertise and experiences range from the public schools to higher education in Virginia, Maryland, Michigan, Africa, and Asia. Her work relates to disenfranchised populations nationally and internationally, other areas of the human sciences, agriculture production of women, and dual household employment. For her contributions to the human sciences and other disciplines, she has served as a consultant, published extensively, and received numerous professional and community awards and recognition.

Joanne Pearson is an emeritus professor of nutrition for James Madison University, Harrisonburg, Virginia. Following retirement in 1998, she was a

Fulbright Scholar at the Technical University in Chisinau, Moldova, in 2001. From 2010 to 2014 she was IFHE vice president, Region of Americas.

Penny A. Ralston is currently a professor, dean emeritus, and director of the Center on Better Health and Life for Underserved Populations, Florida State University (FSU).

A native of Indiana, she received the BS degree from Ball State University and the MEd and PhD degrees from the University of Illinois. She previously served as dean, FSU College of Human Sciences; head, Department of Consumer Studies at the University of Massachusetts; and assistant through full professor, Iowa State University. As a scholar, Dr. Ralston's work has focused on community-based health programs for adults. She is the author of over 65 refereed articles, abstracts, book chapters, and reviews. Dr. Ralston served for nine years on the Florida Biomedical Research Advisory Council and has provided leadership for a statewide effort to develop a research agenda to address health disparities in Florida and to establish the Florida Health Equity Research Institute. She has held many leadership positions with professional organizations and is the recipient of several honors and awards.

Ahlishia J. Shipley is the founder of AJS Relationship Strategies, LLC, a family enrichment consulting firm based in Washington, D.C. Dr. Shipley previously served as a national program leader in the United States Department of Agriculture's National Institute of Food and Agriculture, providing leadership for research, education, and extension in the division of family and consumer sciences in the areas of family life and human development, health and wellness, and family and consumer sciences education. Dr. Shipley has training as both an educator and a researcher, earning a BS in family and consumer sciences education, an MS in career and technical education, and a PhD in family studies, all from the University of Kentucky. All of her experiences have culminated in a sincere appreciation for comprehensive teaching and outreach that is firmly rooted in research.

Amber N. Smith is a native of Washington, D.C. She holds a Bachelor of Arts in interdisciplinary humanities with a museum studies specialization and a Master of Science in child development. Her professional experiences include four years as a substitute teacher and five and a half years as a childcare provider. Ms. Smith is currently serving as a graduate assistant while pursuing a Doctor of Philosophy degree in early childhood education.

Bettye P. Smith received her bachelor's degree from Grambling State University, her master's degree from Northwestern State University, and her Doctorate from The Ohio State University. She was a professor at the University of Georgia. She was a member of Church of the Nations.

Cynthia M. Smith is a retired professor and chair of the Department of Family and Consumer Sciences (FCS) at Alabama A&M University where she is involved in teaching, research, advisement, and the ongoing leadership responsibilities of the FCS Unit. She received her bachelor's and master's degrees from Tuskegee University and her doctorate from The Ohio State University. She is a 2012 graduate of the Food Systems Leadership Institute, Cohort #6.

Nadine Smith is a family and consumer sciences (FACS) teacher in a midsized magnet high school within Baltimore County. She received her Bachelor of Science degree in family and community development from the University of Maryland, College Park, and earned her MA in teaching and leadership from Notre Dame of Maryland University. Currently, she is pursuing her doctorate. After receiving her BS from the University of Maryland she worked a variety of jobs from counselor for Planned Parenthood of Maryland to production manager for Patuxent Publishing.

Danielle C. Stacey is a developmental scientist specializing in learning and instructional design. Danielle earned her PhD in child study and human development from Tufts University and completed her BS in psychology at the University of Wollongong in New South Wales, Australia. She has applied her expertise in educational technology, curriculum development, and assessment methods to assist software developers in the design and evaluation of educational games for elementary and middle school students. She is an advocate for media literacy delivering workshops to parents, educators, and youth and serves on the board of several organizations focused on promoting women in the sport of sailing.

Dana D. Legette-Traylor served the family and consumer sciences department as an assistant professor and program coordinator of the textile, apparel, merchandising, and management program at Virginia State University. Dr. Legette-Traylor had over 20 years of experience as a practitioner and scholar in the discipline. Her credentials include a doctorate in business administration and marketing. She held a Master of Science degree in clothing and textile science with an emphasis in international business and marketing education, and a BS in family and consumer sciences with a concentration in fashion merchandising.

William H. Whitaker Jr. currently serves as the Acting Associate Provost for Academic Affairs for SC State University (SCSU) located in Orangeburg,

South Carolina. Dr. Whitaker is a professor of fashion merchandising and the immediate-past chairperson of the Department of Family and Consumer Sciences at SCSU. His previous experience includes Benedict College, Columbia, SC—School of Education as the assessment coordinator of Teacher Education and assistant vice president for Institutional Effectiveness; Livingstone College, Salisbury, NC—special assistant to the president. Whitaker is active in many professional and learned societies and organizations and is president and CEO of W. H. Whitaker Interiors, a full-service interior design company that specializes in residential and commercial interiors.

Quantanise M. Williams is a Spring 2021 Master of Social Work candidate at the University of Michigan, focusing on interpersonal clinical practice and health. She is also a psychotherapist intern at the Women's Center of Southeastern Michigan and works as a research assistant at Michigan Medicine Department of Psychiatry on the Zero to Thrive Prenatal Stress Study. Quantanise is passionate about using a variety of therapeutic modalities to assist Black women in healing from intergenerational trauma and managing chronic stress. She is currently training to become certified as a Holistic Reproductive Practitioner, through an international holistic health school (By the Moon), specializing in fertility and maternal doula services, reflexology, Usui Reiki, and energy healing.

Wenting Yang obtained her PhD in workforce education from the University of Georgia. Her research interest was to improve job satisfaction by considering cultural factors and coping strategies. She was the doctoral student advised by Dr. Bettye P. Smith and was deeply impacted by Dr. Smith's passion for teaching and love for students. After earning her PhD, Wenting served as a research analyst at the Georgia Department of Education to evaluate teachers' performance, and conducted research regarding teaching effectiveness. She is now a data scientist and actively organizing and participating in career development events.

www.ingramcontent.com/pod-product-compliance
Lightning Source LLC
Chambersburg PA
CBHW022302280326
41932CB00010B/947